A BIBLICAL APPROACH TO

MUSIC

CALEB & KATIE GARRAWAY

A Biblical Approach to Music

Remnant Publishing
Copyright 2019 Caleb & Katie Garraway
Pamphlet Edition 2015.
ISBN: 978-0-9914963-4-1

REMNANT MINISTRIES
215 S. Marion Avenue
Washington, IA 52353

Remnant Ministries is a ministry sent out of the Marion Avenue Baptist
Church. Remnant Ministries seeks to stir up the hearts of Christians around the
world to zealously reach our generation with the Gospel. God has appointed us
to live upon the earth at this time for a reason – so let us get serious, get busy,
and live our lives for him. Both young and old must realize that it is our time to
do our part in reaching our generation, before it is too late!

www.remnantministriesonline.com
calebgarraway@gmail.com
917.412.0059

Scripture quotations are from the Authorized King James Version.

zwü yecti. .

TABLE OF CONTENTS

*"O come, let us **sing** unto the Lord:*
*let us **make a joyful noise** to the rock of our salvation.*
Let us come before his presence with thanksgiving,
*and **make a joyful noise** unto Him....*
For the Lord is a great God,
and a great King above all gods.
*O come, let us **worship** and **bow down**:*
*let us **kneel** before the Lord our Maker.*
***Sing** unto the Lord, **bless** his name;*
***shew forth** His salvation from day to day.*
***Declare** His glory among the heathen,*
His wonders among all people.
For the Lord is great, and greatly to be praised:
He is to be feared above all gods.
***Give** unto the Lord **the glory due** unto His name:*
*O **worship** the Lord in the **beauty of holiness**:*
fear before Him, all the earth."

— Psalm 95:1-3 & 6; 96:2-4 & 8-9 —

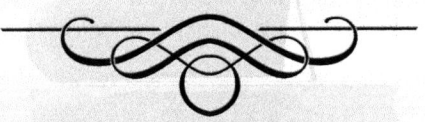

RECOMMENDATIONS

We thank the Lord for the number of dear friends He has given to us over the years through the ministry. Every individual listed below (among so many others that could have been included) holds a special place in our hearts, and we cherish their love and kindness toward our family. We are so grateful for each of them taking the time to read through this book and providing helpful insight, rousing encouragement, and constructive wisdom along the way as we tirelessly worked on producing this book. We thank God that He has allowed us to be co-laborers together with the Gospel and for His glory. The following recommendations are listed in alphabetical order.

In our generation, there is a desperate need for a *Biblical* approach to music. That cry is met within the pages of this book. With clarity and Scriptural authority, you will be introduced to the truths God intended for us to know concerning music. Caleb and Katie have kindred spirits to my wife and I. We count them as some of our closest friends in the ministry and share the same heartbeat in all aspects of doing God's will. They could've chosen to follow the trends of today's "millennials," and no doubt would have been very "successful" at it. That is not who they are. The Garraways are Biblically grounded, incredibly talented, the real deal, and used by God! This book will be a tremendous resource to your church, choir, youth department, and home. Read it, use it, share it. This book is worthy of your time!

— **PASTOR JOSEPH BROWN**
Marion Avenue Baptist Church, Washington, IA

Caleb and Katie Garraway know music, but more importantly they know God! In this book they not only sound an alarm for the wrong kind of music, but they sound the trumpet for the right kind of music. Bible-believing fundamental Christians are in transition right now, and it is NOT a good transition. Caleb and Katie are NOT a part of that movement, and a lot of what is said in this book will explain why. The book will be very valuable as a teaching aid for pastors, teachers, and anyone wanting to know the why's of those who refuse to adopt the world's philosophy in secular and Christian music. We recommend it.

— **EVANGELIST LARRY & RHONDA BROWN**
Founding pastor of Marion Avenue Baptist Church

I've just finished reviewing the Garraway's new book on music. *Excellent, excellent!* It is wonderful, solid, and filled with many examples and practical applications. This book is a valuable resource that can be used over and over again. I heartily recommend it as a great addition to your library.

— **BRO. GLENN CHRISTIANSON**
Music author and arranger
(with Patch the Pirate and Bible Truth Music)

Music is a big deal to God and it should be a big deal to the Christian also. The Garraways lay out *A Biblical Approach to Music* in such a way to challenge the reader to think and evaluate music on a personal level. The questions asked in each chapter advocate for honest response from the reader's heart and life. Caleb and Katie don't try to shove their opinions down the reader's throat. Their points are supported with Scripture, historical facts, and personal experiences, and they are presented in a manner that encourages the individual determination of personal beliefs about music and how to apply those beliefs to life and ministry. This book will be a valuable resource for any Christian musician, pastor, teacher, parent, or layperson.

— BRO. ANTHONY COLLINS
*The Vice President of Operations and
Music Department Chairman of Hyles-Anderson College*

In a day and age in which many churches have put *"no difference between the holy and the profane"* when it comes to music, the Garraways have given a clear, concise, Scriptural, and Spirit-filled approach to Biblical music. It was refreshing to read a book filled with the Word of God and not filled preferential opinions. I personally appreciated the firm stand on the Bible as well as the kind and gracious manner in which Caleb and Katie handled this often difficult subject. This book needs to be used in local churches and Bible colleges across the country. Brother Garraway and his family genuinely live what they preach and sing about. I am honored to give a recommendation for this wonderful book and pray God uses it mightily for His glory!

— BRO. THOMAS DELP
*Minister of Music of Calvary Baptist Church, King, NC
Administrative Assistant and Instructor at Calvary Baptist Bible College*

I am encouraged that there are people within Biblical Christianity willing to brave the arrows from those who are addicted to

Christian pop. It never ceases to stun me how vicious fellow Christians can be on this issue when they are encouraged to simply *think Biblically*. Even if you don't end up in the exact same spot as the Garraways, reading this book will greatly benefit you in your Christian growth.

— **EVANGELIST BEN EVERSON**
Author of "Fusses, Fights & Funerals"

The Word of God is the greatest book; and the greatest music in all of the world is Christian music! I have just finished reading *A Biblical Approach to Music* and highly recommend it to you! Evangelist Caleb Garraway is an energetic, passionate evangelist. I deeply appreciate him and his precious family! I am grateful for his excellent spirit and earnest labor for our Lord!

— **EVANGELIST BYRON FOXX**
Founder of Bible Truth Music

I wholeheartedly and unreservedly recommend *A Biblical Approach to Music* by Caleb and Katie Garraway. This couple, like my wife and me, have united their talents and dedication to the Lord to write this book. I believe it will be a classic for Christians in generations to come should the Lord tarry. The book is a sensible, practical, and Biblical approach to a sensitive subject because it is saturated with documentation and the Word of God itself. It clarifies the difference between right and wrong in a direct but loving way by differentiating *"between the culture around us and the Christ within us."* It is a resource that you will refer to over and over as you seek God's will in the area of music. Because it is full of spiritual truth, it will also encourage you to be faithful to the Lord, not only in music, but in every area of life. This book should be in every Christian's library.

— **DR. FRANK GARLOCK**
Founder of Majesty Music, Inc.

From an early age, Caleb was taught the joys and dangers of music. His father and I carefully taught him the importance of giving God his heart and glorifying Him in all things, especially this area. Warren and I were saved out of a life filled with sinful, worldly music, so we never wanted this type of music in our home.

It is easy to see, as Caleb points out in this book, that contemporary Christian music is just a repackaged form of rock-n-roll, infiltrating churches at an alarming rate. Sadly, it has even influenced people we know and love dearly. I am proud of how Caleb, Katie, and their family stand for truth, when so many are compromising and weakening their convictions. I know Brother Garraway is looking down from Heaven just as proud of our son and his service for the Lord as I am. This book is filled with truth that comes from the passionate and loving heart of Caleb Garraway. I know, because I am his mother.

— MRS. BONNIE GARRAWAY
Reseeding America Ministries

A Biblical Approach to Music is a worthwhile read. It is well researched and covers a myriad of issues concerning appropriate music for conservative Christians and their churches. The Garraways have done a great job of reinforcing their points with scripture as well as the comments of musical experts both saved and secular. It will even be a great tool for my own musical instruction.

— BRO. MIKE HALL
Vice President of Providence Baptist College
Chairman of the Music Department

Evangelist Caleb and Katie Garraway are a lovely, talented couple who have tender hearts towards seeking to please God. It is refreshing to see young people who don't accept the status quo of many of their peers, but look critically at the Scriptures to formulate their own convictions. Their book *A Biblical Approach to Music* is a perfect blending of what the Bible says about music from a preacher's and a musician's perspective. We very much enjoyed reading this diligent work. This will be a great resource for music pastors and senior pastors for years to come. Thank you, Caleb and Katie, for helping this generation with such well-thought-through reasoning!

— RON AND SHELLY HAMILTON
Patch the Pirate and Sissy Seagull

Music is a mighty influence upon us all, positively or negatively. It plays an essential role with God and in the lives of men and his creation (Job 38:7). Music is one of the first things that go wrong in any ministry; therefore, it must be guarded and guided by Scriptural principles (Colossians 3:16). I highly recommend *A Biblical Approach to Music* for many reasons — most importantly, because of its deep Scriptural basis. This book is not the opinion of Caleb and Katie Garraway; it is a stirring testament about godly music that truly glorifies God. This book is an outpouring of the Garraway's life in their faithful service for our Savior. It effectively equips the Christian with a foundational Biblical understanding, answers the questions that many have concerning music, and proves what is acceptable to the Lord.

— DR. CHUCK HARDING
Founder of "Mission To America"

The Garraway's book is one of the most Scriptural and comprehensive works on the subject of Biblical music. It is a must-read for every believer. *A Biblical Approach to Music* covers topics that are left out by others. Along with how the proper music practically applies to our daily lives, this book deals with both the doctrine of music and the power of its influence. You will want this title on your bookshelf as a reminder, reference, and resource.

— PASTOR STEPHEN HENDERSON
Harvest Baptist Church, Manhattan, KS

Over the past few years Megan and I have had the privilege of partnering with Caleb and Katie Garraway on several different projects and have seen firsthand their love for the Lord and their dedication to ministry. We count them as dear friends and are thankful for their conservative, Biblical stance. We are so excited to see others in our generation writing on this profoundly important topic!

— BRO. ADAM MORGAN
President of Majesty Music, Inc.

A Biblical Approach to Music is a joy to read, offering a refreshing Scriptural perspective. I highly recommend it for anyone seeking to study and serve in the music ministry!

— DR. KACY PALMORE
Music Director / Assistant Pastor of Parkside Baptist Church, Mesquite, TX

Caleb and Katie are a unified voice crying out in the wilderness of compromise, carnality, and chicanery! Few (if any) are saying what they are saying about music. My wife and I both agree — this is the best book to date that we have ever read on this subject. In fact, we believe it should be required reading in Christian colleges. We live in the midst of a generation of youth and young adults who demand answers. And Caleb and Katie have given it to them in this book.

The contextual biblical use and application is spot on. The musical insight was educational and fascinating, to say the least. The historical appreciation of hymnody as explained from our authors as well as dipping back into the rich legacy of the great hymn writers and singers such as Sankey and Alexander was in itself a personal revival experience.

The truth (as documented so well in this book) shows that music can be wrong, even when it "feels" so right. And as the Garraways point out again and again, we must be right with God and our music must line up with the Bible. It is so good to have a book like this, which explains the reasons why and how our music should remain Christ-honoring, especially to our teens and young adults.

We are thankful for those who are still writing beautiful Christian music today. But the worldly music that is being pushed on our churches is reminiscent of the story of the "Trojan Horse." The Greeks bearing gifts left the wooden horse full of elite soldiers outside the gate of Troy, and the Trojans foolishly pulled the horse into their fair city. When night had fallen, the soldiers crept out and opened the gates for the attack of the Greeks who destroyed Troy. Fundamental churches have permitted the "Trojan Horse" of "rock music" into our formerly safely-guarded churches, and the churches are rocking and rolling away from holiness, revival, and the perfect will of God.

Carnal "Christian" music has been the proverbial elephant in the room of far too many of the Lord's churches. While many have refused to speak to the issue or, in timidity, have shied away from the subject, the Garraways have, with God's help and guidance, taken a spiritual "elephant gun" and blown away every excuse we may use to justify the wrong kind of music. But on an even more positive note, the Garraways have masterfully written this book to encourage and inspire godly music that will ultimately bring glory and honor to the Lord Jesus Christ (I Corinthians 10:31) and hopefully be a catalyst to national revival (Psalm 85:6).

— DR. JOHNNY POPE
Hopewell Baptist Church, Napa, CA

What a book! What a preacher! What a family! They have a song in their hearts, and it comes out in their lives! Caleb and his family have sung across America and preached in hundreds of churches. You will enjoy this book as it teaches clear music doctrine. Read, meditate on, use, and pass on the truths of this great book. Thank you, Bro. and Mrs. Garraway for all your labor to make this tool available to all of us!

— PASTOR MIKE RAY
Hopewell Baptist Church, Napa, CA

I so appreciate the work that Brother and Mrs. Garraway have put into their new book *A Biblical Approach to Music.* The premise for the need of such a book can be summed up from a closing statement in the chapter on congregational singing, *"God has given the gift of music to every Christian to help us fulfill our chief purpose in life — to glorify God."* I enthusiastically recommend the Garraways and their ministry.

— BRO. ED RUSS
Faith Music Missions

It's always a blessing for a parent to see their children "walk in the truth" they were given. We taught our daughter Katie God's principles for music ever since she was a young girl. We taught her that music is a powerful, universal communicator! Its message goes far beyond the mere words of a song. Yet many Christians seem to be naive and without discernment when it comes to evaluating music as a medium of personal edification or corporate praise and worship. Her mother and I are delighted that Katie and her husband Caleb continue today in the things they learned as youth.

In *A Biblical Approach To Music,* Caleb and Katie are very insightful and intensely practical as they unfold literally hundreds of Scripture passages which articulate the principles that every believer should consider when forming a standard by which to determine whether a particular song or style of music would be acceptable to God. While music is an area of Christian liberty and not every believer will "draw their line" at exactly the same place, this masterful work by the Garraways is sure to aid each reader in his/her understanding of many Bible principles which we can apply to this awesome expression of praise. The book is very simple to understand and quite thorough. It is a must-read for every child of God, especially in the times and culture of today.

— PASTOR VINCENT SAWYER
Victory Baptist Church, Port Charlotte, FL

God's Word is the final authority and the fixed point of reference in the life of every believer. Many today are blinded and deceived by the label "Gospel" and or "Christian" that is placed on titles and genres of music. Through my own personal experiences years ago, I discovered firsthand that a majority of the leading "Southern Gospel" groups look at and treat music as a business, performance, and career more than a ministry to exalt Christ. In a world that is driven by entertainment, Caleb and Katie Garraway are being used of God to declare the Truth of God's Word and its standard on Christ-honoring music. This is a must read for every believer, and a tremendous reference for those involved in the ministry of music.

— PASTOR SETH SICELOFF
Little Elkin Baptist Church, Ronda, NC

Music is one of God's greatest gifts. Yet, it can be one of the greatest areas of division among Christians. Music was created to glorify God, and Satan seeks to rob that glory for himself. The insight Caleb and Katie share in this book is grounded in Biblical truth, and they have taken great care to share the truth absent from personal preferences and traditional pressures. I believe this book will help you solidify in your mind God's purpose and plan for music in the life of a Christian.

— DR. DAVID B. SMITH
Executive Director of Al Smith Ministries

It is with high honour and great respect that I willingly offer my approval and recommendation of *A Biblical Approach to Music*. I was so moved by the content that I was personally convicted and drawn closer to Christ. This book is filled with the Word of God! When read with an open heart and a willing mind, *A Biblical Approach to Music* will bring about change to an individual, a family, a church, and even a nation! It is evident that the authors, Caleb and Katie Garraway, were truly filled with the power of the Holy Spirit while giving themselves to this writing. As one was quoted within the pages of this book, *"Revival of sacred song is the forerunner and first fruits of a general revival of religion in the church of God."* Oh, how we need revival today! This book truly rejoiced my heart, reinforced the truths of God's Word, and strengthened my walk with God. To God be the Glory!

— PASTOR MARK G. SWANSON
Berean Baptist Church, Rockford, IL

In a day of conflicting opinion and contradictory voices, there is a desperate need to get back to the truths of Scripture. *A Biblical Approach to Music* brings us to where our authority begins and ends, the Word of God. I have read many books on the subject of music and this one is the most exhaustive, comprehensive, and documented study on music you will find. I encourage every pastor and every Christian to read it and use it as a resource for discipleship. Further, it would behoove Christian schools and colleges to use it as a textbook on the subject.

— PASTOR WILLIAM TYSON
Woodlawn Baptist Church, Bowie, MD

Caleb and Katie Garraway have done a thorough job of covering a biblical position on music for God-fearing Christians in the twenty-first century. Every issue is backed by multiple Scripture references and applications. This book has been written with families in mind. It should be used by parents as an aid to guide and protect their children from the wiles of the devil. It was also written to warn young people of the great dangers of dabbling in Satan's music, in secular music, but more seriously — the supposedly Contemporary Christian Music of many independent fundamental Baptist churches. All readers must heed the exhortations given in this book, because they are given from God's Word. There may be those who read these pages and do not agree with the premises laid out. I would suggest that they read the book again slowly, maybe one page per day, to let the message sink in and let the Lord speak to them. If this book changes the destiny of one young person, it will have been well worth the effort.

— DR. ADRIAN VAN MANEN

Music Director and Vocal Instructor of Oklahoma Baptist College
(Caleb's voice teacher for eight semesters)

The principles shared in this book about music are outstanding. I believe this book needs to be read by every parent and taught in Bible colleges across America. The contents of this book certainly meet a great need that we have in understanding Biblically-sound music.

— DR. MIKE WELLS

Pastor of Parkside Baptist Church, Mesquite, TX
President of Lone Star Baptist College

This book is true to its title. Rather than reading of the opinions and preferences of an individual, you will find Scriptural principles that provide clarity and direction in the area of music. In a day and age where music is painted as something that is "taboo," Brother and Mrs. Garraway sheds biblical light on the issue, providing practical insight on how to keep the right balance in something that matters a great deal to our Lord. I appreciate the great spirit in which this book was written, and even more so appreciate the effort put in to providing a sound and scriptural approach to music.

— PASTOR NICK WHITE

Victory Baptist Church, Boston, MA

INTRODUCTION

Music is a beautiful gift when used wholesomely and appropriately. It can be described as a flowing composition of tones — or a "singable" flow of sound — consisting of melody, harmony, and rhythm working together to communicate a message that influences our spirit and emotions. It can seemingly evoke any feeling (some good and some bad). Music makes an impression on everyone who can hear sound. Our hearts and minds instinctively respond to happy tunes, reflective scores, inspiring anthems, stirring hymns, majestic orchestrations, and so on.

There are clear principles in the Bible concerning music; after all, God is the One who created it. In Job 38, the Bible says that when God laid the foundations of the earth the angels sang and shouted for joy. Colossians 1:16 teaches, *"...all things were created by Him, and for Him."* God ultimately designed music to be a melodious medium by which we can praise, magnify, and worship Him.

As God's children, we should desire to glorify our Heavenly Father in all things, including our music.

I Corinthians 10:31 exhorts us, *"Whether therefore ye eat, or drink, or whatsoever ye do, do all to the glory of God."* May it be our daily prayer concerning our music: *"Let the words of my mouth, and the meditation of my heart, be acceptable in thy sight, O Lord, my strength, and my redeemer"* (Psalm 19:14).

In Colossians 3, verses 16 and 17 are interwoven with one another. *"Let the word of Christ dwell in you richly in all wisdom; teaching and admonishing one another in psalms and hymns and spiritual songs, singing with grace in your hearts to the Lord. And whatsoever ye do in word or deed, do all in the name of the Lord Jesus, giving thanks to God and the Father by him."* We need to allow God's Word to fill our hearts and completely govern our lives, ultimately influencing us to sing with joy and delight unto God.

Every part of what we say, sing, or seek to do should be done with a grateful heart that desires to bring Him glory. I Corinthians 6:20 teaches us to *"glorify God in your body, and in your spirit, which are God's."* The Lord should be honored through our bodies — our mouths (what we say), our means (what we do), our methods (how we live), and even our music. He should be exalted through our spirits — our minds (what we think) and our motives (why we do what we do). *Can this be said of your life?*

Without Scripture, Rick Warren insisted in his book *The Purpose Driven Church* that: *"The style of worship that you feel comfortable with says far more about your cultural background than it does about your theology. Debates over worship style are almost always sociological and personality couched in theological terms."*[1] No, our music is far more intricate than culture or personality. Though we may have various tastes and preferences, these subjects are certainly theological issues.

God has given us His precious Word to guide us in every aspect of life. It is *"a lamp unto my feet, and a light unto my path"* (Psalm 119:105). Through His precepts we will receive the wisdom and understanding (Psalm 119:104) we need to excellently honor and praise Him with our music, to correctly glorify Him, and to beautifully worship Him in holiness.

However, each of us must personally decide that we are going to *"let the word of Christ dwell"* in our hearts *"richly in all wisdom."* We must determine that His principles are going to direct us. Instead of letting personal preferences lead us to our positions, we need to allow Biblical truth to grow us and develop us so that we might make right, spiritual choices on this matter. All of our preferences and all of our positions should be aligned with Biblical principles. Dedicated believers will determine to follow Christ and not culture or the control of our own flesh.

In writing on the topic of music, please understand that we are not claiming to be a superior authority on the subject — we honestly believe that there are better people suited to write on this subject. This book however was born out of a burden from the Spirit of God and a plea for help from others. It is not a textbook on music theory but a practical, spiritually-rational guide in applying Biblical truths to music.

It started out as a pamphlet covering only a few topics; and once people read it, it encouraged them and strengthened them so much that they asked us to write more on the subject. Hundreds of parents, young people, and pastors specifically and diligently requested that we produce a resource that could help them with a deeper study. Initially, we didn't think we should, since music is such a sensitive issue among so many. (We are just being transparent with you from the start.) But as we prayed about it for some time, the need to do it would not leave us but only intensified. Our hearts became so burdened by God to produce this full-length book — a book that some might criticize us for because of its direct content in places. This book was **not** written to try to convince you to align with our personal positions. No, it is our desire to help give clarity using Biblical principles and wholesome applications for godly music. Would you allow us to simply share what God has been teaching us over the years?

As is the case in every area of the Christian life, *God's Word* should be our sole authority. Music is no exception. Music is given a high priority in Scripture as it is directly connected to the praise and worship of Almighty God, used to bring edification to God's people, and bears witness of the Gospel to a lost and dying world.

But, over time, sinful humanity has twisted what God intended (as they always do), and unfortunately, Christians have begun to adapt more and more to the world's view of music, forgetting what it should be, according to the Bible. We must get back to God's Word and take a Biblical approach to music! All of our music should be examined in light of Scriptural principles, and the musical and lyrical content ought to be consistent with those principles in every aspect of its wording, style, and presentation.

To give you a little context of our background, we have enjoyed lives filled with music, and it has always been a passion of ours. Caleb took music classes and piano/voice lessons all throughout college and traveled on his Bible college's men's quartet for four summers singing in churches all over the country. Katie began piano lessons at the age of five and has developed a great love for music since then as she went on to learn other instruments, write music, teach piano lessons, and take music classes in college. Now that we are married and travel in full-time evangelism, the Lord has allowed us to use our love for music across the country in hundreds of churches to multiple thousands of people, as we have sung together for over a decade and have produced multiple albums. Though we have a wonderful background in music, we will readily admit that we don't know it all.

We would also like to take a moment and publically thank our parents. Katie was blessed to grow up in a pastor's home, with a dad who wisely, passionately, and thoroughly taught the whole council of God, including the topic of music and what the Bible had to say about it. Caleb's parents, before salvation, had much experience with the world's music (his dad had been a DJ in college, and his mom was a dancer). Once saved, they lovingly taught Caleb what they had learned regarding the differences between worldly and Christian music. We are thankful for the teaching we received growing up and their loving investment. We have sought to implement what we learned throughout this book as well.

We have carefully written all this material in a sincere spirit of prayer, seeking to remain sensitive to the Holy Ghost. We understand that there are numerous positions God's people take on this subject. For many, it can be a "hot topic." Various beliefs and opinions are persistently debated and constantly defended in heated discussion. Please take a deep breath and relax. We are not in any way seeking to argue with you. *"Only by pride cometh contention: but with the well advised is wisdom"* (Proverbs 13:10). We have no agenda. We have begged God to give us a spirit of humility and wisdom as we approach this delicate subject. We simply want to encourage you and point you to what God's Word teaches. We also hope that we can effectively give you sensible, Biblical application of the principles regarding music contained in His

Word. We pray that it will be a resourceful blessing to you as we study things together over the next couple hundred pages.

There may be a few things that we discuss in the following chapters that might cause some to think: *"Wow, these guys are looking to make enemies."* But that is not true. We have no personal vendetta or axe to grind with anyone. Some who read this book might even disagree with us on what we present and the conclusions we make. Please understand from the very beginning here that we respect each individual for his opinion, knowing that it is ultimately between a person and the Lord (I Corinthians 4:3-4). We do not answer to each other; we all answer to God (Romans 14:12). Each of us will give individual accounts for the personal choices we make in our music. We may not see "eye to eye" but thank you in advance for letting us transparently share with you from our hearts and from careful study.

Naturally, various Biblical applications and positions God has led us to make will come out in our writing (and we unashamedly stand by them). Again however, the material presented here is not a personal or public attack upon any preacher, church, or ministry. We are not writing the book out of a critical spirit or contentious heart. (God forbid!) It is simply our desire to encourage an increased passion for holiness in music. We sincerely crave for God's people to truly honor the Lord in all things — including music. Again, I Corinthians 10:31 says, *"Whether therefore ye eat, or drink, or whatsoever ye do, do all to the glory of God."* Is God thoroughly glorified with your music?

God's heart is broken in Isaiah 5:12-13: *"And the harp, and the viol, the tabret, and pipe, and wine, are in their feasts: but they regard not the work of the Lord, neither consider the operation of his hands. Therefore my people are gone into captivity, because they have no knowledge: and their honourable men are famished, and their multitude dried up with thirst."* Could it be that there is a lot of "captivity" in our music — to the flesh, the world, and the Devil — because we have not taken the time to understand *"the work of the Lord"* or God's desires and principles for our music?

The Bible has a multitude of passages dealing with the subject of music, but it takes an honest heart to read it. A dishonest heart will refuse the principles and applications of it, will argue their points and personal beliefs, and will even seek to twist Scripture to justify their own positions. As Romans 3:4 exhorts, may we *"let God be true."*

For those truly open to what Scripture says about music, we have found that minimal exhortation is necessary. For a dedicated believer, there should be a natural hunger to fully embrace Scriptural principles; an evident heart's desire to run in the ways of righteousness; and a sweet spirit full of joy and exuberance longing to magnify Christ in the beauty of holiness. *Does this describe you?* But for those who already have their minds made up and desire their own way instead of God's direction, no Biblical reference or application on music will ever be sufficient for them. *Does this describe you?*

This book is not an extensive or exhaustive study on the topic — it is honestly a brief one, compared to all the volumes that have been written on this subject. Yet, we believe that the following content, interlaced with Scripture, can be a helpful, concise tool that the Holy Ghost can use to grow believers and draw His children closer in their walk with the Lord Jesus Christ. We are asking the Spirit to help us recognize what God has to say about music in His Word and speak to hearts. We are praying that the material we share will be an aid to you in making Christ-honoring musical choices and will assist

Christian parents in guiding the tender hearts of their children and grandchildren.

Our purpose in this book is not to be a spiritual "straight jacket" regarding music; but to offer reasonable Bible principles which all believers should consider and apply when determining a standard of music they believe would be *"acceptable to the Lord"* (Proverbs 21:3 and Ephesians 5:10).

The Holy Ghost must be involved in discerning good music from that which is evil. Jesus teaches us in John 16:13-14 that, *"when he, the Spirit of truth, is come, he will guide you into all truth: for he shall not speak of himself; but whatsoever he shall hear, that shall he speak: and he will shew you things to come. He shall glorify me: for he shall receive of mine, and shall shew it unto you."* Would you pray and ask the Holy Ghost to lead and guide you into all truth concerning music? Is your heart open to that?

Of course, He will never lead us to do things that would grieve the Lord or go against God's Word. He will not direct us contrary to Scripture, because the Word of God is the only source of absolute Truth in the entire universe. God's Spirit and God's Word will resoundingly compliment one another. If there is a "spirit" within you that is "opening your mind" or "convincing" you to adopt a more worldly position or carnal stance on music, it is not coming from the spirit of Christ.

I John 4:1 reminds us, *"Beloved, believe not every spirit, but try the spirits whether they are of God."* For generations, there has been a vicious attack on music. However, God's Spirit and Word will never guide our hearts to move farther AWAY from holiness and wholesomeness, but always closer toward it! The Lord is pretty clear in I Peter 1:14-16. Listen to what He declares: *"As obedient children, not fashioning yourselves according to the former lusts in your ignorance: But as he which hath called you is holy, so be ye holy in all manner of conversation; Because it is written, Be ye holy; for I am holy."*

God desires His children to delight their hearts, souls, and minds in music that will glorify Him and not gratify their flesh. He does not want us to fashion our lives after *"the former lusts"* or pattern our lives after the sinful, secular ways of a lost world. Therefore as Christians, we must be walking, talking, and living in the Spirit. He will effectively guide us (if we are yielded to His guiding) according to God's Word. Galatians 5:6 teaches, *"This I say then, Walk in the Spirit, and ye shall not fulfill the lust of the flesh."* We have this promise. We must be sensitive to follow His leadership in our lives. Each of us should earnestly want to live as the Bible teaches.

But if we are not careful, we can become naïve toward the world, the flesh, and the Devil. They have very real tactics that seek to undermine God's holiness and to pervert our music, praise, and worship. May this book strengthen each of us to become more Bible-centered and Bible-minded so that we *"Neither give place to the devil."* (Ephesians 4:27)

Before you read any further, pray and ask God to use this study to mold you more into His image, to draw you closer to Himself, and to develop a greater love and passion for godly music. We strongly believe that Scripture gives God's people clear principles for Christ-honoring, soul-stirring music. Let's study together what the Lord has to say and how application can be drawn from His Holy Word to our lives!

CHAPTER I:

THE PURPOSE
OF MUSIC

There is great joy in knowing that God created music, as He is the One Who formed all things in the beginning (Genesis 1:1). The Bible teaches in Colossians 1:16-17, *"For by him were all things created, that are in heaven, and that are in earth, visible and invisible, whether they be thrones, or dominions, or principalities, or powers: all things were created by him, and for him: And he is before all things, and by him all things consist."*

Furthermore, music was created for His glory and for His pleasure: *"Thou art worthy, O Lord, to receive glory and honour and power: for thou hast created all things, and for thy pleasure they are and were created"* (Revelation 4:11).

God Himself delights in His people through singing. Zephaniah 3:17 mentions, *"The Lord thy God in the midst of thee is mighty; he will save, he will rejoice over thee with joy; he will rest in his love, he will joy over thee with singing."* God sings! How powerful and beautiful His voice must be. One day, we will hear it resound in Heaven! While still here upon the earth, we are encouraged by Him to sing and make a joyful noise: *"Sing and rejoice, O daughter of Zion: for, lo, I come, and*

I will dwell in the midst of thee, saith the Lord" (Zechariah 2:10). God desires His presence to be in the center of our song.

Music was given to man at the moment of creation when *"the morning stars sang together"* (Job 38:7). The Bible provides an explanation for the origin of some musical instruments (Genesis 4:21). The Bible records that God surrounds Himself with angelic hosts and the songs of redeemed sinners (Isaiah 6:1-4; Revelation 14:2-3). A heavenly choir of angels even sang to announce the birth of God's Son, Jesus Christ, to shepherds on a Bethlehem hillside (Luke 2:13).

All of nature is involved in praising God — more than most of us would have probably imagined (Psalm 103:22; 145:10; 150:6)! Isaiah 55:12 shares, *"the mountains and the hills shall break forth before you into singing, and all the trees of the field shall clap their hands."* The stars and breathtaking interstellar space clouds celebrate His glory with praise: *"The heavens declare* [to celebrate and recount] *the glory of God; and the firmament sheweth* [to expound and shew praise] *his handywork. Day unto day uttereth speech, and night unto night sheweth knowledge. There is no speech nor language, where their voice is not heard. Their line is gone out through all the earth, and their words to the end of the world."* The sun and moon, wind and hail, hills and trees, beasts, birds, fish and insects are all urged to praise the Lord (Psalm 148:3-4, 7-10). Wild animals honor Him (Isaiah 43:20). Moreover, Scripture speaks of pastures and valleys "singing." Psalm 65:13 says, *"The pastures are clothed with flocks; the valleys also are covered over with corn; they shout for joy, they also sing."*

All things given to us by God are given for a reason. Colossians 1:16-17 specifically mentions that *"all things were created...for him."* One of the greatest gifts God has given to us is the gift of music. What purposes does the Bible give for music? Here are some thoughts with a sampling of verses to correspond to them. (At the end of the book, when you read through *"A Bible Concordance of Music,"* containing all the relevant verses in God's Word about music, you will see how predominate and obvious these truths are.)

MUSIC AIDS US IN <u>EXALTING</u> ALMIGHTY GOD.

Psalm 100:2 encourages us to *"come before his presence with singing."* As human beings, we are God's crowning creation. As Christians, we are His children. If nature and the angelic host sing praise unto the Lord, don't you think that He longs to hear us worshipping Him, too? Absolutely! God created us to be instruments with the ability to sing and make music.

The children of Israel sang praises unto the Lord for the victory He wrought over the Egyptians at the Red Sea (Exodus 15:1). Joyful worship and instrument playing went before the Ark of the Covenant as it was brought to Jerusalem (I Chronicles 15:16). Music was sung and played in the temple to honor the Lord (Ezekiel 40:44). Songs of worship were offered up to the Lord as the Israelite army marched out to battle against the enemies of God (II Chronicles 20:21). Deborah and Barak led Israel in singing as they rejoiced in God's victory that day (Judges 5:1-31). Many more examples can be found throughout Scripture.

We are taught to *"sing unto the Lord"* (Psalm 30:4). Again, we are exhorted to sing joyfully to the Lord, to praise Him, and to make skillful music unto Him upon our instruments (Psalm 33:2-3). The purpose of music was, and still is, to praise God. This directly implies that our music should be for God's glory and not our own.

Psalm 34:3 joyfully cries out, *"O magnify the Lord with me, and let us exalt his name together."* He is truly worthy! The Bible specifically uses the word "magnify" here, which means that we should *"make large, boast, increase, lift up, and publicly promote"* Jesus. "Exalt" has the same connotation (*"to lift up high"*).

Our lives should be consumed with Christ. For the child of God, there is nothing greater because He is the greatest! Colossians 3:4 reminds us that He *"is our life."* After all, where would we be without Him? Lost! Hopeless! Helpless! According to I Corinthians 15:19, we would be *"of all men most miserable."* Lamentations 3:22 tells us that *"It is of the Lord's mercies that we are not consumed, because his compassions fail not."* When something is magnified, it's made much larger so that it can be easily viewed by many and studied in detail. As born-again Christians, we should be thrilled with the privilege to make Jesus "bigger than life" because He is better than life!

Our music should magnify and exalt Almighty God. Psalm 95:1-3 & 6-7 proclaims, *"O come, let us sing unto the Lord: let us make a joyful noise to the rock of our salvation. Let us come before his presence with thanksgiving, and make a joyful noise unto him with psalms. For the Lord is a great God, and a great King above all gods. ...O come, let us worship and bow down: let us kneel before the Lord our maker. For he is our God; and we are the people of his pasture, and the sheep of his hand."*

The following Psalm starts out by encouraging us: *"O sing unto the Lord a new song: sing unto the Lord, all the earth. Sing unto the Lord, bless his name; shew forth his salvation from day to day. For the Lord is great, and greatly to be praised: he is to be feared above all gods. For all the gods of the nations* are idols: but the Lord made the heavens" (Psalm 96:1-2 & 4-5). Then in verse 9, we are challenged to "worship the Lord in the beauty of holiness" (Psalm 96:9).

Here we find singing, music, praise, and worship interwoven with one another. Another passages declares, "All the earth shall worship thee, and shall sing unto thee; they shall sing to thy name. Selah" (Psalm 66:4). The word "Selah" shows that this truth was something that God wanted us to pause, take note of, and meditate upon. God should be worshipped and praised through our music!

As you read this book, you will notice that we often use the terms "worship" and "praise"; both acts certainly have their appropriate place when used in the right context with music. Today, these words are often used together; although they complement one another, they are two different principles. We believe it is important, here in the very beginning, to define what the Bible means by these words so we don't get confused.

Of course, "praise" and "worship" are not solely reserved to be musical acts. Music is only a small portion of how they should be used in the Christian life. God should be praised and worshipped with our words, in our thoughts, by our actions, through our serving and giving, and so much more! As we use these two terms throughout the book, it is within the context of when it applies to music.

"Praise" is a jubilant expression of admiration; it is a joyful acknowledgement of all that God has done for us. Psalm 135:3 proclaims, "Praise the Lord; for the Lord is good!" Praise is closely intertwined with thanksgiving as we offer back to the Lord sincere appreciation for His mighty works on our behalf. Psalm 98:4 encourages us to "Make a joyful noise unto the Lord, all the earth: make a loud noise, and rejoice, and *sing praise.*" In the New Testament, it was spoken of Jesus: "*And when he was come nigh, even now at the descent of the mount of Olives, the whole multitude of the disciples began to rejoice and praise God with a loud voice for all the mighty works that they had seen*" (Luke 19:37). God has done many marvelous and miraculous things — He is worthy of praise (Psalm 18:3)!

"Worship", however, is not boisterous and exuberant — but quite the opposite, though still filled with joy. As it is mentioned throughout the Bible, it means "*to depress, lay prostrate in homage, fall down flat, or make oneself to stoop in obeisance and reverence.*" According to numerous examples in Scripture, worship is literally bowing down one's head or getting down on one's knees to express from the heart adoration and surrender unto the Lord. Genesis 24:48 is an example. Abraham's unnamed servant, tasked with finding Isaac a bride, shares, "*And I bowed down my head, and worshipped the Lord, and blessed the Lord God of my master Abraham, which had led me in the right way....*" We find several other incidences like this throughout the Word of God (such as Exodus 34:8; Matthew 2:10-12; Matthew 4:8-10; Revelation 22:8-9).

Worship could be described as a sincere expression of contrition before the Almighty, when God's people recognize their own insufficiency, humble themselves before Him in full surrender, and exalt Him in reverence for who He is, not just what He has done. We read earlier that the Bible admonishes us to "*come, let us worship and bow down*" (Psalm 95:6), and to "*worship the Lord in the beauty of holiness*" (Psalm 96:9). Just as praise in music is intertwined with thanksgiving, worship in music should be intertwined with genuine veneration and tender yielding.

II Chronicles 29:26-29 relates the testimony, "*And the*

Levites stood with the instruments of David, and the priests with the trumpets. And Hezekiah commanded to offer the burnt offering upon the altar. And when the burnt offering began, the song of the Lord began also with the trumpets, and with the instruments ordained by David king of Israel. And all the congregation worshipped, and the singers sang, and the trumpeters sounded: and all this continued until the burnt offering was finished. And when they had made an end of offering, the king and all that were present with him bowed themselves, and worshipped." Worship always involves sincere contrition, humility, and reverence in music.

A person could certainly go through the outward motions of "worshipping" the Lord and not be truly engaged in it. But, this an extremely grieving act to God, and it will hinder the outpouring of His presence and power as a result. Psalm 78 testifies of the children of Israel: *"Nevertheless they did flatter him with their mouth, and they lied unto him with their tongues. For their heart was not right with him, …How oft did they provoke him in the wilderness, and grieve him in the desert! Yea, they turned back and tempted God, and limited the Holy One of Israel"* (Psalm 78:36-37 & 40-41).

Don't forget, God sees the heart! *"But the Lord said unto Samuel, Look not on his countenance, or on the height of his stature; because I have refused him: for the Lord seeth not as man seeth; for man looketh on the outward appearance, but the Lord looketh on the heart"* (I Samuel 16:7). God cannot be fooled; He desires and deserves sincere, heartfelt worship.

Exalting the Lord should be the purpose of the congregational singing portion of a church service. Believers should begin together by singing hymns of praise — giving thanks to God and joyfully acknowledging the great things He has done. As the service progresses, the songs selected should transition to hymns of worship so the congregation can individually reflect on who God is in all His greatness and goodness. As believers genuinely *"worship him in spirit and in truth"* (John 4:24), it should generate a spiritual desire within them to become tenderly humble before Him. This will prepare hearts for the preaching of God's Word and the working of the Holy Spirit in their lives.

In our music, there should be a holy mixture of both "praise" and "worship." He is worthy of being Biblically exalted! *Instead of praising and worshipping God the way we want to or the way we think is best, why don't we ask Him, "Lord, how can we appropriately and rightly praise You, exalt You, and magnify Your holy Name in a way that pleases You?"* If we don't have this mindset, over time our attention will no longer be on God, but upon ourselves. Our music will reflect what we like instead of what glorifies Him.

MUSIC HELPS <u>TEACH</u> SPIRITUAL TRUTH AND BIBLE DOCTRINE.

God told Moses to *"write ye this song for you, and teach it the children of Israel: put it in their mouths, that this song may be a witness for me against the children of Israel"* (Deuteronomy 31:19). God had lessons He wanted the Israelites to learn and remember through the generations. He thought it appropriate to use music to communicate and implement these truths within the people's hearts and minds. In addition to this, an entire book of the Bible *(Psalms)* is completely comprised of 150 songs that magnify God for His goodness, describe various aspects of God's attributes and ability, teach doctrine, and convey vital spiritual truths. We believe that this sets an example for us that we should follow today.

The timeless hymns we all sing in church are a treasure trove of doctrinal truth. They are not songs just to "fill up time" in a service. (If that's your view of them, you need a personal revival!) Rather, they ought to be exciting offerings of genuine worship and heart-filled praise directed to our Lord and Saviour, Jesus Christ. Hymns were written, born out of sincere spirituality — many times after a trial or hardship — with the intent of drawing us closer to God. The lyrics are so profound and full of Biblical principles that one cannot help but be stirred and strengthened when they stop and meditate upon their deep spiritual meanings.

Furthermore, it has been scientifically proven that a person will put things to memory more quickly and easily and will retain them longer if they are sung! (It's called Music Related Memory.) Music has a way of clinging to us as barbs on a fishing hook retain a fish. A melody (once learned) will most likely remain lodged in our minds and stay with us for a lifetime. God knew what He was doing when He encouraged Moses and His people to teach and instill truth through the medium of music!

MUSIC ASSISTS US IN REFLECTING UPON WHO GOD IS AND REJOICING IN THE LORD.

In Psalm 98:1-6, we find God's people joyfully singing in celebration for what He had done in their past. *"O sing unto the Lord a new song; for he hath done marvellous things: his right hand, and his holy arm, hath gotten him the victory. The Lord hath made known his salvation: his righteousness hath he openly shewed in the sight of the heathen. He hath remembered his mercy and his truth toward the house of Israel: all the ends of the earth have seen the salvation of our God. Make a joyful noise unto the Lord, all the earth: make a loud noise, and rejoice, and sing praise. Sing unto the Lord with the harp; with the harp, and the voice of a psalm. With trumpets and sound of cornet make a joyful noise before the Lord, the King."*

We believe that it is important to consider what God has done in the past to strengthen us in realizing what God is capable of doing today. After all, our Lord has not changed, and He never will. His power has not withered, His promises have not weakened, and His presence has not waned away over time. He is still capable of accomplishing wonders in our generation! *"Jesus Christ the same yesterday, and to day, and for ever"* (Hebrews 13:8). One of our favorite songs to sing in churches is *"The Great I AM Still Is"*; it is on our album *"Faithful to the Cross"* that we recorded with the Indianapolis Symphony Orchestra. This music, along with many other songs, stirs and strengthens the hearts of people as they reflect upon the truth of Who God is.

The entirety of Psalm 150 crescendos in exaltation of our Great God: *"Praise ye the Lord. Praise God in his sanctuary: praise him in the firmament of his power. Praise him for his mighty acts: praise him according to his excellent greatness. Praise him with the sound of the trumpet: praise him with the psaltery and harp. Praise him with the timbrel and dance: praise him with stringed instruments and organs. Praise him upon the loud cymbals: praise him upon the high sounding cymbals. Let every thing that hath breath praise the Lord. Praise ye the Lord."*

The Bible places an importance upon Christians expressing their gratitude and thankfulness unto God and pouring themselves out before Him with music: *"Sing unto the Lord with thanksgiving; sing praise upon the harp unto our God"* (Psalm 147:7); *"Make a joyful noise unto the Lord, all the earth: make a loud noise, and rejoice, and sing praise"* (Psalm 98:4). It is believed that John Wesley said, *"Singing is as much the language of holy joy, as praying is of holy desire."*

If we are not careful, we will become complacent about the blessings and the goodness of God in our lives. It is so easy to forget about the majesty and the miraculous power of Christ. Music is an excellent tool that can effectively stir us on a frequent basis and excite our hearts to genuinely rejoice in the Lord and worship Him.

When we are in the midst of hardship, music will bring us comfort and correct our focus. David testified in Psalm 77:6-9: *"I call to remembrance my song in the night: I commune with mine own heart: and my spirit made diligent search. Will the Lord cast off for ever? and will he be favourable no more? Is his mercy clean gone for ever? doth his promise fail for evermore? Hath God forgotten to be gracious? hath he in anger shut up his tender mercies? Selah."* The song he sang and the music he meditated upon helped him reflect upon God's character and attributes. It caused him to rhetorically ask questions within his heart that he already knew the answers to: all of which were "No". It calmed him and strengthened him as he willingly placed his life back into a position of faith, rather than giving way to fear and frustration. When fear knocks on the door, answer with faith!

Has godly music ever done that for you? It has brought tears to our eyes in sweet release. In private, it has caused our hands to be lifted up in a holy fashion in prayer and praise unto our God. There is nothing like it! We have heard countless times how music has helped someone through a dark time or a difficult trial.

While sitting in a prison cell, Paul wrote to faithful Christians: *"Finally, my brethren, rejoice in the Lord"*

(Philippians 3:1). And, *"Rejoice in the Lord alway: and again I say, Rejoice"* (Philippians 4:4). Through him, God encourages us: in spite of the sufferings and hardships, rejoice. In spite of the unexpected storms and troubles, rejoice. In spite of the wearying circumstances of what is happening all around you, rejoice. This was the testimony of Paul and Silas as they sat in shackles in the prison's dungeon. In the midnight hour, they sounded out in glorious songs of praise to Almighty God (Acts 16:23-34), and, God used it to do a physical, spiritual, and supernatural work.

A national pastor in Vietnam had spent several torturous years in prison at the hands of the Communist authorities. He was jailed for preaching the Bible and salvation through Jesus Christ. Though he vividly remembered what he endured with his fellow Christian prisoners, he did not focus on that. Rather, he spoke often of the times he was overwhelmed with the joy he experienced in the presence of God.

He said, *"When we were in prison we sang almost every day because Christ was alive in us. They knew we liked to praise God with musical instruments, so they gave every Christian in prison a musical instrument. However, they did not give us violins or mandolins — these were too expensive. Instead, they put chains on our hands and feet. They chained us to add to our grief. Yet we discovered that chains are splendid musical instruments! When we clanged them together in rhythm, we could sing, 'This is the day (clink, clank), this is the day (clink, clank), which the Lord has made (clink, clank), which the Lord has made (clink, clank).'"* He concluded by making this convicting statement: *"Why is it that so many Christians sing only once a week? Why only once? If it is right to sing, sing every day. If it is wrong to sing, don't sing on Sunday."*[2]

Communist captors robbed this preacher and his friends of life's freedoms and dignity. However, these devout Christians focused on what remained and could not be taken away — their joy in the Lord. Friend, if it is good to sing to the Lord when we have everything, then it is certainly good to sing to Him when we have lost it all too!

When we are tempted to give way to discouragement, when we lose our perspective of God, when our faith is weakened from toils and trials, music is a tool that can realign our hearts and minds upon the Lord. Persistently in Scripture, rejoicing and singing are bound together. You can't study one of those two biblical themes without encountering the other. In God's perfect design and understanding of our human nature, He bound the two together for his people. As you study Scripture on this point, you'll notice that sometimes singing brings forth joy and sometimes joy gives birth to singing. Here are a few other passages that show us this:

Psalm 5:11 — *"But let all those that put their trust in thee rejoice: let them ever shout for joy, because thou defendest them: let them also that love thy name be joyful in thee."*

Psalm 9:1-2 — *"I will praise thee, O Lord, with my whole heart; I will shew forth all thy marvellous works. I will be glad and rejoice in thee: I will sing praise to thy name, O thou most High."*

Psalm 68:3-4 — *"But let the righteous be glad; let them rejoice before God: yea, let them exceedingly rejoice. Sing unto God, sing praises to his name: extol him that rideth upon the heavens by his name*

Jah, and rejoice before him."

Psalm 71:22-23 — *"I will also praise thee with the psaltery, even thy truth, O my God: unto thee will I sing with the harp, O thou Holy One of Israel. My lips shall greatly rejoice when I sing unto thee; and my soul, which thou hast redeemed."*

Zephaniah 3:14 — *"Sing, ...be glad and rejoice with all the heart,..."*

As Paul wrote the book of Philippians, his heart was overflowing. He rejoiced amid the uncertain and the unsavory, because his Redeemer lived and he knew that he belonged to the risen Christ who had his best interests in mind. Paul's joy was not anchored in circumstances but in his Saviour, who would never disappoint him or lead him astray.

God lovingly reminds us in I Peter 4:12-13, *"Beloved, think it not strange concerning the fiery trial which is to try you, as though some strange thing happened unto you: But rejoice, inasmuch as ye are partakers of Christ's sufferings; that, when his glory shall be revealed, ye may be glad also with exceeding joy."* God always has a purpose. God always has a plan. There is nothing too sudden that catches God by surprise. *"This is the day which the LORD hath made; we will rejoice and be glad in it"* (Psalm 118:24).

There is nothing too hard that God cannot handle. *"Ah Lord God! behold, thou hast made the heaven and the earth by thy great power and stretched out arm, and there is nothing too hard for thee: Then came the word of the Lord unto Jeremiah, saying, Behold, I am the Lord, the God of all flesh: is there any thing too hard for me?"* (Jeremiah 32:17 & 26-27).

There is no one too broken that God cannot mend, strengthen, and heal. *"To appoint unto them that mourn in Zion, to give unto them beauty for ashes, the oil of joy for mourning, the garment of praise for the spirit of heaviness; that they might be called trees of righteousness, the planting of the Lord, that he might be glorified"* (Isaiah 61:3).

There is no trial too trivial to God that He will not interpose Himself within if He is invited to help. *"Come unto me, all ye that labour and are heavy laden, and I will give you rest"* (Matthew 11:28). *"Casting all your care upon him; for he careth for you"* (I Peter 5:7). There is no storm that God can't carry you through; no bridge that God can't help you cross; and no battle that God can't help you win. Trust God, and never give up!!

If it is a big deal to you, then it is a big deal to Him. The Bible says that Jesus is our interceding High Priest who is *"touched with the feeling of our infirmities"* (Hebrews 4:15). He knows what we are facing. He knows how we are feeling. He knows what we are suffering through. And He knows how we are hurting. The deepest level of worship is praising God in spite of the pain, thanking God during the trials, trusting Him when we're tempted to lose hope, and loving Him when He seems so distant and far away. In our lowest valley, God is our Hope! In our darkest hour, God is our Light! In our weakest point, God is our Strength! In our saddest moment, God is our Comforter. *"Let us therefore come boldly unto the throne of grace, that we may obtain mercy, and find grace to help in time of need"* (Hebrews 4:16).

We have very real needs. But, we have a very real God that is capable of handling those needs... REJOICE! Make a joyful noise! Sing! Just because our lives might be falling apart around us, it does not mean that our faith and our hearts have to fall apart. Why? Because we draw our source of joy, strength, comfort, and victory from the Lord. *"Although the fig tree shall not blossom, neither shall fruit be in the vines; the labour of the olive shall fail, and the fields shall yield no meat; the flock shall be cut off from the fold, and there shall be no herd in the stalls: Yet I will rejoice in the Lord, I will joy in the God of my salvation. The Lord God is my strength, and he will make my feet like hinds' feet, and he will make me to walk upon mine high places. To the chief singer on my stringed instruments"* (Habakkuk 3:17-19).

Jesus is so wonderful — so wonderful that all our challenges, disappointments, and weaknesses pale into insignificance when our hearts and minds dwell on Him. So wonderful that our hearts should leap for joy at just the thought of Him and His goodness! Is this escapism? Are we avoiding our problems by focusing on Jesus when we are disappointed, rather than focusing on the problem itself? No! We are preparing ourselves to face the problems with the right attitude. Colossians 3:15-16 says, *"And let the peace of God rule in your hearts, to the which also ye are called in one body; and be ye thankful. Let the word of Christ dwell in you richly in all wisdom; teaching and admonishing one another in psalms and hymns and spiritual songs, singing with grace in your hearts to the Lord."*

If we don't do this and the peace of God through Christ does not rule in our hearts, we will act and respond in ungodly ways. We can panic, resulting in foolish reactions. We can compromise, resulting in disobedient reactions. We can get too discouraged, resulting in timid reactions. We can become bitter, resulting in ungracious and hurtful reactions. We can be without forgiveness, resulting in a block to experiencing God's love. We can let problems overwhelm us, resulting in gloomy, joyless attitudes. But if we continue to reflect upon Who He is and rejoice in all that He has done through singing (Colossians 3:16), it will inspire us and empower us to go forward with Him according to His will.

Please don't forget that *Jesus is wonderful.* He is bigger than all the challenges we face. He is right there with us, helping us along and giving us His sufficient grace in the time of need. So, may we remember to stop often from our feverish activity to worship the Lord Jesus Christ and praise Him for the salvation He has given us and all His marvelous blessings.

Wonderful grace of Jesus, Greater than all my sin;
How shall my tongue describe it,
Where shall its praise begin?
Taking away my burden, Setting my spirit free;
For the wonderful grace of Jesus reaches me!

Wonderful the matchless grace of Jesus,
Deeper than the mighty rolling sea;
Higher than the mountain, sparkling like a fountain,
All-sufficient grace for even me!
Broader than the scope of my transgressions,
Greater far than all my sin and shame;
Oh, magnify the precious Name of Jesus,
Praise His Name!

Oh, that we would never move away from a life of reflecting and rejoicing in the love, mercy, goodness, and person of Jesus!

It would be fitting to conclude with the lyrics of "Rejoice in the Lord" written by our dear friend, Ron Hamilton. He and his family have faced much in their lives (The Hamilton's are some of our dearest friends), yet they've always had a genuine smile and a godly song. God has used this song to be an encouragement to a countless host of people!

God never moves without purpose or plan,
When trying His servant and molding a man.
Give thanks to the Lord, though your testing seems long;
In darkness, He giveth a song.

O rejoice in the Lord, He makes no mistake.
He knoweth the end of each path that I take,
For when I am tried and purified,
I shall come forth as gold.

MUSIC AIDS IN <u>EDIFYING ONE ANOTHER</u> WITH GOD'S WORD.

The word "edifying" refers to helping, strengthening, and encouraging another. Colossians 3:16 urges us to *"Let the word of Christ dwell in you richly in all wisdom; teaching and admonishing one another in psalms and hymns and spiritual songs, singing with grace in your hearts to the Lord."* In Ephesians 5:18-20, God commands, *"And be not drunk with wine, wherein is excess; but be filled with the Spirit; Speaking to yourselves in psalms and hymns and spiritual songs, singing and making melody in your heart to the Lord; Giving thanks always for all things unto God and the Father in the name of our Lord Jesus Christ;"*

God places a great emphasis upon each of us being *"filled with the Spirit"* so that our music may edify others. The Spirit of truth in us will draw fellow believers closer to Jesus (John 12:32; John 15:26). Without the Spirit's empowering, our music will otherwise become empty, yielding no fruit of *"love, joy, peace, longsuffering, gentleness, goodness, faith, meekness,* [or] *temperance"* as discussed in Galatians 5:22-23.

As in any other area of instruction, exhortation, or correction, our music must be the result of the outpouring of the Spirit's work in our lives from God's Word. If you simply sing because it is expected of you at a particular time in the church service or mechanically sing the special because that's what you are obligated to do, you are merely a robot spitting out information that lacks any of the edifying power which God writes of in Ephesians. Sing to those around you, and in your own heart, with the conscious goal of being the Spirit's mouthpiece through your music.

Twice, God instructs us that our edifying and encouraging music should be that of *"psalms and hymns and spiritual songs."* What did the Lord mean by these?

The book of Psalms is the collection of songs written under the inspiration of the Holy Ghost (see Mark 12:36 and II Peter 1:21) by ancient Jewish leaders such as David, Moses, and Solomon. By God's direction, this divine music became a part of the Bible and was used in personal and congregational singing and worship. The word *"psalm"* means *"song of praise."* Most of the Psalms are directed to the Lord, glorifying and magnifying His might and majesty. Several of them are also faith-filled pleas for God's help. Even when the psalmist cries out his questions and concerns to the Lord, he usually ends with a call to praise God in spite of everything (for example, see Psalm 42:11; Psalm 43:5; Psalm 71:13-14). The psalms are as relevant to our lives as though they were written yesterday. Many people find great comfort in reading and praying through them when they have difficulty finding adequate words to express their hearts to God. We can encourage ourselves and also challenge and extend comfort to those around us by sharing these Bible songs. When the Bible used "psalms" in Colossians 3:16 and Ephesians 5:19, God is encouraging us to specifically sing the Scriptures unto Him. There are a countless number of choruses that contain one or two Bible verses and even entire psalms that have been put to music for individuals and congregations to enjoy singing. This is a healthy and Biblical thing that God wants us to engage in!

A *"hymn"* is a song that gives praise, honor, or thanksgiving to God. Unlike psalms, hymns are not written by divine inspiration of the Holy Spirit and are not considered a part of the Bible. However, it is in reference to songs from our heritage. They often incorporate portions of Scripture and are filled with rich doctrinal truth. Hymns are often metrical poems arranged to be sung corporately. Even in Jesus' day, hymns were part of Biblical worship and music. After the Last Supper, Jesus and His disciples sang a hymn (Matthew 26:30).

The term *"spiritual songs"* is more general. As Christians, we are to express our faith through our music. These songs might not be directed specifically toward God, but they encourage the body of Christ and prompt others toward love and good works. A spiritual song lends itself to a number of things — it might express the joy and need of salvation, revel in the grace of Christ, promote faithfulness, or exalt the greatness and power of God. In short, a spiritual song can communicate a wide variety of sacred themes. "Spiritual songs" also refers to current, doctrinally-correct, Scripturally-accurate, Spirit-filled, non-worldly-sounding songs that encourage and edify. We have been blessed in the 21st century to have many talented composers that have given us a multitude of this kind of music. There is certainly a great need for more godly music in our modern day. God encourages us to engage in this kind of music as individuals and congregations. There is nothing wrong with singing a current song that exalts Almighty God!

MUSIC IS A <u>TOOL</u> THAT CAN ASSIST <u>IN EVANGELIZING</u> THE LOST.

Psalm 40:3 says, *"And he hath put a new song in my mouth, even praise unto our God: many shall see it, and fear, and shall trust in the Lord."* What a thought, that an unbeliever could hear our singing, listen to the Bible truth all throughout the lyrics, catch a glimpse of our born-again testimony, and literally turn from sin and trust in God because of it!

One such example is the enthusiastic soulwinner that caught the attention of R. A. Torrey while Torrey was conducting evangelistic meetings in Ireland in the late 1800's. Torrey fondly related, *"He was constantly bringing drunkards to the front and dealing with them. The story of his [the soulwinner's] conversion was exceedingly interesting. At that time, he was a prisoner in a cell in Belfast. The window of his cell was open. Mr. Ira Sankey [D. L. Moody's song leader] was singing 'Hold the Fort' in another building. The words floated across through the open window into his cell and went home to his heart. There in his cell he accepted Christ under the influence of the hymn, [though] he never saw Mr. Sankey in his life."*[3]

The theme of salvation should be a preeminent one in our music, for one of the purposes of music, as we saw, is to bring the lost to Christ. The redeemed life of a believer is a night and day difference from the shackled life of a lost person. If our music sounds just like theirs, what will show them that they're missing something, draw them in lovingkindness to Jesus, and attract them to God's message of salvation?

After Fanny Crosby wrote the song *"Pass Me Not, O Gentle Saviour,"* it was widely used as a hymn of invitation in revival meetings. A young sailor gave testimony of how he was working on a vessel anchored in a canal while a group of Christians held services in a nearby building called the Mariner's Chapel. They began to sing, *"Pass Me Not, O Gentle Saviour."*

"The words floated out over the water," the man later related, *"And from the tug where I was working I could hear them plainly enough. When they were just going to sing those lines, 'While on others Thou art calling, do not pass me by' a great fear came over me. I thought, 'Oh, if the Lord were to pass me by, how terrible it would be!' Then and there, on the tug, I cried out: 'O Lord, do not pass me by!' And,"* he concluded with a bright smile, *"He didn't pass me by. I am saved."* What a joy that our music could be an instrument that God can use for a lost person to get saved![4]

Ira Sankey tells the story: *"We were holding a prayer-meeting in a lodging house, when a young man came into the meeting in a fun-seeking manner. We sang, prayed, and read out of God's Word, and then the young man asked if we would sing a hymn for him. He chose 'I've Found a Friend.' When we had sung one verse he began to shed tears, and I am glad to say that he gave his heart to God through the singing of that beautiful hymn. The next morning he left the place, but before leaving he wrote me a letter, of which I give these extracts — 'I asked you to sing that hymn, because it was the favorite of my sister, who is waiting for me at the gates of Heaven. I have now promised to meet her there. Please try to always think of me when you sing that hymn!'"*[5]

Music is powerful. It has a powerful impact for either good or evil. We cannot underestimate its potential and its potency! The music that floods into our homes and our ears can be detrimental if it's not pleasing to God. On the flip side, it has equal power to be enriching and uplifting if it's the right kind of music. Throughout everything we do, our lives should be consumed with a quest for purity and godliness. It should be a Spirit-filled and Spirit-led journey. As a result of this, it should leave no room for carnal choices or worldly influences. Our search for Christ-honoring music is vitally important!

CHAPTER II:

THE IMPORTANCE OF MUSIC

As we have studied already, music was designed by God and was introduced to His people as a form of worship and praise and a way to teach spiritual truth from one generation to the next. Music is very important to the Lord. All through the Bible, we can find references to music and singing. At least 500 verses in the Bible directly refer to music and other words associated with it. In the book of Psalms, 55 chapters are written to and for the use of the "chief musician." Well over 2,000 verses compose all of the songs recorded in God's Word. Music is alluded to more in Scripture than even the subjects of Heaven or Hell. We are in no wise saying that it is more important than Eternity, but it does bring to our attention the fact that it is not a small matter or trivial thing to God. This great amount of Scripture devoted to music reveals how important it is to the Lord and how imperative it should be to us as believers.

There are what could be called doctrines of "greater priority" in Scripture — such as salvation by grace through faith, the deity and shed blood of Christ, and other fundamentals of the faith and Bible doctrines. Some will suggest that this book is "majoring on the minors" since music is not considered a doctrine of "greater priority." However, what is in the Bible, is Bible. Doctrine is doctrine. Truth is truth. If it is within the pages of God's Word, it *is* important and needed; it *does* matter!

With as many references to music as there are in the Bible, it proves that *music is not a peripheral issue;* it is a sacred and serious thing to the Lord. Every word and every part of the Bible has come directly from His mouth through His chosen penmen. Anything that God writes in His Word is absolutely crucial and of significance.

II Timothy 3:16 shares that *"All scripture is given by inspiration of God,..."* In other words, all Scripture is God-breathed. Or, more effectively stated: all Scripture is given by the breath of God. God in His sovereignty has breathed out every single word that He wanted written down. Over a period of 1500 years, He used forty specially chosen and prepared godly men as instruments, and He breathed *through* them His words that He wanted penned for mankind. *"For the prophecy came not in old time by the will of man: but holy men of God spake as they were moved by the Holy Ghost"* (II Peter 1:21).

We should be responsible to study what the Lord has written about music — and how other Biblical principles concerning holiness, wisdom, separation, and righteousness should also influence our musical decisions — and then implement these truths into our lives. He has carefully given us these numerous principles so we can glean from them, accurately gain godly discernment, and live solely according to what He teaches within His Word. II Timothy 2:15 reminds us, *"Study to shew thyself approved unto God, a workman that needeth not to be ashamed, rightly dividing the word of truth."*

God desires for His children to be students of His Word. It is essential for spiritual growth!

Let's participate in *"rightly dividing"* by taking a closer look at Psalm 40:3 from the previous chapter: *"And he hath put a new song in my mouth, even praise unto our God: many shall see it, and fear, and shall trust in the LORD."* When Christ saved us, we were given a *"new song"* — and not just a song, but a reason to sing!

Now pondering this in further detail, what should our new song sound like? Where should it come from? Who should it be about? Consider the breakdown of this verse and what the Lord is striving to teach us.

OUR SONG SHOULD BE <u>DERIVED</u> <u>FROM</u> GOD.

The verse says, *"And <u>He</u> hath put a new song in my mouth."* Is the source of our music godly? Is it Scripturally-based? Or are we getting our music from carnal places and secular people? The music that we sing and the tunes that we hum or whistle should be godly songs that cause our hearts and minds to reflect upon the King of kings. The Bible frequently mentions: *"The Lord is my strength and song, and he is become my salvation:"* (Exodus 15:2). Again in Psalm 28:7, *"The Lord is my strength and my shield; my heart trusted in him, and I am helped: therefore my heart greatly rejoiceth; and with my song will I praise him."*

In the midnight hour, the Psalmist rejoiced: *"Yet the Lord will command his lovingkindness in the daytime, and in the night his song shall be with me, and my prayer unto the God of my life"* (Psalm 42:8). The Bible declares in Psalm 118:14-15, *"The Lord is my strength and song, and is become my salvation. The voice of rejoicing and salvation is in the tabernacles of the righteous."* The song of genuine worship and praise will resonate from those who are walking with God and living like Christ.

OUR SONG SHOULD BE <u>DISTINCT</u> FROM THE WORLD.

The verse says, *"a <u>new</u> song in my mouth"*. We will study this more in a later chapter, but let us begin to meditate upon this truth. If an unsaved person walked by your car as you played music with your windows down, would they notice anything different about it, or (not hearing the words but just the music) would they think it no different from their own?

God desires His people — *"khristeeanos,"* meaning *followers of Christ* — to be transformed into the image of His Son, rather than being conformed to this world. Romans 12:1-2 exhorts, *"I beseech you therefore, brethren, by the mercies of God, that ye present your bodies a living sacrifice, holy, acceptable unto God, which is your reasonable service. And **be not conformed to this world**: but **be ye transformed** by the renewing of your mind, that ye may prove what is that good, and acceptable, and perfect, will of God."*

God established His church to be an *"ekklesia"* — a *called out* assembly. If we are to be called out, separate, different from the world, than it stands to reason that our music should be as well. It should have a certain sound that is different from the world's sound. It should be played and sung in the clarity of Biblical truth, cultivated by the holiness of Christ. Yes, it should be distinct!

Furthermore, our music should reflect themes such as redemption (Exodus 15:1), the joy of sins forgiven, (Psalm 32:1-7), consecration (II Chronicles 5:13-14), our future union with Christ (Song of Solomon), triumph through adversity and hardship (Acts

16:23-35), fellowship with God (Colossians 3:16), the Glories of Heaven (Isaiah 51:11), and the attributes of God (Revelation 5:9-13).

We are born again! We are now new in Christ (II Corinthians 5:17), and so should our song! It is to be different, and we should be burdened to share it with this lost world. Isaiah 42:10-12 encourages us, *"Sing unto the LORD a new song, and his praise* [specifically means "a song of praise or hymn of thanksgiving"] *from the end of the earth, ye that go down to the sea, and all that is therein; the isles, and the inhabitants thereof. Let the wilderness and the cities thereof lift up their voice, the villages that Kedar doth inhabit: let the inhabitants of the rock sing, let them shout from the top of the mountains. Let them give glory unto the LORD, and declare his praise in the islands."*

OUR SONG SHOULD BE DIRECTED TOWARD GOD.

The verse says, *"even praise unto our God."* Music should communicate and express a sense of awe and wonder toward the person, power, and promises of God; it should lead our thoughts toward the Lord rather than toward ourselves.

Does your music focus on praising God and bringing glory to Him, or is it more focused on you and making you feel good when you listen to it? The Bible specifies in I Corinthians 10:31, *"Whether therefore ye eat, or drink, or whatsoever ye do, do all to the glory of God."* Furthermore, the Psalmist was overwhelmed and exclaimed: *"I will sing unto the Lord as long as I live: I will sing praise to my God while I have my being"* (Psalm 104:33).

Triumphantly, Isaiah was inspired by the Holy Ghost of God to pen these words: *"Behold, God is my salvation; I will trust, and not be afraid: for the Lord Jehovah is my strength and my song; he also is become my salvation. Therefore with joy shall ye draw water out of the wells of salvation. And in that day shall ye say, Praise the Lord, call upon his name, declare his doings among the people, make mention that his name is exalted. Sing unto the Lord; for he hath done excellent things: this is known in all the earth. Cry out and shout* [sing fervently and authentically], *thou inhabitant of Zion: for great is the Holy One of Israel in the midst of thee"* (Isaiah 12:2-6).

Consider the following encouraging exhortations of Scripture to exalt Almighty God (many others can be found in *"A Bible Concordance of Music"* at the end of this book):

Psalm 9:11 — *"**Sing praises to the Lord**, which dwelleth in Zion: declare among the people his doings."*

Psalm 13:6 — *"I will **sing unto the Lord**, because he hath dealt bountifully with me."*

Psalm 27:6 — *"And now shall mine head be lifted up above mine enemies round about me: therefore will I offer in his tabernacle sacrifices of joy; I will **sing**, yea, I will **sing praises unto the Lord**."*

Psalm 30:4 — *"**Sing unto the Lord**, O ye saints of his, and give thanks at the remembrance of his holiness."*

Psalm 30:12 — *"To the end that my glory may **sing praise to thee**, and not be silent. O Lord my God, I will give thanks unto thee for ever."*

Psalm 33:2-3 — *"**Praise the Lord** with harp: **sing unto him** with the psaltery and an instrument of ten strings. **Sing unto him** a new song; play skilfully with a loud noise."*

Psalm 47:5-7 — *"God is gone up with a shout, the Lord with the sound of a trumpet. **Sing praises to God**, sing praises: **sing praises unto our King**, sing praises. For God is the King of all the earth: sing ye praises with understanding."*

Psalm 98:1-6 — *"O **sing unto the Lord a new song;** for he hath done marvellous things: his right hand, and his holy arm, hath gotten him the victory. The Lord hath made known his salvation: his righteousness hath he openly shewed in the sight of the heathen. ...Make **a joyful noise unto the Lord**, all the earth: make a loud noise, and rejoice, and sing praise. **Sing unto the Lord** with the harp; with the harp, and the voice of a psalm. With trumpets and sound of cornet **make a joyful noise before the Lord, the King.**"*

When you sing (whether it is a congregational song, a church special, or as you go about your day), is it for yourself, for others, or for Jesus? May we thoroughly and genuinely be overwhelmed with God — Who He is in all His might and majesty — and seek to magnify Him and Him alone with the song we skillfully play with our hands or humbly sing from our hearts and lips. He is WORTHY of our praise! We encourage you to specifically sing songs that are directed solely toward Almighty God.

I thank you, Lord, for all You've done,
I don't deserve Your love;
When I was lost, You saw my need,
And left Your home above.

I love you, Lord, I love you, Lord,
Because of Calvary;
I love you, Lord, I love you, Lord,
You're everything to me!

OUR SONG SHOULD BE <u>PUBLICALLY</u> DISPLAYED, DESIGNED TO <u>ATTRACT</u> <u>OTHERS</u> TO CHRIST.

The verse concludes by stating, *"...many shall <u>see</u> it and <u>fear</u>, and shall <u>trust</u> in the Lord."* Is your heart overflowing from the song Jesus placed within? Do you find yourself humming, whistling, or softly singing *"psalms, hymns, and spiritual songs"* as you go about your day, working on the job, shopping for groceries, or running your errands? We are not speaking of being obnoxious or loud, so as to be a nuisance or a disturbance, but we are recommending that just as people might mutter to themselves as they concentrate on whatever it is they are doing, our mutterings could be music. *"O come, let us sing unto the Lord: let us make a joyful noise to the rock of our salvation"* (Psalm 95:1). You never know how a familiar measure of *"Amazing Grace"* might affect or impact someone around you!

The Lord wants His music to be with an authority and majesty that commands attention! Listen to the volume that is created when God asked for us to *"praise Him upon the loud cymbals: praise Him upon the high sounding cymbals"* (Psalm 150:5). When God uses this word *"loud"*, it is obviously not with the intent for the volume to be at harmful levels — He is talking about our music being clearly heard. We certainly have a message that needs to be heard! The word *"loud"* is the Hebrew word *"shema"*, which also means *"announcement, fame, and tidings; intended to be clearly heard."* This indicates it is a sound that should be heard from a long distance away. Our music should be something noticeable — noticeable as something different, something joyous, something holy, something exciting, and something that belongs to God.

The people in our lives around us need to know that Jesus is the Answer! Our songs and music should be a witness to them. In Psalm 138:1-5, David determined, *"I will hope continually, and will yet <u>praise</u> [singing and worshipping] thee more and more. <u>My</u> <u>mouth</u> <u>shall</u> <u>shew</u> <u>forth</u> thy righteousness and thy salvation all the day; for I know not the numbers thereof. I will go in the strength of the Lord God: I will make mention of thy righteousness, even of thine only."*

Do you unashamedly play your wholesome Christian music, even when the unsaved are around? Or do you turn it down or completely off? Are you embarrassed to play Christian music in any scenario? At work, do your co-workers and those around you even know that you are born again? Do you enjoy, endorse, and listen to the world's style of inappropriate music (whether it's "Christian" or secular) with them around? (We understand that many times believers are obligated to work in an environment where they have no control over the music. If this is your situation, we pray that God will grant you the strength, grace, and opportunity to be a shining testimony for Christ where He has placed you.) What kind of music do you listen to with your friends?

If a Christian takes the initiative to play or takes pleasure in the wrong kind of music, it will be a hindrance in his testimony for the Lord. Of course, the lost will mentally note that there is no difference between our music and theirs. May this never be the case! *"For their rock is not as our Rock, even our enemies themselves being judges"* (Deuteronomy 32:31). Even the world knows that Christians are to be different. God wants us to be different. God wants our music to be different!

Psalm 92:1-3 tells us that it is wholesome and spiritually beneficial to be filled with public song: *"It is <u>a good thing</u> to give thanks unto the Lord, and to sing praises unto thy name, O most High: <u>To shew forth</u> thy lovingkindness in the morning, and thy faithfulness every night, Upon an instrument of ten strings, and upon the psaltery; upon the harp with a solemn sound."* Psalm 66:8 encourages, *"O bless our God, ye people, and make the voice of his praise to be heard."*

In Psalm 96:1-9, we are challenged: *"O sing unto the Lord a new song: sing unto the Lord, all the earth. Sing unto the Lord, bless his name; shew forth his salvation from day to day. Declare his glory among the heathen, his wonders among all people. For the Lord is great, and greatly to be praised: he is to be feared above all gods. For all the gods of the nations are idols: but the Lord made the heavens. Honour and majesty are before him: strength and beauty are in his sanctuary. Give unto the Lord, O ye kindreds of the people, give unto the Lord glory and strength. Give unto the Lord the glory due unto his name: bring an offering, and come into his courts. O worship the Lord in the beauty of holiness: fear before him, all the earth."*

On April 10, 1912, the famed *Titanic* sped toward New York. No one knew it would be the *Titanic*'s only journey. When the huge ship with its engines going at full throttle hit an iceberg around midnight four days later, it ripped a large, gaping hole in the side of its hull. The massive liner slowly began to sink beneath the waves for two and a half hours.

Then in an instant it was gone. More than 1,500 people died in that watery grave.

When people realized the ship was truly sinking, panic ensued. The string quartet of the Titanic, lead by their bandmaster Wallace Hartley, immediately played social music on the deck to keep the crowds calm. Eyewitnesses testify that amidst the noise of the fray, Baptist pastor Robert Bateman requested the instrumentalists begin to play *"Nearer, My God, to Thee."*

Wallace Hartley was a devout 33-year-old Christian man, and this was his favorite hymn. When he heard the suggestion of this beloved song, his mind might have instantly gone home and visualized his loving father, Mr. Albion Hartley, who served as the faithful choir director at their local church in Colne, England.

One of Hartley's friends told the *British Weekly* after the tragedy: *"It was the custom of the Bethel church choir leader to choose the hymn after prayer, and Mr. Albion Hartley often selected 'Nearer, My God, to Thee.' The hymn was also a great favorite with his son, the bandmaster of the Titanic, for a cousin mentioned that he would often be kept waiting for Wallace to go and play cricket because he was practicing 'Nearer, My God, to Thee' in variations on the violin."*[6]

On the deck of the Titanic with panicked people thronging about, Hartley gave the order for his men to play with him *"Nearer, My God, to Thee."*

Ellwand Moody, Hartley's friend and fellow musician, told the *Leeds Mercury* (a British newspaper) in April 1912 shortly after the disaster: *"I remember one day I asked him what he would do if he were ever on a sinking ship and he replied, 'I don't think I would do better than play 'Oh God Our Help in Ages Past' or 'Nearer, My God, to Thee.'"*[7]

New York pediatric doctor Alice Leeder, who left on lifeboat 8 at 1:15am, wrote in a letter the next day after she was rescued, *"I shall never forget the sight of that beautiful boat as she went down, the orchestra playing to the last, the lights burning until they were extinguished by the waves. It sounds so unreal, like a scene on a stage."*[8]

One survivor recalled: *"The band played marching from deck to deck,... They began to render hymn tunes and continued to do so to the last. While playing 'Nearer, My God, to Thee' the water was washing over their feet."*[9] Another stated that around 2:05am as they set off on collapsible lifeboat D (one of the last to leave), *"The musicians were up to their knees in water when last I saw them."*[10]

Thomas Patrick "Paddy" Dillon, a coal trimmer on board, was one of the last to leave the ship. When interviewed by a local newspaper in Plymouth, England, he explained that by this time the deck of the Titanic was angled downward at least sixty degrees. After a second explosion, the bow suddenly *"seemed to bob up and then break clean off like a piece of carrot."*[11] The musicians who had been playing with Hartley lost their balance and slid off the deck, along with the ship's captain and others. *"There was one musician left,"* he said with broken voice. *"He was the violinist and was playing the hymn 'Nearer, My God, to Thee.' The notes of this music were the last thing I heard before I went off the deck and felt myself going headlong into the icy water with the engines and machinery buzzing in my ears."*[12]

Hartley must have interwoven a part of his body around some of the sturdy workings on deck to keep himself from collapsing or falling downward. A reporter from the *Witney Gazette*, who interviewed over 100 of the survivors, concluded: *"After his fellow musicians had been washed away* the violinist continued playing 'Nearer, My God, to Thee' until he went under with the ship."[13] His dying testimony would be that of pointing men to Jesus.

Oh! How stirring! The final witness for Christ that Wallace Hartley gave moves us to tears! Would this be our testimony? Are we attracting others to Jesus through our music? Are we ashamed to publicly share our song?

The cross of Christ becomes useless if lips remain silent of the Gospel message or sealed from godly music. May we never cease to "...mention the lovingkindnesses of the LORD, and the praises of the LORD, according to all that the LORD hath bestowed on us, and the great goodness...which he hath bestowed on them according to his mercies, and according to the multitude of his lovingkindnesses" (Isaiah 63:7). We have the message of hope, love, peace, and eternity! We have the Answer! We have the Good News that will save men's souls. It is something worth sharing. It is something worth singing!

CHAPTER III

THE EFFECTS OF MUSIC

A. W. Tozer, an influential preacher and author of yesteryear, wrote in his book *Born After Midnight* in 1959: *"There is about music a subtle charm that no normal person can resist. It works to condition the mind and prepare it for the reception of ideas, moral and immoral, which in turn prepare the will to act either in righteousness or in sin. The notion that music and song are merely for amusements and that their effects can be laughed off is a deadly error. Actually, they exercise a powerful creative influence over the human soul. And their permanent effects will be apparent in our growth in grace or in evil."*[14]

Psalm 40:3, amidst so many other verses in Scripture that could be considered, teaches us that **it is very important to have the right kind of music, the right kind of song, in your life.** Some ask and argue: *"But is music really good or bad?"* Many secular artists and even contemporary Christian groups believe music is amoral, or neutral. In a sense, they are right. A musical note *by itself* is amoral, just as a letter of the alphabet by itself would be amoral. However, as we look at the world around us, we see that indeed, music is its own language.

When musical notes are combined, just as when letters are combined to form words and sentences, a message is produced, communicating a thought or emotion which influences the morality of the one who hears it. Therefore, music is **most definitely** a moral issue.

Henry Wadsworth Longfellow is credited with saying, *"Music is the universal language of mankind."* It is certainly this, going beyond verbal barriers and influencing people — regardless of what culture they're from, what age they may be, or what dialect they actually speak. Because it is a form of language, music can communicate a right or wrong message, just like verbal language can.

God's Word supports this belief through the account described in I Samuel 16 about David's music ministry and its effect on King Saul. Whenever Saul was bothered and restless, David's instrumental playing made Saul feel better and caused the evil spirit that was troubling him to depart (I Samuel 16:23). A "neutral" force could not have done this. David's skillful combination of all the notes that he played unto the Lord for His glory worked as a force of good to drive away the evil spirit and caused Saul's countenance to become happier. This Biblical account indicates that music, apart from lyrics, is not neutral. Music is moral. It definitely is not void of purpose. We would do well to recognize that musical styles are employed to solicit a specific response. Words do not negate the *character* of what is being suggested in the music.

Titus 2:1 instructs: *"But speak thou the things which become sound doctrine:"* This certainly applies when speaking through music. Again, Ephesians 5:19 teaches us that we are to be *"Speaking to yourselves in psalms and hymns and spiritual songs, singing and making melody in your heart to the Lord."*

Music is a powerful tool and a persuasive teacher. Andrew Fletcher (1653-1716), an influential statesman of Scotland, once made the statement, *"I knew a very wise man [who] believed if a man were permitted to make all the ballads he need not care who should make the laws of a nation, and we find that most of the ancient legislators thought that they could not well reform the manners of any city without the help of a lyric, and sometimes of a dramatic poet."*[15] We believe that he who controls the music will control the nation.

Music has a very strong ability to affect people. Think about how doctors are using "Music Therapy" to treat mental and psychological conditions such as depression and anxiety. Ladies will ask for calming music to help them through childbirth. We're sure you have experienced "mood music" in restaurants before. In fast food restaurants, where they want you to order, eat, and leave quickly, the mood music is fast, loud, and upbeat. In a laid back, romantic atmosphere, the restaurant will play slow, soft, often sensual music, to keep the diners relaxed, eating more food and drinking more and more wine (which means big bucks!).

Think about the background music in movies and TV, as they strive to create a desired feeling within the listener — happy, sad, fearful, etc. Did you know that studies have been conducted which show that unborn children in the womb, animals, and even plants can be affected and stimulated, for good or bad, by various styles of music?

David Merrell, a high school student from Suffolk, Virginia, won top honors in regional and state science fairs for his experiment involving mice, a maze, and music. After establishing a baseline of about 10 minutes for the mice to navigate the maze, David started playing music for these mice 10 hours a day, then put them through the maze three times a week for three weeks. Here are his findings: the control-group mice, which did not listen to any music, were able to cut five minutes off their time; the mice that listened to classical music cut 8.5 minutes off their time; and the mice that listened to hard-rock music took 20 minutes longer to navigate the maze. David said, *"I had to cut my project short because all the hard-rock mice killed each other.... None of the classical mice did that at all."*[16]

Music affects our senses. Scientists tell us that when a person hears music, a majority of the brain lights up. There is not anything right or wrong about this; it merely proves that God made our bodies and minds to respond to music.

In their work *Music and Medicine,* Doctors Dorothy Schullian and Max Schoen understood and shared: *"Music, which does not depend upon the brain to gain entrance into the organism, can still arouse by way of the thalamus — the relay station of all emotions, sensations, and feeling. Once a stimulus has been able to reach the thalamus, the brain is automatically invaded."*[17]

Furthermore, Dr. Schoen wrote, *"Music is made of the stuff which is in and of itself the most powerful stimulant known among the perceptual processes. Music operates on our emotional faculty with greater intensiveness and rapidity than the product of any other act."*[18]

National Public Radio (NPR) reports: *"Science all but confirms that humans are hard-wired to respond to music. Studies also suggest that someday music may even help patients heal from Parkinson's disease or a stroke. In her book The Power of Music, Elena Mannes (film producer and six time*

Emmy award winner) explores how music affects different groups of people and how it could play a role in health care.

"Mannes tracked the human relationship with music over the course of a life span. She tells NPR's Neal Conan that studies show that infants prefer 'consonant intervals, the smooth-sounding ones that sound nice to our Western ears in a chord, as opposed to a jarring combination of notes.'

"In fact, Mannes says the cries of babies just a few weeks old were found to contain some of the basic intervals common to Western music. She also says scientists have found that music stimulates more parts of the brain than any other human function. That's why she sees so much potential in music's power to change the brain and affect the way it works. Mannes says music also has the potential to help people with neurological deficits. 'A stroke patient who has lost verbal function — those verbal functions may be stimulated by music,' she says.

"One technique, known as melodic intonation therapy, uses music to coax portions of the brain into taking over for those that are damaged. In some cases, it can help patients regain their ability to speak. And because of how we associate music with memories, Mannes says such techniques could also be helpful for Alzheimer's patients."[19]

Dr. Jay T. Wright conducted a study on the helpful properties of good music and concluded: *"Research at the Walter Reed Hospital over three years showed that WWII U.S. Army soldiers made outstanding improvements with Music Therapy."*[20]

Musicologist Julius Portnoy shares that not only does music *"change metabolism, affect muscular energy, raise or lower blood pressure, and influence digestion,"* but *"it may be able to do all these things more successfully...than any other stimulants that produce those changes in our bodies."*[21] Wow! Music can be such a powerful tool that we would do well to make sure we are using it according to God's Biblical design.

Steven Halpern (Grammy award nominee and widely considered to be one of the founders of New Age music) wrote about the subtle and effective way music communicates to the mind and body: *"All the cells in our bodies are receptors for sound. Although the ear is still given credit as being the major pathway for aural processing, we have a great deal of evidence that the entire body is indeed sensitive to sound. Since this occurs below the level of the mind, it can occur when the mind is not consciously processing the incoming information. ...Another way of looking at the effect of music on us is that music exerts a plagiaristic effect upon the human nervous system. Now remember, we're not even talking about the lyric content at this point. There are a number, shall we say, of 'pre-tuned' channels in the body that we recognize and identify as pleasurable. Simply put, certain combinations of tones and rhythms bio-entertain the body into these states more effectively than others."*[22]

Music has an effect on your body, your heart, and your mind. It *will* influence you and have an impact on you — *either* suddenly or subtly! Researchers have proven that music can have the same effect on your brain as opioids and endorphins, releasing hormones into your body that block pain and induce feelings of pleasure.

We often feel emotions from our heart, but a big part of our emotional stimulus is communicated through our mind. Specifically now, Dr. Daniel Levitin (a cognitive psychologist from the Laboratory for Music Perception, Cognition and Expertise at McGill University in Montreal, Canada) reveals that music is involved in every region of the brain scientists have mapped so far. (Please reference his book *"This Is Your Brain on Music"* originally published in 2006.) Music has a profound impact on one's mind, oftentimes deeply nestling itself within our long-term memory (hence, why we can recall songs from our childhood or from hearing them just a few times).

Research shows that listening to the music you like releases certain chemicals in the brain such as Dopamine. Dopamine has been nick-named the "feel-good hormone" and is a specific neurotransmitter that helps control the brain's reward and pleasure centers. Furthermore, listening to music *with* someone else can also release Prolactin, a hormone that bonds people together. If you sing in a group or with another person, your body releases Oxytocin, which creates feelings of trust. In the past, this is why the military would encourage regiments to sing together. Oxytocin is secreted by the posterior lobe of the pituitary gland, a pea-sized structure at the base of the brain in the thalamus region. It is also the hormone that causes our bodies to respond to music.

Without considering the lyrics or obviously whether the recording artists claimed to be Christian or secular, Professor Manfred Clynes came to the definite conclusion through his experiments that beyond a shadow of a doubt music is *not* neutral and *affects* the human body, mind, and emotions. (You can read of this extensively in his book *Sentics: The Touch of the Emotions* published in 1978 based on the research he conducted. It's some pretty heavy reading! He also wrote a profound chapter in *Music: Physician for Times to Come* compiled by Don Campbell in 1991. Don Campbell's experience in the field of music in health and medicine is nearly unrivaled by any other professional.)

Professor Clynes was incredibly smart as an engineer and extremely gifted as a leading concert pianist of Australia. In the 1950's, after moving to America, he became close friends with Albert Einstein and repeatedly dined in his home. Clynes played for Einstein on his beautiful Bechstein piano. Einstein loved Clynes' playing of Beethoven and Mozart, calling him *"a blessed artist."*

In the 1960's Dr. Clynes invented the CAT computer (not to be confused with the C/T scan) that measures the brain's responses to particular sensory stimuli. What did he find? Regardless if an individual was male or female or if they came from different ethnic backgrounds from across the world, the tests reached the same conclusion. Professor Clynes' studies support that there are musical tones that can induce different emotions such as love, hate, grief, joy, reverence, anger, and so on.

Music will have such a profound impact upon you, and music apart from the words definitely has an ability to manipulate emotions, both positively and negatively. There is music that produces emotions like fear, sensuality, anger, depression, and lethargy. On the flip side, there is music that produces emotions like joy, calmness, peace, worship, and love. Since people have both good and bad emotions, *music can be either good or bad,* depending on which emotions it generates and stimulates.

It is so very important that we, as Christians, have our "spiritual radar" in working order when it comes to music! Leviticus 10:10 says, *"And that ye may put difference between holy and unholy, and between unclean and clean."* There should be a distinction from the world. We are to be different!

If we are not careful, music can provide a passageway for Satan to make a sneak attack upon almost anyone.

Without even realizing it, the listener's mind can be bent to whatever emotional attitude the Devil wants to incorporate. Willem Van deWall, a pioneer in musical therapy, sums it up in this manner, *"Much of what we call irresistible in music is so because we react on this sensory-motor level of functioning."*[23] He also describes how the nerves transmit music's message to the various parts of the body: *"Sound vibrations acting upon and through the nervous system give shocks in rhythmical sequence to the muscles, which cause them to contract and set our arms and hands, legs and feet in motion. On account of their automatic muscular reaction, many people make some movement when hearing music; for them to remain motionless would require conscious muscular restraint."*[24]

There is definitely a subtle psychological effect of music on the brain and the body, and if the Devil can gain access to this, he is able to wreak much havoc upon Christianity and our youth. Through music, Satan's wiles could bypass the spiritual and Scriptural barricades of intelligent reason and enter the citadel of the mind — the great control center of all human decisions and action. There, our flesh can translate sensual musical beats and impressions into inappropriate physical actions through the telegraphic network of nerves reaching every part of the body. May God help us to *"Walk in the Spirit, and ye shall not fulfill the lust of the flesh"* (Galatians 5:16).

In this context, we believe that it is so vital, as Christian parents, to make sure our children are being fed the right kind of music. Unfortunately, you don't have to teach a child to sin, and dancing or wiggling the body in an inappropriate way comes naturally, especially when they are often exposed to music that promotes that kind of movement. It is spiritually detrimental to your child if you are filling his life with worldly-sounding music that would cause him to respond in an ungodly way.

There is something special that God created in music that helps to implant truths into our minds. Christian children's songs can teach many lessons that kids may not otherwise remember. Some songs that we have enjoyed learning teach lessons like sharing, not grumbling, brushing your teeth, and having a gratitude attitude! *(We thank the Lord for how He has used Patch the Pirate!!)* There are also great songs for kids that tell Bible stories (such as Jonah, David, Daniel, and Noah), cementing the stories and lessons in children's minds and hearts through the power of music. Songs straight from Scripture can aid in memorization of God's Word for both young and old!

Studies have shown that classical music can strengthen and stimulate the brain and enhance learning. Play cheerful background music often in your home to contribute to a calm, peaceful atmosphere conducive to your children's mental development and well-being.

Because music can so powerfully affect the way we think, act, and feel, we dare not trust anything outside of Scripture. God does care about music, and there is a right and wrong style of music to God. Many people use the excuse that *"music is only based upon a matter of taste"* in attempts to justify their personal preferences of worldly, fleshly "Christian" music. Then they set their "standard" of music based on those personal tastes. This is unscriptural. Time to get into the next chapter!

CHAPTER IV

DEVELOPING HEALTHY STANDARDS FOR MUSIC

God plainly declares multiple times in Scripture: *"Be ye holy, for I am holy"* (I Peter 1:16). God's positions have not changed, and they never will. He will not bend with the times and become culturally relevant depending on the generation and the ebb and flow of society. He has given a declaration, a command, a truth: *"You need to come up to where I am."* It is neither acceptable nor fitting to bring God and our worship of Him down to our level based on what we esteem to be appropriate. We instead need to bring ourselves (the creation) up to His level (the Creator). Therefore, *"dearly beloved, let us cleanse ourselves from all filthiness of the flesh and spirit, perfecting holiness in the fear of God."* (II Corinthians 7:1).

Of course, there are a number of different styles in music. Just because a style is different doesn't mean it is wrong. And just because it's different and not your style doesn't mean that it's sin. Right and wrong aren't determined by what we like or don't like, but rather by what the Bible teaches by precept and principle.

Congregations and Christians from around the world do not sound or sing alike; rather, they are diverse because of their geographical locations, background, customs, or heritage. Even in America there are a variety of styles — from piano arrangements to a capella, or from full orchestra to bluegrass with guitar, mandolin, upright bass, and banjo. But even within each individual country or culture, there are musical styles that Christians can spiritually discern as acceptable or unacceptable.

An individual's preference of music is between him and Lord. It is not our place to critique and criticize someone if their preference is different from ours within the Biblical context of the principles God laid forth. God has given each of us individual soul liberty with a free will. To further explain, here is how our doctrinal statement words it: *"Every individual Christian has the liberty to believe as his/her own conscience dictates. While we seek to persuade men to choose the right, a person must not be forced into compliance; every person has been created with a free will. The individual soul is answerable to Almighty God and to Him alone. This precludes giving up that independency to a pope, a priest, a system, an organization, a convention, a fellowship, an association, or any other human being. None of these are given the authority to interpose anything whatsoever between the individual believer and God concerning any matter of faith."* Nevertheless, the Word of God should be our sole authority that bridges these different musical styles together into Christ-honoring music.

Keep in mind that standards are to be based on convictions, and convictions are to be based on principles in God's Word. Truth is not what we say it is. Truth is not even what you or I *think* it is. Truth is not relative with what is popular or believed to be right by the majority of society. As defined in the 1828 Webster's American Dictionary, truth is *"conformity to fact or reality; exact accordance with that which is, or has been, or shall be."* No one knows fact or reality (past, present, or future) better than the Lord! Truth is what the Word of God declares it to be.

No one — ourselves included — should have standards just for the sake of having them. We should be able to always explain why we do what we do. *"But sanctify the Lord God in your hearts: and be ready always to give an answer to every man that asketh you a reason of the hope that is in you with meekness and fear: Having a good conscience; that, whereas they speak evil of you, as of evildoers, they may be ashamed that falsely accuse your good conversation in Christ"* (I Peter 3:15-16).

However, it seems that many young people today who grew up in a Christian home are simply keeping the standards that have been handed down to them without really knowing the purpose behind them. Some are even choosing to keep them in fear of being labeled a traitor. This is very dangerous! If we are not careful, standards will be preached and enforced more than the doctrine and purpose behind them are Biblically explained. You need to know <u>what</u> you believe, but more importantly, you need to know <u>why</u> you believe what you believe.

Others (especially in our age group) have simply dropped many standards altogether because they don't want to be associated with the wrong attitude others in the previous generation had about standards. This is a poor excuse. You are responsible for *you*, as Joshua understood in Joshua 24:14-15, regardless of how others may have abused or misused the Bible! We are thankful for the fundamentalists of generations past that have fought hard to protect Christians from being influenced from the world. We ourselves are conservative, true "old-time religion," independent, fundamental Baptists. Nevertheless, it is undeniable that a wrong attitude in a handful within a few "camps" has left a bad taste with some people. This grieves us and breaks our hearts; the Bible says, *"Let not then your good be evil spoken of:"* (Romans 14:16). Our testimonies for truth should be above reproach.

Unfortunately, we have seen a lot of Christians become critical and cynical about standards, while others have become critical and condescending because of their standards. **Both are wrong.** Understand this: a proud person has a critical spirit, and God will have nothing to do with pride (James 4:6)! This is dangerously running rampant across the country in Christianity today. We believe it is vitally important that this subject is addressed before we go any further.

Someone with a critical attitude is prone to complaining, seeing the glass as "half-empty," being upset over unmet expectations, talking about the negative in others, and being overwhelmingly judgmental against those who do not believe or act as they do. Ultimately, it will hinder a person's walk with God, distract him from fulfilling God's purposes for his life, and quench the Spirit's power from resting upon him. Oh, that we would be careful not to engage in this sinful activity!

A critical spirit is always destructive — not constructive. It is not justified anywhere in God's Word. Rather, the Bible directly speaks against it, encouraging people to look within (II Corinthians 13:5) and not to be quick in casting judgment on everybody else (Matthew 7:1-5).

The Bible puts a premium upon having the right **POSITION** and **DISPOSITION.** II Peter 3:14 says, *"be diligent that ye may be found of him in peace, without spot, and blameless."* God is saying, *"Yes, be sure that you're walking right and talking right, but be careful that your spirit is right."*

Philippians 2:14-15 teaches, *"Do all things without murmurings and disputings: That ye may be blameless and harmless, the sons of God, without rebuke, in the midst of a crooked and perverse nation, among whom ye shine as lights in the world; Holding forth the word of life."*

I Peter 2:11-12 & 15 admonishes, *"Dearly beloved, I beseech you as strangers and pilgrims, abstain from fleshly lusts, which war against the soul; Having your conversation honest among the Gentiles: that, whereas they speak against you as evildoers, they may by your good works, which they shall behold, glorify God.... For so is the will of God, that with well doing ye may put to silence the ignorance of foolish men."* In I Peter 2:16, God admonishes us to not use our position for *malicious intent* but rather (as read in I Peter 2:11-12 & 15) to use it as any opportunity to *magnify Christ.*

Unfortunately, so many today have one or the other, but not both. Some have the right positions but their attitude is critical and condescending. They are mean-spirited to those who do not believe as they do, and they are divisive with a petty nature. Others have the right spirit and want to let the love of Christ inspire every motive, but have several wrong positions. NEITHER are right! BOTH are wrong! **We need to have a Biblical stance AND a Biblical spirit.**

You may have noticed the word *"blameless"* mentioned a few times in the verses that we have recently read. Blameless means to be *"above reproach;"* or, when others want to speak bad about you, they can't. They can't because your actions, your words, your stance, your countenance, and your spirit are all in harmony: they are Christ-like and undeniably Bible-centered.

However, when we do not stand for what is right in the right way (i.e. when we have a wrong spirit and critical tongue), we will do more harm than good. We will hinder and hurt the cause of Christ. Truth will be vilified, and Wrong will be magnified.

It's easy to be critical. But it is a carnal, fleshly, unspiritual, sinful thing to do. When you feel the temptation to say something cutting and condescending, follow Christ's clear instruction to take a close look at your own life first (Matthew 7:1-5). Ask God to forgive you of that sin. Ask Him to help you have the right position and disposition as you begin to talk to the other individual (II Peter 3:14). Let your speech be *"seasoned with salt"* (or have a good taste in their mouth — not bitter) and be with grace (Colossians 4:6). Be careful to make it a private discussion between you and that other person — not a public argument in front of others or on social media. Is your spirit and your conversation critical (either cynical or condescending) when it comes to standards?

Everyone has standards. Every company has a code of conduct. Even Facebook has regulations in place to keep themselves and their users within the guidelines of safety, expectations, and privacy. Why is it that a majority of Christians get so bent out of shape over the topic of separation when separation and holiness are clearly taught in the Bible? *"[C]ome out from among them, and be ye separate, saith the Lord, and touch not the unclean thing; and I will receive you"* (II Corinthians 6:17).

The phrase *"be ye separate"* means *"to set off by boundary."* We should set up boundaries in our lives — not because we are better than other people but because we don't want to allow any contamination or corruption to get into our lives. Boundaries and fences are created to set restrictions, keep out undesirables, protect us from danger, and so on. (We are so quick to notice and be cautious about physical danger but so slow, indifferent, and casual about spiritual danger!) Understand that a "wall-less" or "fence-less" lifestyle is going to produce bondage. Proverbs 25:28 declares, *"He that hath no rule over his own spirit is like a city that is broken down, and without walls."* David testified in Psalm 119:45, *"And I will walk at liberty: for I seek thy precepts."* His liberty was only found through finding and adhering to Bible truth.

Every believer should apply the Bible principles he or she is aware of when forming one's personal standard regarding music. Not everyone is going to "draw the line" between acceptable and unacceptable music at exactly the same place. However, every believer should draw the line as their Biblically informed conscience leads as they follow the Holy Ghost. If we are not careful, we can become guilty of adopting and justifying a worldly standard as a result of having a carnal preference of where we *think* we should draw the line, instead of allowing God with His Word and holiness to be the authority.

As mature believers, we must recognize that not everyone will agree with where we draw the line regarding musical standards. And we may not agree with where they draw their line. But we must allow Christian liberty or freedom (we will discuss this in more detail later in the book) for God's people to draw their line as their Biblically informed and directed conscience dictates. We should always be gracious and give people grace to grow — because we all need it! Be patient toward others whose standards differ from your own. *"The patient in spirit is better than the proud in spirit"* (Ecclesiastics 7:8). *"Now we exhort you, brethren, ...be patient toward all men"* (I Thessalonians 5:14).

Though it may not always be easy to know exactly where to draw the line with Christian music, we truly believe that the best place to the draw the line is as *far* from the world as possible. *"If ye then be risen with Christ, seek those things which are above, where Christ sitteth on the right hand of God. Set your affection on things above, not on things on the earth."* (Colossians 3:1-2).

Of course, standards are not the goal of the Christian life — they aren't proof of spirituality. But, they are crucial in helping us stay true to God's Word and will aid us in remaining spiritual. Spiritually-minded people will have standards, but standards don't make people spiritual. Standards with the right motive will draw us away from carnality and closer to Christ. They will help us grow, free from the entanglements of the world and the flesh (II Corinthians 6:17-7:1). Standards are Biblically-tethered guidelines implemented within our lives that we don't wish to break or cross, in order to keep us right with God concerning what He has laid forth in His Word. We need standards. They help us stay focused upon the Lord and keep our hearts from drifting toward what the flesh wants and what the world wishes to allure us with. They will help us honor God and remain faithful to His principles and precepts.

Our standards should be developed from God's Word because it is the only source — the infallible authority — of absolute Truth in the entire universe. As we study His Word and understand what God says (the principle), the Holy Spirit can convince our hearts (conviction) and then we can make a choice about how we will respond to that conviction. We can ignore the prodding of the Spirit and be living in sin, or we can surrender that area to the Lord and make a decision to live right in that area from now on. Thus, our standard is born. We hope the following psalm will be your prayer: *"Make me to understand the way of thy precepts* [or principles]." (Psalm

119:27). We believe that a maturing love toward the holiness of God will create a desire to put standards farther from the "boundary line" and not right on "the edge."

If you have a teachable spirit and a desire to learn, God WILL teach you something! If God teaches you principles of music based on His Word, and the Holy Spirit convicts your heart to do something about what you've learned, we pray that you won't ignore this prodding. May Psalm 119:69b also be your prayer. It says, *"I will keep thy precepts* [or principles] *with my whole heart."* Our fervent desire is that you will obey God's leading and set standards regarding music if you don't have them in your life already. And if you already have standards regarding godly music, may this book continue to encourage you to stand strong in what you believe, knowing that they are not just someone's opinion or "soap box," but they are truly based on conviction which comes from Biblical principles.

Therefore, let us take God seriously when He declared, *"Stand ye in the ways, and see, and ask for the old paths, where is the good way, and walk therein, and ye shall find rest for your souls"* (Jeremiah 6:16). God's people should discover and stay with the timeless truths of the Bible established by the Ancient of Days! God would have us to adhere to the "old paths" — to remain true to the Word of God regardless of the ever-changing world. Culture should not determine our positions and standards; **God's Word** should.

If we truly believe the Bible to be the ultimate source of authority, then we should feel uncomfortable if we are ignoring part of its teachings while following other parts. We do not have the privilege of picking and choosing what doctrine is — God has already established that in His Word.

We're concerned that there are many King Jehoiakim's

in American churches today. This man in the book of Jeremiah was guilty of cutting the parts of God's Word he didn't like out with a pen knife and disregarding them by throwing them into the fire ("out of sight, out of mind," supposedly). The explosion of modern versions has encouraged people to believe what they want (depending on how their preferred translation reads) and has created a tendency to treat every Bible lightly and to look upon none as the final words of God. This growing number of "Christians" who are modifying their views on the inerrancy of Scripture is completely undercutting the full authority of God's Word in our generation. It has given room for personal judgment to "pick and choose" what should be applied and lived by. It is wrong for us to decide which doctrines and principles set forth in the Bible we are going to follow — we are commanded to continue in them all.

The Word of God is NOT a "phone book"! (Do you remember those?) Something that sits in your miscellaneous drawer, only being pulled out to look up what you need when you need it. It is not a "textbook," in which you simply take note of some things in preparation for a test but then later forget about what you studied. The Bible is not to be a "catalog," where you leaf through it to see what might capture your attention and skip over the things that don't interest you. No! No! God's Word is a comprehensive set of doctrine and instructions: *"All scripture is given by inspiration of God, and is profitable for doctrine, for reproof, for correction, for instruction in righteousness: That the man of God may be perfect, throughly furnished unto all good works"* (II Timothy 3:16-17).

God is looking for a generation to rise up that will continue steadfast and unmovable in His Word. A generation that is not complacent about it, or careless with it, or compromising away from it, or calloused about it. No, but a generation that has the conviction of what we learned to sing as children in Junior Church — *"The B-I-B-L-E. Yes, that's the Book for me! I stand alone on the Word of God; the B-I-B-L-E."*

Our positions and preferences should ALWAYS align with God's principles. Hence, by way of application, what should be my standard of apparel? Of music? Of substance use? Of how to raise my children? Of how my marriage ought to be? Of food consumption? Of beauty? Of entertainment? And so on. Well, let us look it up in the Bible and draw directly from Scriptural principles.

Where are the believers in modern-day Christianity that will resolve and proclaim: *"I have chosen the way of truth!"* Not, *"I have chosen the way of trend."* Are you adhering to the "old paths" of God-honoring music?

Whenever a carpenter or a construction worker is putting up the studs and framing a house, he uses a level. If a board or 2'x4' is crooked, what is wrong and what is right? Is the level inaccurate, and the board correct? No. The level is always right. Always. Adjust the board! God's Word is like that level. This world is crooked, and our lives get bent out of shape as we live in the flesh. We need to straighten our lives and fix them according to Bible truth.

Unfortunately, many rebelliously say as the children of Israel did in the end of Jeremiah 6:16, *"We will not walk therein."* This, my friend, is disastrous. When a Christian who knows what is right strays away from what the Word of God teaches or decides to allow his own opinion to supersede what God has commanded, this is **sin** and **compromise** (James 4:17; Jeremiah 6:16; Psalm 119:10; Hebrews 2:1). Billy Sunday preached (as recorded in *The Buffalo Express*; we own the original newspaper) on February 7, 1917: *"The Devil wants you to compromise. He wants you to do things you should not do — things that perhaps you do not consider very bad at first, but you start compromising with the Devil and you are gone."*

The truth is, you always spring a leak before you have a flood. A countless host of pastors have unanimously agreed throughout the decades from what they have personally seen that an individual's, a ministry's, and a church's drifting and compromising begins with their music. We must be careful! The Bible says, *"Therefore we ought to give the more earnest heed to the things which we have heard, lest at any time we should let them slip"* (Hebrews 2:1).

God will never be able to fully bless a Christian, a home, a church, or a ministry that has succumbed to the sin of compromise — the sin of choosing to not follow the whole counsel of God's Word. Beware of this. We live in a society that does not want to wholeheartedly obey. People don't want to *"endure sound doctrine"* (II Timothy 4:3-4). Modern-day Christianity wants to challenge God in everything and justify what it believes to be right, rather than staying away from the gray areas. Determine to stay true to what the Bible teaches and apply it to your life!

The fact remains: unscriptural music is unscriptural music regardless of our personal preferences, justifications, or opinions. If the Holy Ghost convicts you in this area of music, pray about it and seek His face as to what standard (or boundary) He would have you develop in your life. Holiness matters. And in no area is this truer than in the area of our worship and praise unto Almighty God.

We are to *"worship the Lord in the beauty of holiness"* (Psalm 96:9). If your music whether in your car, your home, your church service doesn't meet God's standards of beauty and holiness, don't call it worship, because it's not. Holiness is not what you or I decide it is based on our personal preferences. It is determined by God's position and God's precepts. There is certainly room for different application of Bible principles as we seek to glorify God in our music. However, we must commit ourselves to following the clear commands of the Bible, drawing out Bible principles surrounding those commands, and ordering our lives around those principles. We cannot start with our preferences and try to find Scripture verses to support them.

None of us will ever "arrive" or attain a status of perfection while upon this earth. This does not mean we have the right to live care-free lives, with no standards whatsoever, thinking, *"I'm never going be perfect or know exactly what God wants on the issue, so I'll just disregard it and enjoy life my way."* If we are not careful and if we do not remain vigilant, we will begin to let things slip. We will drift further away from our close, intimate walk with God as we slowly become closer and more intimate with sin. We ought to constantly evaluate our lives and passionately desire to always align ourselves with Bible truth. If it comes to our attention that we have allowed questionable things to enter into our music, we should be humble and willing to remove those things that could hinder our closeness with God.

What we should be asking ourselves is, *"What does the Bible teach?"* Do our tastes for music reflect the holiness of God and the wholesomeness that is taught within God's Word? Oh, that God's people would be willing to immerse themselves in the fullness of Scripture, comprehend what it teaches and then make God's position their position. Music is greatly important to Him, and the Bible gives us multiple applicable guidelines for how it should be.

CHAPTER V:

CHARACTERISTICS OF GODLY MUSIC

There are a number of Biblical principles that ought to be applied to the area of music, as in the other areas of our Christian life. By way of introduction, a key truth to remember is that *everything* should be done to the honor and glory of God (I Corinthians 10:31; Colossians 3:17). Every time you pop a CD into the player, put headphones on your ears and scroll through the albums on your iPod, or step up to sing/play a song in church — sincerely ask yourself, *"Will this please the Lord? Does this make Jesus happy or disappointed? Am I going to glorify God through what I'm about to do or will He be grieved?"*

We were once genuinely asked by a youth pastor: *"So do you guys have music that you would approve of for using in church but then have music you would listen to outside of church, even though it might not be necessarily appropriate for a church setting?"* He was curious where we stood on this issue. Our tender response was, *"No,"* and we do not believe that any Christian should either. We then proceeded to Scripturally remind our dear brother how that everything we do as God's children should bring Him glory. After all, the Lord dwells with us continually, not just when we are at church or in a service.

A few passages teach us of this sobering truth: *"Know ye not that ye are the temple of God, and that the Spirit of God dwelleth in you?"* (I Corinthians 3:16). *"What? know ye not that your body is the temple of the Holy Ghost which is in you, which ye have of God, and ye are not your own? For ye are bought with a price: therefore glorify God in your body, and in your spirit, which are God's"* (I Corinthians 6:19-20). *"And what agreement hath the temple of God with idols? for ye are the temple of the living God; as God hath said, I will dwell in them, and walk in them; and I will be their God, and they shall be my people"* (II Corinthians 6:16).

Honestly, why *should* God's people listen to music that is unfit to use in church — whether it be a cinematic soundtrack in a short film showed during the service, a song in a skit, prelude music of any kind, or a special that is sung by the choir or from behind the pulpit? It is impossible to straddle the fence, hold the hands of two different music philosophies, and go forward in life. Jesus reminds us of this in Matthew 6:24.

Could it be that this is exactly what is happening today in 21st century Christianity? Are we guilty of participating in the sin of segregation? Are we striving to pursue the "sacred" but also the "secular"? Have we compartmentalized life into "church" things and "non-church" things? This ought not so to be, because *everything* we say and do (even as we go about our day, engage in our hobbies, and run our errands) ought to be "spiritual" — it **all** should bring honor and glory to the Lord!

The Bible says in I Corinthians 10:13, *"Whether therefore ye eat, or drink, or whatsoever ye do, <u>do all to the glory of God.</u>"* (We are praying that God would sear this verse into your mind by the time you are through reading this book.) Colossians 3:17 teaches us something similar: *"And whatsoever ye do in word or deed, do all in the name of the Lord Jesus, giving thanks to God and the Father by him."* Our personal music should glorify and praise Him! The Psalmist reflected, *"The Lord is my strength and my shield; my heart trusted in him, and I am helped: therefore my heart greatly rejoiceth; and with **my song** will I praise him"* (Psalm 28:7).

Psalm 69:30-31 declares something rather unique: *"I will **praise** the name of God with **a song**, and will magnify him with thanksgiving. This also shall please the Lord better than an ox or bullock that hath horns and hoofs."* Our personal song of worship and praise means more to the Lord than our public sacrifice. Let that truth sink in!

Psalm 51:14-17 also alludes to this: *"Deliver me from bloodguiltiness, O God, thou God of my salvation: and **my tongue shall sing aloud** of thy righteousness. O Lord, open thou my lips; and **my mouth shall shew forth thy praise**. For thou desirest not sacrifice; else would I give it: thou delightest not in burnt offering. The sacrifices of God are a broken spirit: a broken and a contrite heart, O God, thou wilt not despise."* God is more interested in a truly humble heart and a dead-to-self spirit that magnifies Him and exalts Him in genuine Christ-honoring music than a visible display of offering or sacrifice.

Music is a medium of worshipping God. The worship and praise of God should be our goal when we produce music (singing/playing in a church service) and when we listen to music. He is certainly worthy of it! We can see a direct correlation between music and worship in Revelation 5: *"And* when he had taken the book, the four beasts and four and twenty elders fell down before the Lamb, having every one of them harps, and golden vials full of odours, which are the prayers of saints. **And they sung a new song, saying, Thou art worthy** to take the book, and to open the seals thereof: for thou wast slain, and hast redeemed us to God by thy blood out of every kindred, and tongue, and people, and nation; And hast made us unto our God kings and priests: and we shall reign on the earth...**Worthy is the Lamb** that was slain to receive power, and riches, and wisdom, and strength, and honour, and glory, and blessing. And every creature which is in heaven, and on the earth, and under the earth, and such as are in the sea, and all that are in them, heard I saying, Blessing, and honour, and glory, and power, be unto him that sitteth upon the throne, and unto the Lamb for ever and ever. And the four beasts said, Amen. And the four and twenty elders fell down and **worshipped** him that liveth for ever and ever."

Do we worship God through our music? Are we consumed with an awe and wonder of His power and majesty? Do we respect and have a whole-hearted acceptance of how He wishes our music to be? With all of this in mind, let us take a closer look at some more characteristics our music should have.

OUR MUSIC SHOULD BE PROPERLY <u>ORDERED</u> AND <u>BALANCED</u>.

I Corinthians 14:33 teaches us that *"God is not the author of confusion, but of peace."* His will for our lives is to *"Let all things be done decently and in order"* (I Corinthians 14:40). This most definitely applies to music.

II Chronicles 5:13 says, *"It came even to pass, as the trumpeters and singers were **as one**, to make **one** sound to be* *heard in praising and thanking the LORD.*" Chaos, disorder, and confusion are characteristics of the world's music (if you don't agree, try turning on a random radio music station and listen to what comes blasting out of your speakers!). These characteristics should never be present in a Christian's music.

God has created and ordained for things to be done decently and in order. Everything we do, say, wear, and yes, even listen to should reflect the holiness and order of our Heavenly Father. Our music should not be chaotic with loud disarray or even with an obnoxious overdriving beat that distracts from the melody. Notice the example found in II Chronicles 5:12-13 that supports this:

> "*Also the Levites which were the singers, all of them of Asaph, of Heman, of Jeduthun, with their sons and their brethren, being arrayed in white linen, having cymbals and psalteries and harps, stood at the east end of the altar, and with them an hundred and twenty priests sounding with trumpets:) It came even to pass, as the trumpeters and singers **were as one, to make one sound** to be heard in praising and thanking the Lord; and when they lifted up **their voice** with the trumpets and cymbals and instruments of musick, and praised the Lord, saying, For he is good; for his mercy endureth for ever: that then the house was filled with a cloud, even the house of the Lord.*"

Satan wants the exact opposite of what the Lord desires. If God wants decency and order, the Devil will call for inappropriateness, havoc, disorder (things to be out of order or not in their natural place), and chaos. Satan will even call for it and seek to manipulate this ever so softly and subtly.

When the Devil can have his way, when the world subverts the authority of Scripture, and when the flesh gets riled up in its self-will and pride, there will be confusion. James 3:16 alludes to this, *"For where envying and strife is, there is confusion and every evil work."*

I Corinthians 14:15 teaches us: *"What is it then? I will pray with the spirit, and I will pray with the understanding also: I will sing with the spirit, and I will sing with the understanding also."* God desires for His servants to be knowledgeable about music — *"with the understanding also"*!

There are many different aspects to music (such as timbre, dynamics, tempo, articulations, texture, and form), but the main three components of music are — the melody, the harmony, and the rhythm.

The **MELODY** is the main tune of a song, the "singable" flow of sound. It is the "main voice" that should stand out from everything else. According to the Bible, it is what feeds the spirit and what should be primarily used in our worship and praise of the Lord. Ephesians 5:18-19 says, *"And be not drunk with wine, wherein is excess; but be filled with the Spirit; Speaking to yourselves in psalms and hymns and spiritual songs, singing and making <u>melody</u> in your heart to the Lord."* Notice that God emphasized that we ought to make *"melody"* in our hearts unto Him. He could have said anything He wanted here, because He is God, the Sole Authority of Truth. But, He did not recommend *"harmony"* or *"rhythm"* or any other part of music — He chose *"melody."*

HARMONY (usually with the parts of alto, tenor, and bass) appeals to our mind; numerous studies have revealed this to be true. Scientists have discovered that musical harmony triggers a consistent firing pattern in certain auditory neurons of our brain, and that "pleasant" blends carry more information in our minds than "harsh" ones. Harmony has been proven to bring mental clarity and comfort. However, harmony should always be subject to the melody. An example of harmony is found in Ephesians 4:16 where the phrase *"fitly joined together"* comes from the same word from which we get the word harmony. Harmony is the most complex aspect of music that appeals to the mind of man. It is the alto, tenor, or bass; these are the parts that appeal to our soul or our mental processes. It adds interest and variety; but, since it is not necessary to impart the spiritual content, it must be subject to the melody.

RHYTHM is the "beat" that appeals to the body. The body is full of rhythm. Your heart beats in rhythm, you walk in rhythm, and so on. Music would be chaotic and completely unorganized if it was void of rhythm. It is that which gives order to music, if it is controlled through the appropriate time signatures, measures, and beats per measure. While rhythm can get out of hand (even in a church service while singing very sacred words) and destroy a song's ability to honor God, it is also a necessary element to keep music advancing in an orderly and meaningful way. However, rhythm should not dominate. As we read in Ephesians 5:19, the Bible implies that melody should be what's most prevalent in our music.

Another way to describe rhythm is like the pulse of your body. Too much pulse or an erratic one reveals your heart to be sick. No pulse reveals your heart to be lifeless, rendering the body dead. But a balanced pulsed shows the heart and body to be well. So it is with music. Too much, erratic, or unnatural rhythm and the music is "sick." No rhythm and the music is "dead." Balanced rhythm and the music is "well."

The melody feeds the <u>spirit</u>, the harmony feeds the <u>mind</u>, and the rhythm feeds the <u>body</u>. God designed for the melody to be the preeminent part of music because the spirit is to be nurtured and cultivated over the mind and body. A song that features the melody, with accompanying harmonies (that don't overpower the melody) and a rhythm that aids and supports the melody, has the correct order and balance. On the other hand, an unbalance of rhythm overtaking the melody of a song is not natural, right, or Biblical. Our focus should be that of *"Speaking to yourselves in psalms and hymns and spiritual songs, singing and making melody in your heart to the Lord"* (Ephesians 5:19).

In Isaiah 51:3, we find God sharing that He will come to encourage His people and that He will bring with Him joy, gladness, thanksgiving, and melody (not harmony or rhythm), *"For the Lord shall comfort Zion: he will comfort all her waste places; and he will make her wilderness like Eden, and her desert like the garden of the Lord; joy and gladness shall be found therein, thanksgiving, and the voice of melody."*

The world's music and even contemporary "Christian" music tends to be unbalanced. The rhythm is so pronounced, loud, and driving, that often the actual true "music" of the song can't even be heard or recognized. Make sure your music doesn't feed the flesh and appeal to the body foremost, and then secondarily feed the mind and spirit.

Unfortunately, many Christians determine music to be godly or ungodly based upon their perception, rather than on musical principle found in Scripture. They base their music standards on what they like and what appeals to them (their flesh). They say, *"It makes me feel so good"* or *"it moves me."*

Andrew Murray (1828-1917) was a power-filled preacher, example, and author on prayer and humility. He wrote: *"Between the life of feeling and the life of faith the Christian has to choose every day. Happy is he who...chooses not to seek or listen for feeling but only to walk by faith...preoccupied with the Word...with God Himself and Jesus His Son. Feeling seeks and aims at self; faith honors God. Faith pleases God and shall...witness in the heart of the believer that he is acceptable to God."*[25]

Faith versus feeling. In the arena of music, faith is represented by taking responsibility to search the Scriptures in determining godly music. If feelings were intended as the litmus-test to determine what music one listens to or performs, God would have left out all of the hundreds of references about music in His Word. Feelings, not submissive to the authority of Scripture, will one day eventually override what Scripture teaches us to apply to our music. Our feelings and tastes might and will conflict with Scripture! Why? Because we are fleshly and human. We are prone to wander and become carnal if the flesh is not brought into control on a daily basis. *"I keep under my body, and bring it into subjection: lest that by any means, when I have preached to others, I myself should be a castaway"* (I Corinthians 9:27).

Many defend their musical preferences under the apologetic of feelings, but we must submit our personal desires, preferences, and perception to the authority of God's Word. There's nothing wrong with liking music, but ask yourself, why do you like it? What is being appealed to? Does God like it? Is it nourishing your spirit and mind first and foremost? Or is it feeding fleshly lusts?

Now that you're saved, the music of your new life as a Christian should sound completely different from what was part of your life before Christ. I Peter 2:9-11 says, *"But ye are a chosen generation, a royal priesthood, an holy nation, a peculiar people; that ye should shew forth the praises of him who hath **called you out of darkness** into his marvellous light:*

*Which in time past were not a people, but are now the people of God: which had not obtained mercy, but now have obtained mercy. Dearly beloved, I beseech you as strangers and pilgrims, **abstain from fleshly lusts**, which war against the soul."*

As a believer, you've been chosen, or called out. You are special to God! And you've been saved for a purpose: to show forth His praises. If your music appeals to the fleshly lusts that war against your soul, it is wrong. It should be avoided. We cannot show forth the praises of God with music that appeals to the flesh. It is so important to have the proper order and the right priorities as to what gets "fed" when listening to music.

Perhaps you know that your flesh does have a stronghold in the area of music. Ask God to help you overcome it. If you have a weakness in the area of music, raise your standard and be extra safe. Choose the best and what you know is right rather than settling for what *might* be acceptable. As the cliché goes, *"when in doubt, don't."* Friend, if you are sincere in your pursuit of what's godly, Christ will take away your fleshly desires and give you a desire for the right kind of music.

OUR MUSIC SHOULD BE <u>JOYFUL</u>.

Psalm 100:1-2 are familiar verses on the topic of music and joy. *"Make a **joyful** noise* [a triumphant shout!] *unto the Lord, all ye lands. Serve the Lord with gladness: come before his presence with **singing**."* Colossians 3:16 tells us that we should be *"singing with grace in [our] hearts to the Lord."* Many times in Scripture, especially in Isaiah, you will find that God encourages us to "break forth" into singing.

"Therefore the redeemed of the Lord shall...come with singing unto Zion; and everlasting joy shall be upon their head:

they shall obtain gladness and joy; and sorrow and mourning shall flee away" (Isaiah 51:11). This is describing a people who are fired-up and jubilant over the things of God! *"Behold, my servants shall sing for joy of heart"* (Isaiah 65:14). We should be the same way in our singing — genuine from the heart with excitement and enthusiasm. After all, we don't have to sing — we GET to sing! God has placed this song in our hearts. We have heard the joyful sound of His love, grace, mercy, goodness, faithfulness, promises, provision, *and so much more* — and we should **love** singing about it with all of our hearts! It is a privilege to praise the King of kings!

Let's study what the Bible teaches in Psalm 89:15 — *"Blessed is the people that know **the joyful sound**: they shall walk, O Lord, in the light of thy countenance."* God's hand of favor will be upon those who correctly engage in Biblically joyful music.

The word *"know"* that God used here has a three-fold meaning. It describes a people who DISCERN (understanding what God teaches and what is truth), DISTINGUISH (seeing the difference between what's right and what's wrong), and DO (engaging only in what will please the Lord and enable a Christian to grow spiritually). Can this be said of you concerning your music? Are you discerning what God would have you to do according to His Word? Are you distinguishing the various styles of secular and sacred music that are out there today and only participating in the kinds that honor and glorify God?

"The joyful sound" mentioned in this verse is talking about *"a battle cry of marching unto triumph"* and *"a spiritually impulsive shout of jubilance."* Both definitions have been derived from the Strong's Concordance description of the Old Testament Hebrew *"teruwah"* used here. This is

clearly teaching us that our music should have a victorious cadence to it *("Onward, Christian Soldiers", "Stand Up! Stand Up for Jesus!", "Victory in Jesus", "Dare to be a Daniel", and many more),* and it should be full of vitality *("Amazing Grace", "And Can It Be?", "Wonderful Grace of Jesus", "Isn't the Love of Jesus Something Wonderful?", and countless others)*!

Our music should have a holy excitement, a Heavenly energy, and a hallowed exuberance. God is CERTAINLY worth getting excited about in the appropriate way! The Bible says that if this is the case, we *"shall walk, O Lord, in the light of thy countenance."* Our dispositions will be happy and bright. Our faces will contain a natural glow of God's glory. Oh! God is looking for our music to be joyful!

Whenever you are given the opportunity to sing (whether you are singing a special song in front of everyone or just singing as a congregation to the Lord), make sure you are reflecting on the words and are singing with joy. Put a smile on your face and mean what you're singing! When you find yourself whistling or humming a tune while you go about your day, may it resonate from a heart filled with happiness!

As Christians, we need to be careful not to let our lives and our churches lose this. If we are not vigilant, we will! Among the various styles of music found in independent Baptist churches today, a couple of extremes are "High Church" music and what we will call "Gospel Church" music. (Some of you might have just lowered the book and thought, *"Well, I can't believe they just went there."* Please bear with us! There must be a balance….)

We have found "High Church" music to be very formal. There certainly is a time and place for that — but, a constant diet of it will render a church's music to become sterile and void of any emotions whatsoever. This style can quickly create a rigid atmosphere with a somber sound. The congregational singing is usually participated in with sobriety. Very few in the congregation or the choir smile. The faces of those singing the special music (usually reserved to an "elite" few or those who are highly trained) sometimes look as if they are creased in agony or that something is troubling them. What? This is not the *"joyful sound!"*

We believe wholeheartedly that music should be professional and that we should render unto the Lord our best. That's a Biblical principle! But God is not interested in us going to the extreme so that our music becomes lifeless and sterile. God wants us to smile, be joyful, thrilled, excited, and exuberant in awe of His majesty! He encourages us: *"And whatsoever ye do* [including our singing and church music], *do it heartily* [with gusto and vitality], *as to the Lord, and not unto men"* (Colossians 3:23).

Another extreme is the "Gospel Church" music style. We have found it to be more informal (sometimes a little too much). A by-product of this style is that it can quickly become too casual and lose the magnificence that God is truly worthy of. There tends to be more of a nonchalant atmosphere in the service with trite singing and music that has lost its weight and wonder. If it gets out of control, the congregational singing will often be accompanied by a honky-tonk genre of piano playing. It has a tendency to yield a greater emphasis upon outward emotions rather than a spiritually emotional connection of the song with the Lord. There is *nothing* wrong with emotion, but it must have its proper place. If emotions become manifest — and this has happened frequently in our revival meetings, it must be the result of the Holy Ghost's moving and working and not a manufacturing or a manipulating of the flesh. We believe true *"joyful sound"* music will generate this at times! But please do not mistake *"the joyful sound"* for something that would fit into a worldly scene or something that must be generated by the flesh and worked up to create some sort of "excitement."

We are in grave danger when we fail to conform to the holy nature of our God and worship Him as He wants to be worshipped. The Bible says, *"Give unto the Lord the glory due unto his name; worship the Lord in the beauty of holiness"* (Psalm 29:2). There needs to be a balance — there should be a spirit of reverence and a spirit of rejoicing!

We should keep the song service high enough to honor the King of kings, yet common enough to encourage praise-filled singing from every child of God. For instance, the church pianist should at times play evangelistically and triumphantly if he/she is able to. Sometimes a more *reflective* style is more appropriate. (Remember: balance.) A church should create a small orchestra if possible to let members who know how to play musical instruments join in with the congregation as vibrant accompaniment. Have an occasional key change in the congregational singing before the final verse. Smile! Remember Who God is! Smile! Reflect upon His might and majesty! Smile! Rejoice that God *"is above all, and through all, and in you all"* (Ephesians 4:6)! We should meditate upon the words that we're rendering unto the Lord in song and sing every word from the heart! Because the Lord is worthy of our best, we should prepare each special as an individual offering unto Him. Church services should be saturated with music that praises His name and pleases Him! God is looking for our music to be joyful!

God is also looking for everyone to be involved. Psalm 149:1 says, *"Praise ye the Lord. Sing unto the Lord a new song, and his praise in the <u>congregation</u> of saints."* We also believe it is healthy for churches to allow any qualified member who is willing to sing to be given the opportunity to offer a music special unto the Lord — and not to a select talented few. The Bible exhorts us in I Corinthians 12:23-25, *"And those members of the body, which we think to be less honourable, upon these we bestow more abundant honour; and our uncomely parts have more abundant comeliness. For our comely parts have no need: but God hath tempered the body together, having given more abundant honour to that part which lacked: That there should be no schism in the body; but that the members should have the same care one for another."* Some of the most honorable songs we have ever heard in our lives have come from trembling lips which may mar a note or two as they desperately search for an adequate way to sing: *"Thank you, Lord, for saving my soul!"*

May II Chronicles 29:30 be our testimony: *"And they sang praises with gladness, and they bowed their heads and worshipped."*

OUR MUSIC SHOULD BE RENDERED UNTO GOD WITH THE BEST OF OUR ABILITY.

God is only worthy of our best and the highest quality. He is interested in *excellence* not the earthly, the average, or entertainment. Revelation 4:11 teaches us that He *"is worthy to receive glory and honour and power"* in our music. One thing that we stress to young people and church members in our revival meetings across America is that the Lord does not deserve a "half-hearted" Christianity; He delights in a "whole-hearted" Christianity!

One time we posed the question to a host of young people in the midst of a Christian school revival: *"What song do we have to sing as a congregation that will actually cause you to sing at full volume?"* Most of them had sung rather timidly and quietly; the congregational hymn of that morning, *"The Old Rugged Cross,"* sounded dreary and uninspiring — as if most of them were completely unfamiliar with it. But a majority of them had grown up in church and knew how the song went, some even had it memorized. We began to share with them a renewing and a refreshing view of Calvary and the love of Christ. God did a great work in that very service. At the end of the message, not one seat was occupied, and the altars were flooded. Many surrendered their lives to Christ that day! After the invitation, we sang *"The Old Rugged Cross"* again, and this time it was naturally and joyously at "full volume." Their faces radiated with joy what was being resonated from their hearts.

Ecclesiastes 9:10 exhorts us, *"Whatsoever thy hand findeth to do, do it with thy might;"* Whether singing or playing an instrument, God is worthy of our best with exuberance — not a distracted, "ho-hum" mediocrity! Do you praise the Lord nonchalantly, or with nothing held back?

I Chronicles 13:8 documents, *"And David and all Israel played before God **with all their might,** and with singing, and with harps, and with psalteries, and with timbrels, and with cymbals, and with trumpets."* This was a lively service! They sang and played various instruments with *all* their *might*. However, it was not a liberal service!

The *"might"* mentioned here does not mean that they simply just blew harder or strummed more forcefully. Rather, they put forth every bit of prowess, competence, volume, endurance, and refinement that they possibly could. It was to the best of their ability! Whether it was a softer song of reverential reflection (sometimes less is more) or a bombastic arrangement that thrilled the soul, it was something offered from the heart in their best way. Meek, timid, somewhat-depressing musicians would do well to spend a few days in the company of David's singers and instrumentalists!

Notice these others passages: *"Praise the Lord with harp: sing unto him with the psaltery and an instrument of ten strings. ...play skilfully with a loud noise"* (Psalm 33:2-3).

"Sing aloud unto God our strength: make a joyful noise unto the God of Jacob. Take a psalm, and bring hither the timbrel, the pleasant harp with the psaltery" (Psalm 81:1-3).

"Make a joyful noise unto the Lord, all the earth: make a loud noise, and rejoice, and sing praise. Sing unto the Lord with the harp; with the harp, and the voice of a psalm. With trumpets and sound of cornet make a joyful noise before the Lord, the King" (Psalm 98:4-6).

OUR MUSIC SHOULD HAVE A CLEAR MESSAGE, BEING DOCTRINALLY SOUND.

Our music should not be vague in terminology. Remember what Psalm 40:3b said about our song? *"Many shall see it, and fear, and shall trust in the Lord."* Our message in song should be clear enough that someone listening could understand, be comforted, convicted, or converted through the message. Avoid vague references to God (saying "Him" or "You" and never using actual names for God, which is common in Contemporary Christian music). Avoid loud backbeats (we will discuss this in the next chapter), piano clanging, or overwhelming orchestration that distract from (and often cover up) the words and vital message of the song. Avoid sliding around on the notes — this causes confusion in the listener and can distract them from being convicted by the words of the song or drawing closer to God in worship through the song. Beware of your music clouding or drowning out the message.

Is our music well-written? Is the music doctrinally correct and theologically sound? Beware of twisting a truth from Scripture to make it fit a melody line. Believe it or not, many of the greatest songwriters back in the day were pastors and those who were theologically trained! Hymns were deep and rich with Bible truths. Each song was like a sermon, teaching, admonishing, edifying, and convicting hearts.

Today, many songs have become trite, repetitive, and Scripturally shallow. Audiences seem to care more about whether the tune has a nice, catchy melody and how it makes them feel, rather than what the song will teach them or how the song will lend to exalting God. We believe the Lord is pleased when we place a priority on choosing music that holds rich truths and a message in song that can feed hungry hearts and aid in praising His Name more Biblically.

The lyrics of the songs we listen to and sing should be based upon Scriptural principles, edifying our hearts and magnifying Almighty God. Psalm 119:54 says, *"Thy statutes have been my songs in the house of my pilgrimage."*

Also, we believe it is worth noting (while meditating upon the statement *"he hath put a new song in my mouth"*) that there is _nothing_ _wrong_ with using new music or songs in public worship and congregational singing — and there is certainly nothing wrong with singing the songs of old. Israel continued to sing the songs from Moses celebrating deliverance from Egypt generations after their freedom, as well as singing the current, solid, godly psalms and songs David and musicians were composing. Ultimately, Psalm 19:14 should be our fervent desire: *"Let the words of my mouth, and the mediation of my heart, be acceptable in thy sight, O Lord."*

We know that our music should match the character of God, *"for the LORD JEHOVAH is my strength and my song"* (Isaiah 12:2). Our music should reflect Psalm 99:5 — *"Exalt ye the LORD our God, and worship at his footstool; for he is holy."* He is worthy of it! The style of music (even a part from the words) should be that which best expresses the holy and righteous character of God. For example, it seems obviously unfitting and out of character to sing or play *"Holy, Holy, Holy"* to a trite disco beat or a carnal rap beat.

Too many times, we may find ourselves enjoying music, even Christian music, for what it *sounds* like and not what it *says*. If we really stop and focus on the words of the songs we sing/listen to, are they truly Biblical? Are they doctrinally sound? Colossians 3:16 says, *"Let the word of Christ dwell in you richly in all wisdom; **teaching** and **admonishing** one another in psalms and hymns and spiritual songs, singing with grace in your hearts to the Lord."* Our song's lyrics should teach and admonish — they should confront our minds and thinking with Biblical truths.

We encourage you: strive to listen to and sing songs that are filled with Christ-honoring, worshipful, doctrinally-rich lyrics and also have godly music accompanying them that doesn't detract from the words or cause an impulse for worldly emotions or movements.

OUR MUSIC SHOULD BE SUNG AND PLAYED FROM THE HEART.

We have already hinted at this truth under the previous section about our music being a *"joyful sound."* God delights in hearing our songs that are brought before Him genuinely, sincerely, and authentically. Psalm 135:3 teaches us, *"Praise the Lord; for the Lord is good: sing praises unto his name; for it is pleasant."* This brings God great joy and pleasure. In Psalm 147:1, the Bible encourages: *"Praise ye the Lord: for it is good to sing praises unto our God; for it is pleasant; and praise is comely* [suitable or fitting]. *"*

Every time we sing those beautiful words *"In my heart there rings a melody,"* it brings a smile to our face! Could it be that as Elton M. Roth (who lived from 1891-1951 and was a well-known musician of his day) composed this song, he understood that the location of the *"new song"* that the Lord gave us is from our heart? Absolutely! *"It was while assisting with evangelistic meetings in Texas on a hot summer day in 1923, that the words and music for this hymn suddenly came to him. Mr. Roth recalled, 'That evening I introduced the song by having 200+ boys and girls sing it at the open air meeting, after which the audience joined in the singing. I was thrilled as it seems my whole being was transformed into song.'"*[26]

As Ephesians 5:19 exhorts that we should be *"singing and making melody in [our hearts] to the Lord,"* God expects the heart to be filled with the sound of His song! When our worship is overflowing from this, our lives will encourage others to know this same joy in the Lord also.

Whether you are playing an instrument for the Lord or singing a special or congregational song in church, play and sing from your heart! Play for the Lord, not for men. Colossians 3:23 says, *"And whatsoever ye do, do it heartily, as to the Lord, and not unto men."* Have the right heart motives for why you are singing or playing in church. It's not a performance; it's a service for the Lord.

Many people are too nervous to sing or play an instrument in church and we wonder if it's because they are too busy worrying about how they think they'll sound or what others will think if they make a mistake (performance focus). Be thankful for whatever ability God has entrusted unto you, and ask Him to use you to be a blessing to others (service focus) as you worship and praise Him!

Play and sing with *humility*, for the Lord, from your heart, and you'll be surprised at how God will take your small talent and multiply it for His glory! When singing hymns in church or special music in front of a congregation, focus on the words being sung and mean them from your heart. Every time you sing the name of God without thinking about it and meaning what you're saying, you are actually taking *His name in vain* and breaking one of the Ten Commandments (Ex. 20:7)!

May we not be guilty of being like the children of Israel as recorded in Psalm 78:36-37, *"Nevertheless they did flatter him with their mouth, and they lied unto him with their tongues. For their heart was not right with him."*

Every once in a while, we should discreetly, individually, stop singing in the middle of a verse or a chorus of a congregational song and genuinely ask ourselves, *"Do I really believe this? Am I being real? Am I truly meaning what I'm singing to the Lord?"* It is spiritually healthy to inspect our hearts and make sure what we say, do, and sing is sincerely coming from our hearts! This is what pleases the Lord.

OUR MUSIC SHOULD <u>ENCOURAGE</u> THE HEART AND <u>REFRESH</u> THE SPIRIT.

Our music should edify, encourage, and build up other believers spiritually. I Corinthians 14:26 reminds us, *"How is it then, brethren? when ye come together, every one of you hath a psalm, hath a doctrine, hath a tongue, hath a revelation, hath an interpretation. Let all things be done unto edifying.*" God specifically states in I Thessalonians 5:11, "*Wherefore comfort yourselves together, and edify one another.*"

When we offer up heart-felt praise unto God through music, our reflecting and rejoicing will be a blessing to those around us because it will strengthen their focus of God, their faith in God, and their fervency for God. The book of Psalms is filled with Biblical songs that serve as wonderful examples of what our music should be like — songs about God's love and mercy, the Bible, the power of God, His attributes and character, His presence in our trials, His unending goodness, and so much more.

In this way, God can use our music to be a ministry unto others through encouragement and edification. The Lord instructs us that we should be "*teaching* [to instruct] *and admonishing* [to put in mind] *one another in psalms and hymns and spiritual songs, singing with grace* [a happy sweetness that benefits others] *in your hearts to the Lord*" (Colossians 3:16). Each time any of us sing a special, play an offertory, make an album, or share a song — it should be to honor our Great God and help others. What a blessing!

We believe that this is important to note: Musicians in the Bible were considered ministers (servants) through song. Music was a ministry. There are numerous examples of this throughout Scripture, one such case is II Chronicles 7:6, which says, "*And the priests waited on their offices: the Levites also with **instruments of musick** of the Lord, which David the king had made to praise the Lord, because his mercy endureth for ever, when David **praised by their ministry**; and the priests **sounded trumpets** before them, and all Israel stood.*"

Fascinatingly, most of the evangelist duos in America's revival history (D. L. Moody and Ira Sankey, D. W. Whittle and P. P. Bliss, R. A. Torrey and Charles M. Alexander, Billy Sunday and Homer Rodeheaver, etc.) considered the preacher to be the "minister of sermon" and the song leader/choir director/soloist (he wore three hats in one) to be the "minister of song." Both were viewed as equally important. Each of them believed that their mighty endeavors would not be a success without both being passionately engaged in the yoke as *"labourers together with God"* (I Corinthians 3:9).

The Lord ordained the ministry of music, and He expected musicians to be thoroughly involved in the work of God. Nehemiah 11:22-23 share with us, *"The overseer also of the Levites at Jerusalem was Uzzi the son of Bani, the son of Hashabiah, the son of Mattaniah, the son of Micha. Of the sons of Asaph,* **the singers were over the business of the house of God.** *"* Today, people involved with the music ministry should not just sing specials or play instrumentals in the services; they should be actively involved in the work of the church as key members!

This ministry of music is so vitally important because (as we will see in greater detail in the next section), God will speak to His people through the catalyst of music. II Kings 3:14-16 relates a distinctive account: *"And Elisha said, ...But now bring me a minstrel. And it came to pass, when the minstrel played, that the hand of the Lord came upon him. And he said, Thus saith the Lord,..."*

The right kind of music can have a profound spiritual impact upon a congregation and individuals in preparing their hearts for the encouraging and edifying preaching of God's Word. We have witnessed this, without fail, in our meetings as we sing what God would have us to offer up to Him. We consider providing special music to be a sacred ministry. We pray about what specific songs God would have us to bring. We are continually sensitive to His Spirit's leading. Sometimes we do not have peace until we get into the service. Without fail, God has always led us to the right ones to prepare hearts and strengthen believers. It is incredible how music tenderizes and opens the hearts for God to do a work!

Singing music is not a flippant thing to us, because it is a Biblical ministry, and we know music has the power to lift up a fallen spirit and encourage a saddened heart. Discouragement and depression are like a self-feeding cancer that drains the life out of a soul. Such was the case with King Saul. Yet, in I Samuel 16:23 we find an example of his spirit being refreshed by David's music: *"And it came to pass, when the evil spirit from God was upon Saul, that David took an harp, and played with his hand: so Saul was **refreshed** [physical health], and was **well** [emotional health], and the evil spirit departed from him [spiritual health]."* David's music affected the body, mind and spirit of Saul.

"Refreshed" refers to a physical healing (body). *"Was well"* speaks of an emotional healing (mind). And when the *"evil spirit departed,"* we see a spiritual healing (spirit). Music has the power to do all of this! Music therapists passionately claim: *"For years, studies have proven that the right kind of music has the power to relieve mental suffering."*[27] But, just as music can be influential for good, it can also be for bad. Play the dark, moody, satanic music of the world and the opposite effects will take place in your body, mind, and spirit.

Interestingly, David was not brought before the king for his ability to sing — rather for his ability to play music upon his harp. This teaches us something unique. Music that can refresh our spirits and uplift our hearts is not limited to the words of a song; it can be found in the very *melody* that is being played.

When life is hectic and you feel frazzled, this is an opportune moment to listen to Christian instrumental music so you can meditate and reflect upon the Lord. It will help you continue to *"walk in the Spirit."* It will strengthen you to re-center your methods and motives to reflect that of Christ. I Corinthians 6:20 encourages us to *"glorify God in your body* [your actions], *and in your spirit* [your attitudes], *which are God's."*

Sometimes music with words can distract a person while they are trying to work at their desk or on the job, but beautiful instrumental music of hymns will cause you to spiritually meditate upon the theme of the song while your mind can stay sharp and focused. It will "charge your batteries"! Consider having wholesome Christian music playing softly in the background as you go about your day and especially in your home.

OUR MUSIC SHOULD <u>INVITE</u> THE <u>WORKING</u> OF GOD'S PRESENCE.

What a *privilege* it is to *"praise ye the LORD: for it is good to sing praises unto our God; for it is pleasant; and praise is comely"* (Psalm 147:1). We believe that church services are not complete without the opportunity to *"sing unto the LORD with thanksgiving; sing praise upon the harp unto our God"* (Psalm 147:7). Blending a mixture of our best ability and volume unto the Lord creates a wonderful dynamic as all of God's people vibrantly praise the Lord by singing *"unto Him a new song"* and playing *"skillfully with a loud noise"* (Psalm 33:3). What an honor it is that He has allowed us to *"make a joyful noise unto the LORD"* and *"come before His presence with singing"* (Psalm 100:1-2).

As we come before Him, our music should be a fervent and fragrant invitation for the Lord to manifest His presence. In II Kings 3, Jehoshaphat needed council and wisdom from the Lord. He asked, *"Is there not here a prophet of the LORD, that we may enquire of the LORD by him?"* (II Kings 3:11). When Elisha came before him with the others present, the man of God paused and required that they first *"now bring me a minstrel. And it came to pass, when the minstrel played, that the hand of the Lord came upon him. And he said, Thus saith the Lord, Make this valley full of ditches"* (II Kings 3:15-16). God spoke to His servant in this instance through the catalyst of music. By following the advice given from Heaven, the people witnessed the Lord accomplish a great victory on their behalf that day. God did a mighty work! Godly music, worship, and praise were the very things that drew out the working presence of God.

In our meetings, we have experienced many times how the message of the music has so incredibly nurtured and stirred the hearts of God's people that, after we sing, Caleb will preach from his heart for a few moments as God directs him, while Katie continues to play softly on the piano. There is often a very evident, visible need to have a time of public prayer. People have been so spiritually moved, convicted, broken, or comforted through the working of God's presence from the music that they just *have to* talk to the Lord. As the call to prayer is given, many people instantly flood the altar — some with tears — to meet with God and pour out their hearts before Him. Invitations have lasted from twenty minutes to over two hours with men, women, teenagers, children, and whole families gathered together in God's presence. There is wailing and sobbing. People get saved. Sins are confessed.

Lives are surrendered to the Lord. Relationships are healed and mended. Prodigals return home. Revival breaks loose.

What we are describing here through what the Bible teaches us is not to be confused with the fleshly emotionalism or the "feel-good" sensation that Contemporary "worship" music produces. Much of the carnal modern music in churches today generates a charged emotional excitement that is mistaken for a genuine godly experience. When the Lord moves and speaks to hearts through godly music, it is not something that can be manipulated or manufactured by men — though many have tried to pseudo-create the effects of it. This sort of Heavenly working is only possible through the mighty moving of the Holy Spirit of God, as He powerfully manifests Himself to His people.

Notice the carefully recorded account of what took place with God's people in II Chronicles 5:11-14 as a result of their God-honoring music: *"And it came to pass, when the priests were come out of the holy place: (for all the priests that were present were sanctified, and did not then wait by course: Also the Levites which were the singers, all of them of Asaph, of Heman, of Jeduthun, with their sons and their brethren, being arrayed in white linen, having cymbals and psalteries and harps, stood at the east end of the altar, and with them an hundred and twenty priests sounding with trumpets:) It came even to pass, as the trumpeters and singers were as one, to make one sound to be heard in praising and thanking the Lord; and when they lifted up their voice with the trumpets and cymbals and instruments of musick, and praised the Lord, saying, For he is good; for his mercy endureth for ever: that then the house was filled with a cloud, even the house of the Lord; So that the priests could not stand to minister by reason of the cloud: for the glory of the Lord had filled the house of God."*

As this happened, King Solomon and the throngs of God's people who had gathered there were overwhelmed with how the Lord manifested Himself. The entire congregation stood before Him; Solomon stood in front of the people, *"spread forth his hands"* (II Chronicles 6:12), and cried out for some time in humble prayer to the Lord.

"Now when Solomon had made an end of praying, the fire came down from heaven, and consumed the burnt offering and the sacrifices; and the glory of the Lord filled the house. And the priests could not enter into the house of the Lord, because the glory of the Lord had filled the Lord's house. And when all the children of Israel saw how the fire came down, and the glory of the Lord upon the house, they bowed themselves with their faces to the ground upon the pavement, and worshipped, and praised the Lord, saying, For he is good; for his mercy endureth for ever. Then the king and all the people offered sacrifices before the Lord" (II Chronicles 7:1-4).

The entire powerful experience of God meeting with them began with godly music! While music forces no "magical" incantation upon God, it is part of the way in which He operates. Music can open the channel for His special visitation. Oh, how we should long for that! Now in the church age, we believe that immersing a congregation in godly, Christ-honoring music will pave the way for this very profound work of the Holy Spirit.

However, this is something that is not limited to a congregation only. As Psalm 63 teaches us, the same effect can accompany individuals on a daily basis. *"O God, thou art my God; early will I seek thee: my soul thirsteth for thee, my flesh longeth for thee in a dry and thirsty land, where no water is; To see thy power and thy glory, so as I have seen thee in the sanctuary"* (Psalm 63:1-2). That is why God encourages us: *"And be not drunk with wine, wherein is excess; but be filled with the Spirit; Speaking to yourselves in psalms and hymns and spiritual songs, singing and making melody in your heart to the Lord;"* (Ephesians 5:18-19).

It should be the daily desire of every believer to be filled with God's presence. This is only possible by being completely dead to selfish ambition and remaining yielded to the Spirit. God would not have us to be intoxicated with alcohol, but He wants us to be completely enraptured and captivated with Him and by His presence alone. We are told to be under the influence and control of the Holy Spirit.

As we are *"singing and making melody"* throughout the day, it should be a personal, joy-filled reflection of His majesty and a fervent offering from our hearts directly to God's heart, inviting Him to be completely involved with our lives. We should diligently seek God's leadership in the details of our day. After all, Jesus reminds us: *"for without me ye can do nothing"* (John 15:5). We are in need of God! Otherwise, we can make a mess of things really quickly.

As we sing and listen to the right kind of music, it will cause our minds to be more centered on our Saviour rather than ourselves. It will influence us to not rush ahead and do what we think is best or right for a certain situation, but it will produce a longing for God to give us the appropriate insight to make the correct choice in our daily decision making. Our godly music can make His involvement a reality throughout the day! As the chorus of *"Like a River Glorious"* puts it: *"Stayed upon Jehovah, hearts are fully blest! Finding, as He promised, perfect peace and rest."*

CHAPTER VI:

THE DANGERS OF "ROCK" MUSIC

I Corinthians 14:33 teaches us that *"God is not the author of confusion, but of peace."* His will for our lives is to *"Let all things be done decently and in order"* (I Corinthians 14:40). This most definitely applies to our music.

As we have studied, music has a great potential for good and godliness. It is a precious sweet-smelling fragrance that we can offer up before God in honor of His majesty and glory. But we must understand that music has the same profound capacity for evil. Charles M. Alexander (known as the "Prince of Gospel Singers" and considered to be the successor of Ira D. Sankey in evangelistic music) *"realized, to an unusual degree, the rivalry of Satan in the matter of music, which God had ordained for praise of Himself, and, which, when perverted to other uses, may ruin, rather than upbuild, human character."*[28] We will read of his passion and love for Gospel hymns in Chapter 11.

In this lengthy chapter, we are going to discuss in detail the hazardous influence and effects that rock music has had upon our generation and upon Christianity. We believe that "rock-n-roll" is not *"just another style of music."* We believe that it is a tool devised by Satan to stir rebellion, create a questioning of values, and usher in a casual, carnal attitude toward the things of our Holy God.

WE HAVE AN ADVERSARY

The Bible describes how the Devil *"as a roaring lion, walketh about, seeking whom he may devour"* (I Peter 5:7). He should not be underestimated; he is a crafty conniver! Remember, Satan wants the exact opposite of what the Lord desires. God calls for decency and order; the Devil wants inappropriateness, chaos, and disorder (things to be out of order or not in their natural place). He is roaming subtly and stealthily — watching and waiting for clever opportunities to infiltrate and influence our music. He is vicious with a vehement desire *"to steal, kill, and destroy"* (John 10:10).

Satan desires to destroy all things that were intended to be holy. Satan will do anything he can to taint our worship and praise that we offer unto God. Without a doubt, Satan wishes to turn our music into a wretched vileness of disgusting stench before the Lord. We must not be *"ignorant of his devices"* (II Corinthians 2:11b)! If we go on naively, he will *"get an advantage of us"* (II Corinthians 2:11a). Have you let your guard down? Have you given place to the Devil? Will you let him influence you? Have you let him infiltrate your music?

Ezekiel 28:13 speaks about Satan with these words: *"the workmanship of thy tabrets and of thy pipes was prepared in thee in the day that thou wast created."* Satan was originally created to be an angelic being of praise and adoration to God; he was essentially a living musical instrument. But, he turned all that potential for beauty inward and fell victim to his own pride and ambition. (Perhaps this explains why many people are so easily enthralled by sensual music and the fleshly expression of it — they become victims to their own pride and carnal desires.)

Now that he is consumed with evil, Satan despises to hear God's children joyfully sing anthems of praise unto Him. He is passionate about defiling, redefining, diluting, and destroying the wholesomeness and holiness of our music. Just as he subtly slithered up to Eve in the Garden of Eden when she was least expecting it and arrogantly asked (as recorded in Genesis 3:1-6), *"Yea, hath God said,"* Satan is *still* attempting to put a question mark where God has put a period. He is working overtime trying to distort music and Christian music. The Devil has his own style of music, and sadly, it has infiltrated modern-day Christianity.

The purpose of this chapter is to enable the Christian to no longer be naive toward Satan's tactics and ultimately strengthen each individual to *"Neither give place to the devil"* (Ephesians 4:27). Satan is a crafty mastermind behind the scenes — conniving to emotionally pull people away from God through the power of music. We believe that *rock-n-roll music and its styles* are the wrong kind of music and are manifested works of darkness, designed to gratify the flesh and bring about carnality.

Sacred musician Tim Fisher has warned: *"Rock music appeals to the flesh. Through beat, volume, and repetition, the music is designed to appeal to our sensual nature. Its victims admit that rock music is often more addictive than drugs. It has the power to split families and churches and to alienate teenagers. It grabs hold of our bodies and dulls our minds."*[29]

Frank Garlock (founder of Majesty Music and the man God used to stand against rock music in fundamentalism in the 1960's and 1970's) boldly declared: *"Rock music, by its inherent nature, its associations, its atmosphere, its proponents, and its results, has shown itself to be the enemy of decency, morality, and spirituality. I believe that those who try to use this music are ignorant of the devil's devices and have been duped into thinking that this is the way to reach teens for Christ."*[30]

Listen to the plea given by a Christian young man to a host of youth workers at the Moody Bible Institute decades ago: *"It wasn't a question of whether the music was right or wrong, because that did not matter to me. Somebody could have come up to me and said, 'This worldly music that you have now given yourself over to is wrong.' However, I would not agree with him.*

"After years of rebellion and doing things that were very damaging to myself and to those around me, I finally got back under my parents' authority and God's plan for music.

"I saw that rock music, rebellion, and immorality were hooked together, and that only when you get rid of the wrong music can you get rid of the immoral desires and wrong feelings to which I was in bondage.

"As I talk with others about music, they tend to argue, just as I did. However, when it comes right down to it, I can look them in the eye and say, 'Are you experiencing victory in your life morally?' After talking to hundreds that listen to this music, not one has said to me, 'Yes.'

"I bring you a plea, a cry from my generation, from the generation that was brought up in this music, and for the next generation that is coming along — stop this music! Help us! Or a moral decay will overwhelm us — such as we have never known before!"[31]

Rock music is an enemy to godly music. By way of

application, the Bible plainly says in Deuteronomy 32:31: *"For their rock is not as our Rock, even our enemies themselves being judges."* Here are some important things we should ask ourselves before we continue. Who first started using rock music? Was it churches and Christians schools, desiring to portray God's love and holiness in a better and sweeter way? Or was it a lost world that found a new medium and style to convey their lustful craving for sex, drugs, and rebellion? Why did they choose the rock style of music? Was it chosen randomly, or was it the appropriate accompaniment for their lifestyle choices? These are things that we are going to address and evaluate in the following pages. Once we understand the true nature of rock music (whether it is portrayed softly or harshly in music), should a Christian incorporate it in their music in any fashion?

THE HISTORY OF ROCK-N-ROLL

According to secular sources (not the independent Baptist slant on it), **rock-n-roll** is a genre of popular music that originated and evolved in the United States during the late 1940's and early 1950's[32] prior to its surging development by the mid-1960's into *"the more encompassing international style known as 'rock music'."*[33] There is general agreement that it arose in the Southern United States (a region that would produce most of the major early rock-n-roll performances) through the meeting of various influences that embodied a merging of the African musical tradition with European instrumentation.[34]

Rock-n-roll music emerged in the early 1950's from a culmination of musical styles[35] such as jazz, boogie woogie, gospel, and jump blues (an up-tempo style of blues, usually played by small groups and featuring saxophone or brass instruments. It was popular in the 1940's and was a precursor of R&B and rock music.[36]), along with country music.[37] While elements of what was to become rock-n-roll can be heard in blues records from the 1920's[38] and in country records of the 1930's,[39] the genre did not acquire its name until the early 1950's through the music of Chuck Berry, Buddy Holly and others, with Elvis Presley emerging by the latter part of the decade as its "King."[40]

The Rock-n-Roll Hall of Fame openly presents on their website and in their museum [there will be some repeated information here, but it is worth noting what they claim.]: *"Rock-n-roll is a form of popular music that emerged in the United States in the late forties and early fifties. But rock-n-roll's roots can be tracked back centuries to drum beats in Africa and Celtic folk music in Europe. As people from these regions immigrated to America, they brought their music with them, and as they were exposed to each other's music, they began to incorporate different styles.*

"The more immediate roots of rock and roll lay in the so-called 'race' music, and 'hillbilly' music, or county-western of the Forties and Fifties. Other significant influences include blues, jazz, gospel, boogie-woogie, folk and bluegrass.

"The actual phrase 'rock and roll' emerged as code words for sexual intercourse in blues songs. In 1922, the words 'rock and roll' appeared on a record for the first time. That record, Trixie Smith's 'My Daddy Rock Me (With One Steady Roll),' went on to inspire other blues songs. In the thirties, the words were also used to described rhythms and musical beats, as in Duke Ellington's 'Rockin' in Rhythm.' In 1947, blues shouter Wynonie Harris recorded 'Good Rockin' Tonight,' which went to number one [bestselling song].

"Over the past five decades-plus, rock-n-roll has evolved in many directions. Numerous styles of music — from soul to hip-hop, from heavy metal to punk, from progressive rock to electronic — have fallen under the rock-n-roll umbrella."[41]

Rock music historians go on to tell us that in the earliest rock-n-roll styles, either the piano or bluesy saxophone with string bass was typically the lead instrument; most performances were drummerless. But these instruments began to be replaced or supplemented by guitar, organ, and drums by the 1950's to provide rhythm.[42] The beat of rock music is essentially a dance rhythm[43] with an accentuated backbeat, which is almost always provided by drums.[44]

This brings us to a very important topic of discussion. What is "backbeat"? Is it good? Is there anything "wrong" with it?

BACKBEAT DEFINED

Universities worldwide teach *"The Rule of Accent"* or that the accent of music naturally lands on the first and third beats in 4/4 time and the first beat in 3/4 time. This is a law of nature (just like gravity is a law of nature) and was established by our Creator. *(What is the natural rhythm of the human heart beat? Isn't it X x X x?)* Accenting the second and fourth beats in 4/4 time and accenting the third beat in 3/4 time creates a backbeat which defines the essential and inherent core of rock music. Even Mickey Hart of the *"Grateful Dead"* pointed this out in a NPR (National Public Radio) interview.[45]

As our dear friends Ron and Shelly Hamilton (Patch the Pirate and Sissy Seagull) have taught: *"Normally, music written in 4/4 time has a rhythm based on the strong beats 1 and 3 — count 1 2 3 4* [with emphasis on the bold numbers].

*Rhythm with an emphasis on the beats 1 and 3 is universally thought to create a natural feel. In contrast, the rock beat often has an emphasis on the weak beats 2 and 4 — count 1 **2** 3 **4**."*[46]

Listen to a John Philips Sousa march. The strong on-beat rhythm makes a person want to march or tap his foot in time to the music. Now, there is nothing wrong with this because that is the way God meant for it to be. However, the emphasis of the second and fourth beats (instead of the first and third) seeks to elicit a fleshly emotional and sensual response.

Syncopation should not be confused with backbeat; because in its original sense, syncopation does not actually quite mean that. Rather, it is a temporary shift off the beat. It is *"a momentary contradiction"* in a note from the beat to emphasize something in the music and then immediately return to the on-beat again. Playing a note ever so slightly before, or after, a beat is another form of syncopation because this produces an unexpected accent. Could a song become overly syncopated? Certainly. Our music should not have an offbeat or backbeat emphasis. All things must have their balance and our music should be *done decently and in order"* (I Corinthians 14:40).

Ron and Shelly Hamilton explain further that *"all syncopation, however, does not result in rock music. 'The Hallelujah Chorus' is syncopated, with the 'jah' of 'Hallelujah' landing on an off beat (the '&' of '3'). Matching the rhythm of the word 'Hallelujah' in music with how the word flows rhythmically when you say it also creates a natural feel. 'The Hallelujah Chorus' is not rock music! Occasionally syncopated rhythms in a melody do not create a 'rock feel.' But when the rhythm of a piece of music is characterized by a constant and overemphasized syncopation or driving rhythm, the music does take on a 'rock feel.'"*[47]

Backbeat is a term used to describe a continuous heavy accent on beats 2 and 4 (in 4/4 timing, for example) in music. It is a displacement of the rhythm, causing the naturally strong beats to become weak and the weak ones to be emphasized as strong. Rock music and backbeat goes against nature itself. This is wrong, because we find in Scripture that God intends for His creation to follow what He originally designed. By way of application, consider the principle taught: *"For this cause God gave them up unto vile affections: for even their women did change the natural use into that which is against nature:"* (Romans 1:26). *"Doth not even nature itself teach you, that, if a man have long hair, it is a shame unto him?"* (I Corinthians 11:14).

Backbeat generates a defiant sound, counteracting the normal way of how God created rhythm to flow. This emphasis is obnoxious rebellion. In secular music, this backbeat has become very popular for the rebellion it instills. (We will read some quotes about this over the next few pages.) Such "anti"rhythm is musically confusing and should be avoided.

There are various kinds of rhythm "gone wrong." While our study does not outline each distinction, suffice it to say that whenever the on-beat is obscured in relation to the backbeat, the rhythm has lost its proper cadence as God designed and has most definitely gone wrong.

Should a Christian then employ this same style of rhythm in their music? Well, why would God actively endorse and sanction something that violates the order of what He originally established? He certainly wouldn't, and a rock-styled music cannot be the right kind of accompaniment for godly music or the soundtrack of a Christ-honoring life. But unfortunately, you can readily find this same violation in an overwhelming majority of recorded Contemporary Christian Music and Southern Gospel Music songs and soundtracks. Is this "fine" with God and acceptable to the Lord?

THE SENSUAL ESSENCE OF ROCK

Rock music and the backbeat it generates not only is unnatural (defying the natural law of rhythm that God originally instituted), but it also lends itself very evidently to being provocative and arousing the sensual/carnal. If you don't believe us, read on and observe what the world's top rock musicians and educators (past and present) have to say about this beat, and *you* decide.

Bill Haley (one of America's first rock musicians) said: *"I felt that if I could take a tune and drop the first and third beats and accentuate the second and fourth, and add a beat the listeners could clap to as well as dance, this would be what they were after."*[48]

Elvis Presley (the "King of Rock and Roll" who was popular from 1954 until his sudden death from prescription drug abuse in 1977) declared: *"It's the beat that gets to you. If you like it and you feel it, you can't help but move to it."*[49]

Grammy-Award winning singer/songwriter Robert Palmer wrote in his book *Rock & Roll: An Unruly History*, "I *believe in the transformative power of rock and roll. This transformative power inheres not so much in the words of songs or the stances of the stars, but in the music itself — in the sound, and above all, in the beat."*[50]

John Lennon (co-founder of the Beatles) said in the *Rolling Stone* Magazine on February 12, 1976: *"Because it is primitive enough...it gets through to you its beat. Go to the jungle and they have the rhythm and it goes throughout the world and it's as simple as that.*"[51]

Jan Berry of *Jan and Dean,* a popular rock and roll duo in the late 1950's into the mid 1960's, stated, *"The throbbing beat of rock provides a vital sexual release for adolescent audiences."*[52]

Steve Lawhead (an advocate for the use of rock rhythm and styles in Christian music) even acknowledged, *"Rock music can make it easy for you to go somewhere you want to go, but know you shouldn't."*[53]

Bob Dylan (a major figure in rock music and pop culture for more than fifty years) laughingly mentioned to an interviewer in 1965: *"If I told you what our music is really about, we'd probably all get arrested."*[54]

Allan Bloom, a professor of sociology at the University of Chicago, specified in his work *The Closing of the American Mind: "This is the significance of rock music. I do not suggest that it has any high intellectual sources. But it has risen to its current heights in the education of the young on the ashes of classical music, and in an atmosphere in which there is no intellectual resistance to attempts to tap the rawest passions…. But rock music has one appeal only, a barbaric appeal to sexual desire — not love. Rock is all there is. The words make little difference. They may be explicitly sexual or even religious — it all is eroticism."*[55]

Simon Frith, a British sociologist who specializes in popular music culture and is a former rock critic, wrote in his book *Sound Effects* in 1981: *"Rock expresses the body with a directly physical beat and an intense emotional sound. It is the beat that commands a directly physical response. We respond to the materiality of rock's sounds, and the rock experience is essentially erotic."*[56]

Jimi Hendrix (widely considered to be the greatest secular guitarist in musical history) was quoted in his biography by David Henderson to have said: *"Perhaps it is sexy, but what music with a big beat isn't?"*[57]

Frank Zappa, leading electric guitarist and record producer known as "The Oracle of Rock Music", wrote in *Life* Magazine on June 28, 1968, *"The big beat matches the body's* [sensual] *rhythms. Rock and Roll has largely been seen as a form of rebellious music for just about as long as it has existed. It radiates a secret message: 'You can be free. You can get away with it. Look, we're doing it!'"*[58] But Almighty God — the Author of Truth — has openly stated that *"rebellion is as the sin of witchcraft."* (I Samuel 15:23). To have rebellion-rooted music or styles is just as wicked as worshipping Satan himself. God, help us!

Rock music, by its very history, nature, and character, is unholy. To attempt to use it *"to glorify God"* is blasphemous. Rock music began as a rebellious, sensual style of music, and it remains that today. Trying to unite a holy message with the unholy music of the world is an abomination in the eyes of God. We believe that it is offensive to Him — and it should be equally offensive to those who genuinely love God and seek to obey His Word.

Time Magazine boasted in its report on January 3, 1969: *"By its very beat and sound, Rock has always implicitly rejected restraints and has celebrated freedom and sexuality."*[59] Paul Kantner, American rock-n-roll musician, openly stated: *"Our music is intended to change one set of values to another — free minds, free dope, free bodies, and free music."*[60]

Malcolm McLaren, clothing designer and "respected" rock band manager, declared: *"Rock-n-roll is pagan and primitive, and very jungle, and that's how it should be! The moment it stops being those things, it's dead. The true meaning of rock...is sex, subversion, and style.*"[61] Rock bassist Gene Simmons of *Kiss* said on ABC's *Entertainment Tonight* on December 10, 1987: *"That's what rock is all about — sex with a 100 megaton bomb — the beat!!*"[62]

Even if someone doesn't personally think that backbeat is sensual, the fact alone that a majority of worldly musicians say that it is should steer God's people away from it altogether. Honestly, any form of rock music is raw carnality at its core. It is the music of the flesh and leads a person to worldliness or wickedness.

The Bible teaches us clearly: *"Abstain from all appearance of evil"* (I Thessalonians 5:22). *"Let no corrupt communication proceed out of your mouth, but that which is good to the use of edifying, that it may minister grace unto the hearers"* (Ephesians 4:29). *"And be not conformed to this world: but be ye transformed by the renewing of your mind."* (Romans 12:2). *"Set your affection on things above, not on things on the earth. For ye are dead, and your life is hid with Christ in God. When Christ, who is our life, shall appear, then shall ye also appear with him in glory. Mortify therefore your members which are upon the earth."* (Colossians 3:2-5). *"But fornication, and all uncleanness, or covetousness, let it not be once named among you, as becometh saints; Neither filthiness, nor foolish talking, nor jesting, which are not convenient: but rather giving of thanks"* (Ephesians 5:2-3). *"For God hath not called us unto uncleanness, but unto holiness"* (I Thessalonians 4:7). Should we continue?

These are not suggestions to be entertained; they are commands to be obeyed. This is but a scratch on the surface of what God says to us and how He desires for us to live. May the Lord help us to not walk in the flesh but walk in the Spirit and obey His Word, drawing nigh unto Him with worship that is *"in spirit and in truth"* (John 4:24), and not *"in flesh and in trend."*

ROCK MUSIC AND THE BODY

As we continue to move forward, do you remember our discussion in Chapter 3 about the effects music has on an individual? Without a doubt, rock-n-roll and backbeat has a profound impact on a person's body. We will leave it up to you to determine whether it is healthy, wholesome, and holy or not.

Hal Zeiger (rock music advocate and movie producer) commented as he reflected back when rock music first became popular: *"I realized that this music got through to the youngsters because the big beat matched the rhythms of the human body. I understood that. I knew it and I knew there was nothing that anyone could do to knock that out of them. And I further knew that they would carry this with them the rest of their lives."*[63]

The natural rhythms of our hearts (and some even propose our biological molecular cells) are in tune with the natural accent of music (This is *"The Rule of Accent"* that we mentioned earlier taught worldwide in universities, printed in textbooks and found in treatises). These bio-rhythms allow us to "feel" and keep music in time. Even those with no understanding of bio-rhythms can still tell the difference between music that creates a "fight or flight" release of adrenaline as it attacks the natural heartbeat versus music that flows with your bio-rhythms making you relax.

Steven Halpern (one of the founders of New Age music) wrote: *"When you realize that much of Pop music is built around a bass drum pattern that has been getting increasingly louder in relation to the melody and other aspects of song, you have an inkling of just how pervasive this artifact of our culture is. Much like the air we breathe, we have been so inundated with this beat, massaged for years without even being aware of it, that we don't notice the subtlety of its power.*

"Not only that, but the actual pulse pattern that is used in most contemporary music, be they AM or FM varieties, hard or soft Rock, is actually counter to the naturally occurring heartbeat. Dr. Sheldon Deal, a nationally known chiropractor and author, and by no means an old fuddy-duddy categorically putting down rock-n-roll, demonstrated the effect of the standard Rock beat on muscle strength of the body.

"Using tests basic to kinesiology, he showed that the rhythm arrangement that we hear all the time in pop music has a definite weakening effect on a subject's strength. This effect held true WHETHER THE SUBJECT LIKED THE STYLE OF MUSIC OR NOT. In other words, how one 'felt' about the music, tastewise, was irrelevant in terms of how the body 'felt'. A common denominator cutting through most subjective reactions is that of sexual arousal. There are electrical changes in conductivity that manifest themselves on the surface of the skin as well as internally. These are easily measured by the same kind of apparatus that is used in lie detectors."[64]

Furthermore, according to Dr. John Diamond (a respected physician from Australia who practiced medicine in New York) and his extensive research that he revealed in his 1989 book *Your Body Doesn't Lie,* there is a specific beat in most rock music that is detrimental to your health. It will suppress your thymus gland, reduce your immunity, weaken your muscles, and potential affect your organs.

"With the ears completely blocked, the body still responds

to sound. This is because we 'hear' not only with our ears, but also with our bodies. Several years ago, my research on the effect of music took an unexpected turn. Shopping in the record department of a large NY store, I became weak and restless. The place was vibrating with rock music. Later, I tested the effect of this music.

"Using hundreds of subjects, I found that listening to rock music frequently causes all the muscles in the body to go weak. The normal pressure required to overpower a strong deltoid muscle in an adult male is about 40-45 pounds. When rock music is played, only 10-15 pounds is needed. This is far more serious than 'just' a weakening. When a muscle tests weak in the clear, the energy problem is even more severe. Every major muscle of the body relates to an organ. This means that all the organs in our body are being affected by a large proportion of the popular music to which we are exposed each day.

"I have also demonstrated that when the weakening beat is played, the phenomenon called 'switching' occurs — that is, symmetry between the two cerebral hemispheres is lost, introducing subtle perceptual difficulties and a host of other early manifestations of stress. The entire body is thrown into a state of alarm. This has been observed clinically hundreds of times.

"What characteristics of...rock are responsible for this weakening effect? Careful listening to and examination of many rock records suggest that a common characteristic is a backbeat. The weakening rhythm is apparently counter to the body's normal physiological rhythm.

"Of the well over 20,000 records of all types of music that I have tested, I have found only two instances in classical music that produce muscle weakness. One is at the conclusion of Stravinsky's 'Rite of Spring' and the other at the conclusion of

Ravel's 'La Valse.' In both cases the composer was attempting to convey chaos and has done it quite successfully.

"'La Valse' begins as a typical waltz, but ends as a parody as it disintegrates into a crescendo of dissonance. Certain conductors try to maintain the steady pulse of the waltz, and at the climax of these conductors' renditions, test subjects are not weakened. Other conductors, however, take a much more satirical view of the music and deliberately break up the pulse at the end; here the subject's muscles indeed test weak."[65]

It is true!! Rather than a waltz-like beat pattern that reflects the heartbeat and the rhythm of one's body, rock music employs an unnatural sequence. Altering the rhythm from what God originally intended it to be has dire consequences to a person's physical, emotional, and spiritual well-being.

If rock music and backbeat pose significant threats to our bodies, then why do Bible-believing Christians implement them within their music? It makes no sense. Maybe some have never been taught? Others possibly allow it in their music because their flesh likes it and they are mistaking a carnal "feel-good" emotion for a genuine godly experience? Possibly there are those who engage in it because of pride and rebellion, thinking *"There is nothing wrong with it! I don't care what you think. This is my kind of music."?* We do not know. But this is an area that our hearts are so burdened about, and we believe that God's heart is broken over it as well. Scripture teaches us very carefully to *"grieve not the holy Spirit of God"* (Ephesians 4:30) and to *"quench not the Spirit"* (I Thessalonians 4:19).

If our bodies are the temple of the Holy Ghost, then why would a person consider harming it or abusing it? God is appalled that we would engage in such a thing: *"What? know ye not that your body is the temple of the Holy Ghost which is in you, which ye have of God, and ye are not your own? For ye are bought with a price: therefore* **glorify God in your body, and in your spirit, which are God's***"* (I Corinthians 6:19-20).

DRUMS — ARE THEY GOOD OR BAD?

So many people get flustered over the discussion of drums. To begin, we want to be clear. A drum is not evil or wrong by itself — just like a piano or a flute are not either. Can drums be used correctly? Definitely. Those who decry using instruments that could possibly create rhythm would do well to study the Bible a little closer before ignorantly presuming that God is anti-rhythm or is against any instrument that generates a rhythm. In fact, He encouraged the use of hand clapping (Psalm 47:1; Psalm 98:8; Isaiah 55:12, etc.), cornets (small finger cymbals; see II Samuel 6:5 and II Chronicles 15:14), timbrels (similar to the tambourine; see Exodus 15:20, Psalm 68:25, Psalm 81:2, etc.), and cymbals (Psalm 150:5) — all of which must be used in their proper context and place.

In God's Word, we also find many tempo-generating instruments. *"And David spake to the chief of the Levites to appoint their brethren to be the singers with instruments of musick, psalteries and harps and cymbals, sounding, by lifting up the voice with joy"* (I Chronicles 15:16). Psalteries (of the harp family) cannot physically be thrummed without generating a beat. Cymbals, obviously, have an immediate influence on the rhythm of a song. And today, even the piano (one of the most-popular musical instruments in the world and practically in every Bible-believing church) is classified as a stringed percussion instrument, hence tempo-generating. *(See footnote for explanation.)*[66]

We find it very fascinating that though drums existed

prevalently in Bible times, they are not specifically referenced or even acknowledged within Scripture. We are not trying to manipulate the Bible to say something as a result of this; but God's Word places a greater emphasis upon instruments that can generate *melody* and not rhythm when making music. Here are a few examples out of many that could be given: *"Upon an instrument of ten strings, and upon the psaltery; upon the harp with a solemn sound"* (Psalm 92:3); *"...we will sing my songs to the stringed instruments all the days of our life in the house of the Lord"* (Isaiah 38:20); and *"I will sing a new song unto thee, O God: upon a psaltery and an instrument of ten strings will I sing praises unto thee"* (Psalm 144:9).

We completely understand the determination not to give any space for the rock-n-roll backbeat (it is certainly wrong). However, we must be careful to resist the knee-jerk reaction to conclude that all rhythm is ungodly. Rhythm is never supposed to dominate. As we have already studied, the Bible implies in Ephesians 5:19 that melody should be what is most prevalent in our music.

We are not opposed to drums; we are opposed to the use of drums in an inappropriate way. The problem therein lies in what it is used for and when the emphasis of the rhythm goes wrong. As we have already studied, rhythm itself is not bad — God made it! It brings order, structure, and cadence to music (in 4/4 timing, the beat is found and counted in each measure 1 2 3 4, 1 2 3 4, and so on). Rhythm is not wrong unless it is misused.

So that brings us to the question: can drums be used inappropriately and for evil? Yes, absolutely — just like any other instrument, such as a jazzy piano in a bar or a silky flute used for ethnic dancing. However, we must be careful! I'm sure we can all agree that the drum-set is used more than any other instrument to pound out the backbeat in rock-n-roll music. No other instrument in the world has been used more to produce unnatural, fleshly rhythms than the drum. Consider its history. Drums have been around for thousands of years. The first images of drums we find date to around 2200 B.C. and were used for dancing and for worshipping false gods. Music of Baal worship has actually been deciphered from ancient fragments found in Greece and was reconstructed by modern-day musicians. This pagan music defined the need to pound out unnatural rhythms on drum-like instruments. In Africa, India, the Caribbean, and South America, drums have been heavily used to conjure up spirits and permit demon possession.

Of course, not all drums were designed for these uses. Some served as a means of communication over distances and others to provide a cadence for soldiers marching to battle. In the European culture, drums and other percussion instruments were mainly utilized to generate a rhythm for orchestral music. However, they did not have a major emphasis in the orchestra.

Frank Garlock explained: *"How much rhythm is too much rhythm, as thought of from a numerical perspective? The typical symphony, such as the Boston Symphony Orchestra or the Chicago Symphony Orchestra, includes approximately one hundred musicians. Three to four of them are responsible for the rhythm as they play the percussion instruments like the timpani, bass and snare drums, cymbals, triangle, bells, and several other rhythmic devices. Since the percussion instruments do not perform much of the time, it can be concluded that <u>less than four percent of the orchestra is responsible for the basic rhythm</u>. It might be argued that all of the instruments play some part of the rhythm, but this only makes the analogy* *between rhythm and the pulse stronger. All parts of our bodies are affected by the pulse, but it is the pulse itself which gives the body its basic rhythm. In addition to this, it must be remembered that just as the spirit, mind, and body are interrelated, so are the melody, harmony, and rhythm. One cannot exist without the other two.*

"The conventional secular or Christian rock group has a slightly different blend. Typically there are four basic instruments: the rhythm guitar, a bass guitar, an array of drums, and the lead guitar. Although the guitar can be a beautiful instrument used for melody, harmony, and rhythm — in rock groups it is mainly used to magnify the offbeat rhythm or to accentuate the driving rhythm. At best, the sound which comes from the typical rock group is <u>seventy-five</u> <u>percent</u> <u>rhythm</u>."[67] Hence, the instrumentation and the music is way out of balance!

The modern drum kit was developed in the vaudeville era during the 1920's and became the central part of jazz. Its purpose was to provide syncopation for music to help it have a greater swing and dance feel at clubs and lounges. A man by the name of Chick Webb (known as "the daddy of them all" by legendary rock drummers) was the first to usher in this sound and style. From that time, because of the "life" it brought to music, many emulated what he started and developed it over the last century to what we have today.

Sun Records founder Sam Phillips (who recorded some of the first rock & roll hits, including Elvis' first recording in 1954) understood the power of rock music. Reminiscing many years later about why it became such a social phenomenon, he said, *"It all came out of <u>that</u> <u>infectious</u> <u>beat</u> and those young people wanting to feel good by listening to some records."*[68] The *"infectious beat"* that Phillips is talking about (and what so many others referenced in the quotes we have already seen in this chapter) came from the drum-set of the rock band.

We **must** handle rhythm with caution, for an imbalance of it can immediately transform a song into an ungodly noise. The beat of rock music appeals to the flesh — that's why so many people like it. I John 2:16 says that *"the lust of the flesh...is not of the Father, but is of the world."* The music we use and listen to should seek to glorify God, not entertain people or satisfy fleshly desires.

We CANNOT dismiss the facts that there is an <u>addictive quality</u> to backbeat and the fleshly excitement of rock-n-roll styled music. A good feeling does not equate to Biblical edification. True edification is always in conformity to God's Word. Backbeat from drums can be hard or soft, fast or slow, loud or quiet, but it is still "infectious" rock music nonetheless.

A DOORWAY TO THE OCCULT

The Bible exhorts that we are to be *"warning every man, and teaching every man in all wisdom; that we may present every man perfect in Christ Jesus:"* (Colossians 1:28). We want to be careful how we present the following contents, but we believe that it is critically important to note. For multiple centuries throughout history, drums and certain beats they can produce have been specifically associated with the kingdom of darkness. Ultimately, rock music can be a door to the occult world via percussion.

Mickey Hart (drummer for the *Grateful Dead* and considered to be one of the greatest experts in drums) traveled the world researching the power of drums. Though he is clearly not a Christian, what he discovered should serve as a sobering wakeup call to believers. In *Drumming at the Edge of Magic*, he wrote of his findings:

"Everywhere you look on the planet, people are using drums to alter consciousness. I've discovered, along with many others, the extraordinary power of music, particularly percussion, to influence the human mind and body.... I know that it's possible to ride the rhythms of a drum until you fall into the beginnings of trance. When I'm drumming, I like to get as close to this state as I can. There have been many times when I've felt as if the drum has carried me to an open door into another world."[69]

This book and a few others he has written based on decades of research are very chilling and eye-opening about the "spiritual" history of percussion. Through them, he has proved in excruciating detail the connection of rock music and backbeat with paganism, spiritism, and demonism. He shares with the reader his startling revelations:

"Years ago, I thought shamans were like stage magicians, using all sorts of tricks and ventriloquism to fool people into believing they had special powers. Now I know better. The word 'shaman' is used to describe individuals who can enter into a trance in order to communicate with the spirit world."[70]

Hart then described throughout a majority of his work that Asian, African, Caribbean, South Pacific, and Brazilian cultures (among others) all have the same spiritual connection around the drum. He unbiasedly arrived to the conclusion after his vast interaction with these cultures that *"the spirits ride the drumbeat."*[71]

He went on to further explain: *"Shamans are drummers — they're rhythmists, they're trance masters who have understood something fundamental about the nature of the drum. [They used drumming] to summon the spirits or the gods down into the body of someone, usually a dancer. This is known as possession trance. The classic example is voodoo, where the spirits are said to descend and mount the bodies of the dancers and ride them like horses."*[72]

Pearl Primus, an expert on voodoo, says: *"The drummers keep up a terrific throb and beat which very easily takes possession of the sensibilities of the worshippers. Observers say that these drums themselves are able to bring a person to a place where it is easy for the 'loa' [spirit] to take possession of their bodies — the defenseless person is buffeted by each stroke as the drummer sets out to 'beat the loa' into his head."*[73]

Other unsaved rock musicians have also observed this association of rock-n-roll with voodooism as well. The famous British drummer Rocki (who has recorded with many renowned groups such as the Rolling Stones, Spooky Tooth, and Ginger Baker) understood that the music of Jimi Hendrix, one of the "greatest" guitarists in rock history, was akin to voodoo rhythms. Note the following amazing statement from Hendrix's biography: *"He [Hendrix] had gotten a chance to see Rocki and some other African musicians on the London scene. He found it a pleasure to play rhythms with them. They would totally get outside, into another kind of space that he had seldom been in before.*

"Rocki's father was a voodoo priest and the chief drummer of a village in Ghana, West Africa. Rocki's real name was Kwasi Dzidzornu. One of the first things Rocki asked Jimi was where he got that voodoo rhythm from. When Jimi demurred, Rocki went on to explain in his halting English that many of the signature rhythms Jimi played on the guitar were very often the same rhythms that his father played in voodoo ceremonies. The way Jimi danced to the rhythms of his playing reminded Rocki of the ceremonial dances to the rhythms his

father played to Oxun, the god of thunder and lightning. The ceremony is called voodooshi."[74] Stunning!

Mickey Hart shared in his own writings: *"You don't want to be possessed by just any spirit, so great care must be taken that only the correct spirit takes up residence. The way this is accomplished is with the drum. Particular rhythms are supposed to attract particular spirits. An 'Orisha'* [what possessing spirits were called in Africa] *only comes when he hears his rhythm."*[75]

"When the shaman reaches that door (of the spirit realm), he sings his songs and the spirit allies come, often taking up abode in his drum. Percussive noise might be helpful in inducing trance, but it was rhythmic entrainment that enabled the shaman to actually move into this spirit world. This, I think, is the drum's function. That is mentioned in almost all accounts.[76] *I awoke to the fact that my tradition — rock-n-roll — did have a spirit side.*[77]

"Drums have two voices. One is technical, having to do with the drum's shape, material, and the standard way it's played. Technique gives you this voice. It takes commitment and apprenticeship to learn how to find a drum's sweet spot. But once you do, the potential arises for contacting the drum's second voice — the spirit side of the drum.[78] *The voice of the drum is a spirit thing."*[79]

He then transitioned to discuss how tribal music influenced America. (You will see how this corresponds with some of the things we already mentioned.) *"I think it's safe to say that Africans are probably the most rhythmical, in the sense that an awareness and appreciation of rhythm is the mainstay of their culture.*[80] *When the slave ships began plying the waters between the New World and West Africa, everyone thought they carried just strong, expendable bodies. But they were also carrying the form of drum rhythms that could call down the 'Orisha' [possessing spirits] from their time to ours.*[81] *New Orleans was the area in America where the 'Orisha' established a strong foothold.*[82] *And out of this came jazz, the blues, the backbeat, rhythm and blues, rock-n-roll — some of the most powerful rhythms on the planet.*[83]

In our personal study, we found it incredibly fascinating that when the first African slaves in America were reached with the Gospel and became Christians, because of their background and familiarity with the instrument, they understood the evil power and influence that drums could have. These born-again believers actually forbade the use of drums in their services! A notable authority on American soul music went on to say: *"Historically, these African Americans had drawn the line between particular instruments and practices; they permitted tambourines, for instance, but NOT DRUMS."*[84]

Mickey Hart continued to share the origins of rock music: *"The backbeat emerged, first appearing in those New Orleans brass bands — African rhythms and African sensibility channeled through the unfamiliar instruments of the American marching band — and in the syncopated ragtime. The front line of these bands consisted of trumpet, clarinet, and trombone, but sitting in the back, propelling this new beat, was an invention that to my mind rivals those of Henry Ford and Thomas Edison. I speak, of course, of the drum-set."*[85]

"I remember exactly what I was doing when the backbeat first affected me, making me want to dance, dance, dance. I was working in a public pool as a junior lifeguard and the older lifeguards had the radio tuned to a station that played 'race' music. Little Richard. Chuck Berry. Elvis. Buddy Holly. It was irresistible, this music. It just drew you in. You had no choice.[86]

"*In Africa, musicians are never possessed by the spirits they call down with their rhythms, so what possesses our audiences I can never know. But I feel its effects. From the stage you can feel it happening — group mind, entrainment, find your own word for it — when they lock up, you can feel it; you can feel the energy roaring off them. We have learned if we patiently feed the rhythms, if we manage to vibrate in time, to resonate, then the big wave will come.*[87] *I have seen masses and masses of people going into trance.*"[88]

Thinking back to his days as bass player in "*Bill Haley and His Comets*" during the 1960's before he got saved, Louis Torres said: "*I recalled the effects of the music I once helped produce in nightclubs. I remembered seeing sensuality, uncontrolled emotions, rebellion, violence, and what I would now call devil possession. I heard people on drugs blurt out 'Wow!' as they experienced highs stimulated by our music. I also saw extreme lethargy. I confess with shame that our ability to produce these different reactions and sensual responses to our music filled us with glee. Yes, we knew we were manipulating people's minds.*"[89]

Juan Carlos Pardeiro, who also has been saved and turned from his former life, recalls what it was like at his rock concerts: "*In my youth, I was a nationally famous rock star in Uruguay, my home country. God has brought me a long way. I especially remember a particular evening long ago....*

"*The air was warm and radiant; the screams could be heard several blocks away. Thousands of cars overflowed the parking lot of the huge stadium. Inside, the voices of the wild audience mingled with the screeching of electric guitars and the lead singer's intense yelling. Smoke rising through colors flashing from the strobe lights, along with the fans' frenzied dancing, helped create a bewitching atmosphere. Every*

movement the rock stars made was watched by thousands of
intently adoring eyes. As the sounds burst from the stage, a
wave of screaming and uncontrolled crying flooded back.

"From the outside, the scene in the stadium resembled a
cage of demons. Inside, the sensual atmosphere made everyone
lose command of self-respect and sanity. Everyone was caught
up in a single torrent of emotions, as if guided by invisible
hands toward an abyss of endless ecstasy. Everyone, that is,
except the lead singer. He was there watching it all, unable to
understand it. I was that lead singer. I was a major cause of the
madness."[90]

In conclusion, Mickey Hart stated: "When I play a drum,
I'm looking for transcendence, I'm looking for uplifting of
consciousness. I'm looking for the groove. I'm looking for the
feeling. I'm chasing it, constantly.[91] Your mind is turned off,
your judgment wholly emotional. Your emotions seem to
stream down your arms and legs and out of the mouth of the
drum; you feel light, gravity-less, your arms feel like feathers.[92]

"None of my friends talked about shamans, and yet that's
what we were all trying to become, without knowing it. We
were intent on the thrill that came from playing in these
dangerous spaces."[93] Whether a drummer is consciously aware
of this or not, Hart believes from all his vast studies that rock
drummers through their beat are rhythmically "standing" at
the doorway of the spirit realm and calling for spirits to come.
Yikes! This should give CHILLS! As he referenced, this is a
"dangerous" place, and it should be no place for a child of God.
The Bible teaches that a Christian should have no fellowship
with darkness and that we are to "Abhor that which is evil;
cleave to that which is good" (Romans 12:9).

What we have just painstakingly and carefully shared
with you is not "the rabid ramblings of some wide-eyed

ignorant Baptist preacher" as some might critically accuse. No, a majority of this has come directly from a renowned rock musician who knows more about drumming than perhaps any other person on the planet.

There are great dangers in rock music! There are the great dangers in utilizing the drum inappropriately and incorrectly. There are great dangers in having backbeat in our music. It is wrong, and it is a direct association with evil.

In 1978, Little Richard (whose music and charismatic showmanship laid the foundation for rock-n-roll) shocked the world when he openly admitted: *"Rock-n-roll doesn't glorify God. You can't drink out of God's cup and the devil's cup at the same time. I was one of the pioneers of that music, one of the builders. I know what the blocks are made of because I built them. My true belief about rock-n-roll — and there have been a lot of phrases attributed to me over the years — is this: I believe this kind of music is demonic. A lot of the beats in music today are taken from voodoo, from the voodoo drums. If you study music in rhythms, like I have, you'll see that is true."*[94] **Wow! Powerful!** Little Richard specifically brought up *"beats,"* *"drums,"* and *"voodoo"* tied with rock music. Wasn't it startling to see the connection? And he saw the connection back in 1978!

Grammy-Award winning singer/songwriter Robert Palmer (whom we have already quoted once) wrote in his book *Rock & Roll: An Unruly History:* *"The idea that certain rhythm patterns or sequences serve as conduits for spiritual energies, linking individual human consciousness with spirits, is basic to traditional African religions, and to African-derived religions throughout the Americas. And whether we're speaking historically or musicologically, the fundamental riffs, licks, and drum rhythms that make rock-n-roll can ultimately be traced back to African music of a primarily spiritual or ritual nature. In a sense, rock-n-roll is a kind of 'voodoo'.*"[95]

Rock-n-roll takes great pride that its rhythm and drum techniques come from this <u>very</u> <u>same</u> <u>style</u> <u>of</u> <u>music</u>. Repeating Malcolm McLaren, listen to what he believed: *"Rock-n-roll is pagan and primitive, and very jungle, and that's how it should be!"*[96]

As we read earlier from the Rock-n-Roll Hall of Fame's website: *"Rock-n-roll's roots can be tracked back centuries to drum beats in Africa and Celtic folk music in Europe."*[97] It was a merging of the African musical tradition with European instrumentation.

John Lennon (co-founder of the Beatles) stated in the *Rolling Stone* Magazine on February 12, 1976: *"Because it is primitive enough, it gets through to you its beat. <u>Go</u> <u>to</u> <u>the</u> <u>jungle</u> and <u>they</u> <u>have</u> <u>the</u> <u>rhythm</u> and it goes throughout the world and it's as simple as that."*[98]

It is understandable for a lost world to implement these sort of rhythms, because the Bible says, *"But the natural man receiveth not the things of the Spirit of God: for they are foolishness unto him: neither can he know them, because they are spiritually discerned"* (I Corinthians 2:14). However, once a child of God understands the difference between the right and wrong uses of rhythm or the drum, there is no excuse. To disregard it is a form of rebellion. Christians have no business going to a pagan culture and imitating their music styles. We are called to be different! *"But ye are a chosen generation, a royal priesthood, an holy nation, a peculiar people; that ye should shew forth the praises of him who hath called you out of darkness into his marvellous light:"* (I Peter 2:9).

There are physical and spiritual dangers in rock music. There are physical and spiritual dangers in utilizing the drum inappropriately and incorrectly. There are physical and spiritual dangers that we open ourselves up to (including our families, our children, and our churches) by having backbeat in our music. Dear friend, please understand! It is wrong, and it is a direct association with sin and evil!

ROCK-N-ROLL IN THE CHURCH

In the November, 1982, issue of the *Contemporary Christian Music Magazine,* one of the feature articles was entitled, *"Rock Artists Look at Gospel Music."* Here are a few disturbing quotes to consider from it:

"Contemporary Christian music is what we call a pop sound, yet with gospel lyrics. But any song that people would normally dance to — because of the beat — is now coming into the churches. Everyone is not comfortable with God, but contemporary music is a way of making them comfortable."
— William King of the "Commodores"

"Christianity is a point of view that's been around for a couple thousand years, and over the last few years it's been quite good at adopting contemporary styles of music. I'm not terribly religiously motivated, but I'm sure that Contemporary Christian music is going to become more commercial because the better the music is, the better it is going to get sold."
— Laurence Juber, lead guitarist for former Beatles vocalist Paul McCartney

"To me, Contemporary Christian music is the station that I tune in on the radio, thinking that I'm hearing secular music because it sounds so hip — until I catch the words and realize the lyric has a slightly different intent. I'm happy to see that Christian music is moving into the 20th century, and that in some cases, the distinction between Christian and secular music

is being blurred." — Alan O'Day, pop rock sensation and composer

In his book *"Why Should the Devil Have All the Good Music?"*, Frank Edmonton (a "Christian" DJ who broadcasted on rock stations and a heavy promoter of Contemporary Christian music) wrote: *"'Jesus music'* [what Contemporary Christian music was originally called] *has emanated from people for whom rock music has been a natural language."*[99] Later on, he acknowledged that "Christian rock" entered the churches — not through Christian musicians who sought to glorify the Lord — but mainly through unsaved, secular rock performers who sought to capitalize on religious themes.

Today we find a variety of so-called worship services having a huge dependency upon the use of drums and rock rhythms. Dan Lucarini, a former contemporary praise leader who led two churches from a sacred to a contemporary stance, warns about rock drums in his book *"Why I Left the Contemporary Christian Music Movement: Confessions of a Former Worship Leader."* Lucarini describes how he purposely led churches incrementally away from the traditional music. Lucarini associates the drum set with the final stage in this process: *"When the drum set finally appeared on the platform, I believe the church reached the steepest and most dangerous part of the slope. More than any other instrument, a drum set is the key instrument of contemporary music styles."*[100]

God's Word teaches us plainly: *"Proving what is acceptable unto the Lord. And have no fellowship with the unfruitful works of darkness, but rather reprove* [expose] *them"* (Ephesians 5:10-11). We are seeking to prove through this chapter what is *"acceptable unto the Lord"* by revealing what is not. Sadly, over the past century, there has undeniably been a great blending of carnal music with Christian music, and it is a grievous thing to mix the two. God strives to reason with us in II Corinthians 6:14-15, *"what fellowship hath righteousness with unrighteousness? and what communion hath light with darkness? And what concord hath Christ with Belial? or what part hath he that believeth with an infidel?"* The answer is: **NONE.**

As God's children, we should not even remotely associate with darkness. We strongly believe that Christians should not associate with rock-n-roll and the inappropriate use of drums. It is darkness! **We should be opposed to the use of drums when they produce rhythms that go against God's natural design (backbeat), that are sensual in nature, and that are associated with the demonic.**

Some may rationalize the adaptation of rock-styled music in their personal music or worship music. Others may defiantly excuse away the implementation of backbeat, thinking that it's cute, fun, and okay. No. It is wrong! There is a great plague of this sweeping across Christianity today. The same drum style of rock music has infiltrated the church and Christian music and forms the backbeat in Contemporary Christian music and mainstream Southern Gospel music. (We will discuss more about these two Christian genres in the next chapter.) This corruption is *tragic.*

Christian "rock" music is essentially the attempt to unite Christian words to beat music. Thus, it is a yoking together of the spiritual and the carnal. The words intend to glorify God, but the beat appeals to the flesh, even to sensuality. The words say one thing — the music says something else. This is wrong. How can we as Christian possibly engage in this music or implement its style in our worship when God has commanded us to *"come out from among them, and be ye separate, saith the Lord, and touch not the unclean thing"* (II Corinthians 6:17)?

Furthermore, the Bible says: *"As obedient children, not fashioning yourselves <u>according</u> <u>to</u> <u>the</u> <u>former</u> <u>lusts</u> in your ignorance: But as he which hath called you is holy, so be ye holy <u>in</u> <u>all</u> <u>manner</u> <u>of</u> <u>conversation</u>* [conduct or lifestyle]; *Because it is written, Be ye holy; for I am holy"* (I Peter 1:14-16).

We must understand that sin is still sin, regardless of its context. There is never a permission given for it in the Bible. Lying is still lying, in spite of the intent or purpose. Robbing a bank is still robbing a bank, in spite of the motive or reasonable use of the stolen funds. Backbeat is still backbeat — in spite of how tactfully or tastefully one may think it has been implemented or performed in music. God says, *"Ye did run well; who did hinder you that ye should not obey the truth? This persuasion cometh not of him that calleth you. A little leaven leaveneth the whole lump. I have confidence in you through the Lord, that ye will be none otherwise minded:"* (Galatians 5:7-10a).

Could it be that Christians have become so immersed, desensitized, and conditioned to rock music and its styles? Since it is everywhere around us (in the malls, in restaurants, at our jobs, on television in movies and cartoons, on the radio, at theme parks, etc.), have we allowed our conviction against it to weaken over time? Do we find ourselves slipping and drifting, now considering that it is not "that bad" if there is simply a "soft" backbeat in our music?

The old illustration of a frog in boiling water is an accurate parallel of the church and the world today. If Bible-believing and Bible-living churches were rapidly thrust into sensual, carnal music, they would jump out if it immediately and turn away from it as fast as possible. However, if fleshly secular musical influences were slowly introduced and their "heat" was gradually turned up — the church could become oblivious to its devastating effects until it is too late. Frank

Garlock of Majesty Music warns, speaking from experience with what he witnessed over decades, *"If a church starts using Contemporary Christian music, it will eventually lose all other standards."*[101]

As A. W. Tozer declared, *"It is time this generation learned that there is nothing smart about wrongdoing and nothing stupid about righteousness. We must stop negotiating with evil. We Christians must stop apologizing for our moral position and start making our voices heard, exposing sin for the enemy of the human race which it surely is, and setting forth righteousness and true holiness as the only worthy pursuits for moral beings."*[102]

I Thessalonians 5:5-6 exhorts us: *"Ye are all the children of light, and the children of the day: we are not of the night, nor of darkness. Therefore let us not sleep, as do others; but let us watch and be sober."* Rock music has subtly crept into so many churches, and Christians have been blind and asleep to its true nature for far too long. It is time to awake! It is time to arise! It is time to get active!

May God sincerely help us to *"Abstain from all appearance of evil"* as is commanded in I Thessalonians 5:22. Could it be that we are spray-painting "Ichabod" over churches, ministries, homes, and lives as a result of this open and blatant acceptance of worldly practices in what should be worshipful praise to our God? Absolutely.

Recently, a Contemporary Christian musician who played in several different bands at his mega-church commented, *"It's all about the heart of worship. God can enjoy a distorted guitar as well as a clean guitar. Especially when you're playing it for him."*[103] But God is not interested in our offering of worldly music unto Him.

Though many Christians may justify the carnality in

their music, it does not suddenly make it "okay" with God. In response to worldly music on the part of Israel, the Lord said through his prophet Amos, *"Take thou away from me the noise of thy songs; for I will not hear the melody of thy viols"* (Amos 5:23). Could it be that God is saying the same thing today with various styles of our "Christian" music and worship? Soberly, we believe so.

CONCLUDING COMMENTS

There are various observations that we have made in this chapter that may not be popular or accepted by some of the brethren. Please understand — we are not striving to be mean, contentious, or disrespectful. It is our genuine desire to be real, transparent, honest, and thorough with you about all of this in as concise a manner as possible. We pray that this chapter has been an eye-opener to the dangers of rock music and how it is influencing Christian music!

To apply Biblical principles regarding lifestyle choices and personal positions, one must exercise judgment. God is passionately looking for a generation of Christians that will actively engage in this: *"Run ye to and fro..., and see now, and know, and seek in the broad places thereof, if ye can find a man, if there be any that executeth judgment,"* (Jeremiah 5:1). Where are the Christians in this generation that will courageously rise up with holy conviction and determine to honor God with their music?

Judgment in its most basic definition is *"to form a conclusion about something."* May it be our heart's desire unto the Lord: *"Teach me good judgment and knowledge: for I have believed thy commandments"* (Psalm 119:66). And, *"Hear my voice according unto thy lovingkindness: O Lord, quicken me according to thy judgment"* (Psalm 119:149). We need God's wisdom and discernment in order to know what we should do in our lives that will glorify and magnify Him!

With all that we have studied in this chapter, certainly enough applicable Biblical principles and proven evidences about rock music and backbeat have been given to show that it is unnatural, sensual, and linked to darkness — therefore, not pleasing to the Lord. It is understandable that this is very difficult for some to acknowledge because of the strong pull this music has on the flesh and the appetite it generates. We are not striving to be critical or "judgmental" (as some would possibly accuse us of being); we are simply putting forth spiritually discerning "judgment."

We are not judging the hearts and motives (as only God can) of those who listen to the wrong kinds of music (that's between a person and the Lord), but we are standing to judge (point out) the wrong kinds of music — rock-n-roll and its styles with interruptive backbeat (whether it is "Christian" music or not). Of course, we seek to speak *"the truth in love"* (Ephesians 4:15) and with gentleness and meekness (II Timothy 2:24-26; Titus 3:2). The Bible encourages each of us: *"And let us consider one another to provoke unto love and to good works: ...exhorting one another: and so much the more, as ye see the day approaching"* (Hebrews 10:24-25).

If you have a number of rock music albums or Christian music that has been influenced by the "rock" style, you should *destroy* them and *replace* them with good, wholesome music. Christians should strive to only perform and listen to music that honors our Lord and Saviour Jesus Christ. There is a vast amount that *does* please the Lord! If you do not have an appetite for the right kind of music, then begin to pray and ask God to create one within your heart. He certainly can! In

Ezekiel 36:25-27, He promises, *"Then will I sprinkle clean water upon you, and ye shall be clean: from all your filthiness, and from all your idols, will I cleanse you. A new heart also will I give you, and a new spirit will I put within you: and I will take away the stony heart out of your flesh, and I will give you an heart of flesh. And I will put my spirit within you, and cause you to walk in my statutes, and ye shall keep my judgments, and do them."*

Though it might sound a bit radical, it is a Biblical principle to destroy bad, tangible influences. Acts 19:18-20 shares with us: *"And many that believed came, and confessed, and shewed their deeds. Many of them also which used curious arts brought their books together, and burned them before all men: and they counted the price of them, and found it fifty thousand pieces of silver. So mightily grew the word of God and prevailed."* The wrong kind of music, movies, materials, and so on should be destroyed instead of sold or given away so that they will not harm anyone else that gets their hands on it. As in the case of those described in the book of Acts, God will bless as a result! There are multiple passages and testimonies in the Old Testament that reveal God's favor upon those who rejected what was wrong, broke down the evil, and turned toward the Lord. God even encourages in Isaiah 1:19, *"If ye be willing and obedient, ye shall eat the good of the land:"*

But are we radical enough to embrace this truth and sincerely *"turn from our wicked ways"* (II Chronicles 7:14)? II Corinthians 10:5-6 directly exhorts: *"<u>Casting down</u>* [to lower with violence, demolish, pull down, destroy] *imaginations, and every high **thing*** [speaking of anything tangible or intangible that has the power to elevate itself] *that exalteth itself against the knowledge of God,..."* God can certainly give us the strength to overcome any vice of wrong music! We can overcome it *"because greater is he that is in you, than he that is in the world"* (I John 4:4).

God has nothing against our music having "life" to it (after, all our music should be joyful)! But not "life" the way the world would describe it. This is contrary to Scripture. Romans 8:6 says, *"For to be carnally minded is death; but to be spiritually minded is life."*

Our lives should be void of rock music. It is absolutely true: *"their rock is not as our Rock"* (Deuteronomy 32:31). May God help each of us to stay away from its influence and infiltration and determine to remain with Christ — only engaging with music that honors Him! As we get into this next chapter, we are going to ask ourselves some further questions about music and dig a little deeper into what godly music ought to be.

CHAPTER VII

QUESTIONS TO ASK YOURSELF WHEN ANALYZING YOUR MUSIC

We can never ask ourselves too often, *"Does my music glorify God?"* We have sought to bring this to your attention time and again throughout this book. This is so vital! Again let us read and meditate upon the words: *"Whether therefore ye eat, or drink, or whatsoever ye do, do **all** to the glory of God"* (I Corinthians 10:31). Colossians 3:17 exhorts us: *"And whatsoever ye do in word or deed, do all in the name of the Lord Jesus, giving thanks to God and the Father by him."*

Music was intended by God to be a vehicle of worshipping, magnifying, exalting, and glorifying Him and His truth. For instance, Psalm 66:1-4 encourages, *"Make a joyful noise unto God, all ye lands: Sing forth the honour of his name: make his praise glorious. Say unto God, ...through the greatness of thy power shall thine enemies submit themselves unto thee. All the earth shall worship thee, and shall sing unto thee; they shall sing to thy name. Selah."*

Psalm 95:1-3 & 6-7 proclaims, *"O come, let us sing unto the Lord: let us make a joyful noise to the rock of our salvation. Let us come before his presence with thanksgiving, and make a joyful noise unto him with psalms. For the Lord is a great God, and a great King above all gods. ...O come, let us worship and bow down: let us kneel before the Lord our maker. For he is our God; and we are the people of his pasture, and the sheep of his hand."*

Jesus declared in John 4:23-24, *"But the hour cometh, and now is, when the true worshippers shall worship the Father in spirit and in truth: for the Father seeketh such to worship him. God is a Spirit: and they that worship him must worship him in spirit and in truth."*

Our selection of the music we listen to or offer to God is a spiritual one. It should be based upon principle (truth), not our preference. The music that we listen to should draw us closer to the Lord and continually cause our hearts and minds to be turned toward Him. It should set our spirit toward His Spirit and ground us more upon truth! Frequently, the phrases *"unto the Lord," "unto Him,"* or *"unto our God"* are found in the Bible when music is mentioned.

As we previously studied, music can affect us. Two certified music therapists observed: *"A favorite song can get you into the mood for a social event, help you through the last mile of a long race, make standing in traffic tolerable, inspire you, or just make you feel good all over."*[104]

All of these things ought to be spiritual activities to the believer — the Lord certainly would want us to be socially cheerful (Romans 12:18), applying ourselves to the best of our ability (Ecclesiastes 9:10), patient and free of frustration (Ecclesiastes 7:8 & Philippians 4:6-7), visionary (Proverbs 29:18), and joyful (Romans 15:13). As we mentioned earlier, we *must be careful* to not segregate our life apart from God. Everything we do should be with Him in His presence. We are supposed to be *"continuing instant in prayer"* (Romans 12:12), *"praying without ceasing"*

(I Thessalonians 5:17) and *"praying always"* (Ephesians 6:18). This describes more than just having a prayer life, but enjoying a life of prayer and continual interaction with Almighty God in all that we say and do.

Many Christians listen to classical music or symphonic soundtracks (sometimes through Pandora radio) while they are at work or at home to aid in the mood of the atmosphere. Music like this softly playing in the background helps create a streamlined, stress-free environment where much can be accomplished. If music like this helps you accomplish tasks or stay calm and stress-free, God is pleased and honored and can receive the glory for it!

Let us be sure though that if we are listening to some "secular" music, we are heavily considering three key factors: the purpose of the music, the style of the music, and the content of the lyrics (if there are lyrics). Does it meet the standard of Philippians 4:8? Does it belittle or uphold godly values such as honesty, purity, and integrity? What message is it conveying? Is it musically appropriate and Biblically sound? Will it encourage and strengthen you emotionally and spiritually? Does it have a form of rock music in its instrumentation (whether jazz, country, oldies, etc.) that goes directly against what God established?

If any song glorifies what opposes God, a Christian should not listen to it. If anything leads you to think about or get involved in something that does not glorify God, it should be avoided. We recommend that a great majority of your music be Christian music (vocals and instrumentals). After all, we are saved! We should always seek to feed our soul and nurture our spirit. *"If we live in the Spirit, let us also walk in the Spirit. This I say then, Walk in the Spirit, and ye shall not fulfil the lust of the flesh"* (Galatians 5:25 & 16). Again, walking with God should not be a hit-and-miss thing; it can be a delightful 24/7 thing!

An excellent, free source we thoroughly enjoy using is *"Abiding Radio."* It is an online radio station that also has an app on iTunes and Google Play. On the app you can select different "channels" or "styles" of Christ-honoring music — ranging from vocals and choral to instrumental only, wholesome bluegrass, seasonal (depending on the time of the year), and music for children. Another great app is *"Faith Music Radio"* which plays wonderful Christian music recorded throughout the years by our dear friends Ed Russ and David Chamberlain at their studio, Faith Music Missions. Of course, there are several other good, wholesome apps and online stations that have been developed by Independent Fundamental Baptists that you could listen to (such as *BTM Radio* by our good friend Evangelist Byron Foxx of *Bible Truth Music*). There are more ample sources of godly music today than *ever* before! Praise God for that!

As Christians, we are members of two worlds — the spiritual and the material. Each of us have a choice to make: to engage in music that is pleasing to God because it ennobles character and spiritual growth or to defile our minds, hearts, and souls with music that will arouse lust and fleshly desires or impulses.

The two music therapists we quoted from before continued in their observation: *"Music is an art form that people respond to all day with their hearts, minds, bodies, and spirits. Music defines our likes, dislikes, physical appearance, mood and means of expression, and it fosters close communication with our peers. One of the most poignant gifts of music is its ability to elicit the most tender emotions. In this way, **it communicates directly to our hearts and souls**."*[105]

God's Word puts this last statement into proper perspective in Proverbs 23:7 — *"as he thinketh in his heart, so is he."* Since music does communicate directly to the heart and soul, the matter of what is being communicated should be of the utmost importance to every believer. With this in mind, let us consider some thought-provoking questions about the music we daily engage in and listen to.

IS MY MUSIC WORTHY OF GOD'S DIGNITY?

Psalm 7:17 says, *"I will praise the Lord **according to his righteousness**: and will sing praise to the name of the Lord most high."* Does your music fit the nature of God and His Word? For instance, many Gospel songs in particular can tend to have trite words and a honky-tonk "saloon style" of accompaniment that definitely doesn't magnify God and exalt His majesty. Music that fits a bar scene (whether it is from the Old West to the jazzy slinky music of the nightlife atmosphere of today) is not fit to glorify our holy God. Nor does its style suit His holy and righteous character. The Lord isn't the God of a carnival or saloon. He is a God of wonder, beauty, dignity, peace, and holiness among MANY other things! Do your songs in both lyrics and musical accompaniment style portray those qualities? As was just mentioned, beware of putting trite music to a song filled with deep, theologically sound lyrics. The music's character and style should be consistent with the message it claims to convey.

Furthermore, Ephesians 3:21 declares, *"Unto him be glory in the church by Christ Jesus throughout all ages, world without end. Amen."* I Timothy 1:17 pronounces, *"Now unto the King eternal, immortal, invisible, the only wise God, be honour and glory for ever and ever. Amen."* There are many other passages throughout the Bible that proclaim this same thing. We cannot forget that God is worthy of glory in all things. He does not deserve to be ashamed by what we listen to, embarrassed by how we sing, or ridiculed by the worldly instrumentation that we have callously called "acceptable." He is GOD, and He deserves dignity!

Music is not a peripheral issue with God; it is a sacred and serious thing. Long ago, the angels cried, *"Holy! Holy! Holy!"* before God (Isaiah 6:3). Those same angels are still singing, *"Holy! Holy! Holy! Lord God Almighty, which was, and is, and is to come."* (Revelation 4:8). Today though, it seems that from both pulpits and pews, the attitude towards our worship and praise of God has decidedly more become that of: *"Ho, hum. Ho, hum. Ho, hum,"* We have shrugged our shoulders, thinking it is not that big of a deal. It is a big deal to God, though.

He is passionate about our worship and praise of Him! A half a dozen times in Scripture, we find that, *"Thou shalt worship no other god: for the Lord, whose name is Jealous, is a jealous God:"* (Exodus 34:14). He desires to be glorified and praised in holiness.

Philippians 4:8 says, *"Finally, brethren, whatsoever things are* true, *whatsoever things are* honest, *whatsoever things are* just, *whatsoever things are* pure, *whatsoever things are* lovely, *whatsoever things are of* good report; *if there be any* virtue, *and if there be any* praise, *think on these things."* So much worldly "Christian" music involves words that don't honestly convey Biblical truths or a right perspective of our holy God. This music is sung to worldly instrumentation and beats that cause impure bodily movements and unlovely behavior in God's presence.

We can't help but picture a Christian "rock" concert, where people are dancing around, lights are flashing (making it look more like a nightclub scene than a reverent, church-like worship scene). Fans at the concert are more worried about getting their album signed by the performer after the concert than worshipping the God the musicians are supposedly singing about. We don't want to have any part of that and we don't believe God has any part in it either, since it goes against the things mentioned in Philippians 4:8 that we are supposed to think about and dwell on.

To take it even further, how do we know if music is "acceptable to God," as seen in Ephesians 5:10 which says, *"Proving what is acceptable unto the Lord"*? Well, ask yourself, *"Could it be sung in God's presence in Heaven? Would Jesus walk into the room and listen to it or put my headphones on and enjoy it?"* So much worldly music — rock, rap, pop, hip-hop, salsa, metal, punk, reggae and country (among many others) — is literally Satanic. Every day, people who feed their ears, minds, and hearts with it have gone out and committed murder or suicide because of the influence that music had on them. It is not worthy of God's dignity!

Colossians 3:1-2 teaches: *"If ye then be risen with Christ, seek those things which are above, where Christ sitteth on the right hand of God. Set your affection on things above, not on things on the earth."* Verses 5-6 admonish us: *"Fornication, uncleanness, inordinate affection, evil concupiscence, and covetousness, which is idolatry: For which things' sake the wrath of God cometh on the children of disobedience:"* We must soberly understand that God will have no part in it.

Unfortunately, a lot of Christian music is performed in such similar styles as the world because performers and churches are trying to gain larger audiences and please bigger crowds. Again, some might argue, *"But my music has Christian words! Jesus would listen to it."* Yet your music sounds just like the music on an unsaved person's ear buds. Is our music good, wholesome, and acceptable to God?

We are to *"come out from among them, and be separate, and touch not"* (II Corinthians 6:17) the *"unclean"* elements or the ordinances of the world. God cannot make it any plainer or simpler: *"And be not conformed to this world:"* (Romans 12:2). Only music with the right *balance* (where the words are right *and* the music is right) can be acceptable to God and worthy of His dignity.

IS MY MUSIC SUNG OR PLAYED <u>SENSUALLY?</u>

Romans 13:14 says, *"But put ye on the Lord Jesus Christ, and make **no provision for the flesh**, to fulfill the lusts thereof."* What does my music appeal to — the flesh or the spirit? What does the vocalist sound like? Is the singer's voice breathy and "intimate-sounding," making you feel more like you are in a movie love scene rather than worshipping in the presence of our holy God?

We all certainly enjoy the hymn *"Amazing Grace,"* but only the versions that have not been secularized or sensualized. Believe it or not, there is a right way and wrong way to sing and play even the simplest of songs. Don't excuse a sensual voice performing your favorite hymn just because it's your favorite hymn.

We are not speaking about "grace notes" (an extra note added as an artistic embellishment though not essential to the harmony or melody) or the use of "portamento" (meaning "carriage" or "carrying"; a purposeful slide from one note to the other). These and other musical "ornaments" can be utilized skillfully and conscientiously without evoking a sensual feeling. We are speaking against husky, guttural, heavy scooping, breathy, and raspy singing. The identical methods employed by the world to make a sensual sound are being used by many popular Contemporary Christian music and Southern Gospel music vocalists. Yet many Christians either do not realize it or deliberately ignore the fact that this is no longer God-honoring — but pure, sensual, flesh-gratifying fleshliness. Unfortunately, this type of singing has also crept its way into the style of some independent Baptist Millennial singers and other strong Bible-believing musicians. When we hear people singing with this sort of secular style, there is no denying the kind of music artists who have influenced them or whom they are seeking to emulate.

The whispery, breathy moan is a secular technique giving a feeling of closeness. Sociologists note that there are essentially three zones in which most interaction takes place. The *social zone* (about one arm's length) is considered a comfortable distance in which most conversation and communication take place. The *personal zone* is closer and is viewed as appropriate for dear friends or family members. The last zone is the *intimate zone*. This space — considered to be a space of one or two inches and includes touching — should be reserved only for one's spouse and is extremely private.

When was the last time you had a four or five minute conversation with a member of the opposite sex (other than your spouse) only one to two inches apart? Answer: It took place the last time you listened to any one of the popular secular or Christian vocalists who employ the whispery, breathy technique. It may have been a one-way conversation, yet it took place within your intimate zone.

As Mrs. Shelly Hamilton wrote, *"A Christian woman*

would never dream of speaking to another woman's husband with the breathy, sultry vocal quality so often demonstrated by female pop icons. Yet, in many churches, it has become acceptable for a female vocalist to 'bless' the congregation in this way."[106] This inappropriateness should not be in God's house.

What is the primary purpose of a microphone in any facility? It is to amplify the sound for satisfactory hearing. Its purpose is NOT to gain and project intimacy. Many musicians do not use the microphone correctly! If you think we're crazy, observe most entertainers or even "Gospel" singers and see how they clutch and caress the microphone. However, the microphone is not to blame — it is the singer's fault.

A microphone is an inanimate object that could be used for good or evil purposes. We enjoy what our dear friend and music author Ben Everson has to say about this matter: *"There was a time when handheld microphones were considered an evil thing. Some people prefer not to use handheld microphones or other types of microphones in their churches for various reasons; and that is between the individual congregation, the pastor, and the Lord. But is it the microphone itself that is wrong? Is a handheld microphone or a lapel microphone or a headset inherently evil? The only thing a microphone does is take a person's voice and amplify it so that everyone in the room can hear. I can preach a sermon through that microphone, or I can start swearing through it. The microphone itself isn't right or wrong; it's what a person is saying through that microphone that carries morality.*

"Some people say microphones off the stand are sensual. I disagree. I think a microphone on the stand emphasizes any movement of the body in contrast to the stationary microphone stand. I'm much more at ease holding the microphone because I can allow it to become a natural extension of my arm without it

becoming a focus and, therefore, a distraction. A microphone on a stand means I can't even turn my head without rotating my body. That's distracting.

"...While it is true that you can use a microphone to accentuate sensual styles of singing, it has much more to do with the way someone is singing in the first place than the proximity to the mouth. I routinely sing an inch or less away from the mic. The microphone will exaggerate (amplify) anything that is going on in my mouth. So, for example, if I have a lot of spit in my mouth, that might be distracting to hear so I really work on that. If my voice cracks or creaks, it will be exaggerated. Sensual sounds are created in the singer and simply amplified by the microphone. It isn't the fault of the mic!"[107]

Fleshly, sensual, worldly music cannot and will never please the Lord. God's Word is clear in Romans 8:6-8: *"For to be carnally minded is death; but to be spiritually minded is life and peace. Because the carnal mind is enmity against God: for it is not subject to the law of God, neither indeed can be. So then they that are in the flesh cannot please God."*

The sound of the voice suggests what a singer truly means. Through it, a secondary message is being conveyed to the listener besides just the words they hear sung. Jesus said in Matthew 12:34, *"...out of the abundance of the heart the mouth speaketh."* When you sing, what sort of message are you sharing? Ephesians 4:29 declares, *"Let no corrupt communication proceed out of your mouth, but that which is good to the use of edifying, that it may minister grace unto the hearers."*

There is no doubt that there are many different singing styles; God is not looking for us to be robotic — we are all created differently! But, we must determine if the style we are engaging in mimics anything sensual. God's people aren't to imitate the world or copy its "sound." God wants the melody we make to glorify Him and to be pure and not sensual (Ephesians 5:19). Galatians 5:24 states, *"And they that are Christ's have crucified the flesh with the affections and lusts."*

II Corinthians 7:1 admonishes believers to *"cleanse ourselves from all filthiness of the flesh and spirit, perfecting holiness in the fear of God."* (Perfecting holiness or completing Biblical purity, living a life that is Christ-like and Christ-honoring with a genuine reverence and respect for Who God is.) As we talked about before, God desires us to always be feeding the spirit, NOT the flesh. Does the style we use match the sacredness of the words which we sing?

IS MY MUSIC <u>WORLDLY?</u>

I John 2:15-20 exhorts every believer: *"Love not the world, neither the things that are in the world. If any man love the world, the love of the Father is not in him. For all that is in the world, the lust of the flesh, and the lust of the eyes, and the pride of life, is not of the Father, but is of the world. And the world passeth away, and the lust thereof: but he that doeth the will of God abideth for ever."*

God's Word teaches us here that worldliness should not be part of a Christian's life. When a statement like that is made, people can immediately become defensive and demand, *"Just wait a second! What's your definition of worldliness?"* The "world," as spoken of in the Bible, is that organized cultural system which is anti-God in philosophy, purpose, and practice. James 1:27 exhorts, *"Pure religion and undefiled before God and the Father is this, To visit the fatherless and widows in their affliction, and to keep himself unspotted from the world."*

What is worldliness in music? How can melody, harmony, and rhythm be considered worldly? It is so when it has been born out of this **corrupt cultural system** (nightclubs, ballrooms, taverns, lounges, karaoke sing-alongs, and other places where society congregates to feed the flesh) with **corrupt means** (backbeat and unnatural rhythm or instrumentation) for a **corrupt purpose** (fulfilling fleshly appetites or eliciting sensual responses).

Surely you know what the world's version of music sounds like. We can't avoid it, unfortunately, as it blasts in restaurants, grocery stores, on TV, from car radios, and more. If we are not to love the world or things in the world, why do we try and justify music that, apart from some "spiritual" words, sounds just like the music of the world? Oh, that God's people would be humble and honest enough to acknowledge the worldly things that make Christian music tainted and unclean!

If our children went outside during a rainstorm and rolled around in the mud, they would be pretty dirty, wouldn't they? When they came in the house, if all we did was put clean clothes on them instead of cleaning all the mud off of them first, would they be clean or would they still be dirty? They would still be dirty! Covering up the dirt doesn't take it away!

In a similar way, putting good words to worldly music doesn't make the song acceptable to God. He wants both the lyrics AND the music to please Him and not reflect the world. Good lyrics and bad music do not please God. Right and wrong can't fellowship. Christ's words and the Devil's music don't mix.

The Bible adamantly declares that God wants no part with the world. *"Ye adulterers and adulteresses, know ye not* that the friendship of the world is enmity with God? whosoever therefore will be a friend of the world is the enemy of God" (James 4:4). If we are choosing to "buddy up" to the world in our music, whether the lyrics are good or not, we are choosing to become the enemy of God. This must not be ignored.

Worldliness should not be acceptable or excusable, because separation is still taught in the Bible! God would have us to be set apart from this world and the things of this world. He reminds us in II Corinthians 6:14-18 that just as light and darkness are opposite and Jesus and Satan aren't friends, His children should not try to figure out ways to conform to secularism and culture. We were made to be different. He wants us to be sanctified — set apart from wickedness and worldliness so that He can use us to the maximum for His glory. He plainly says, *"Be ye not unequally yoked together with unbelievers: for what fellowship hath righteousness with unrighteousness? and what communion hath light with darkness? And what concord hath Christ with Belial? or what part hath he that believeth with an infidel? And what agreement hath the temple of God with idols? for ye are the temple of the living God; as God hath said, I will dwell in them, and walk in them; and I will be their God, and they shall be my people. Wherefore come out from among them, and be ye separate, saith the Lord, and touch not the unclean thing; and I will receive you, And will be a Father unto you, and ye shall be my sons and daughters, saith the Lord Almighty."*

God expects our entire testimony to be separate from this world. We should not do anything this world does that is considered in the least bit *questionable*. God commands: *"Quench not the Spirit. Despise not prophesyings* [don't scoff at Bible preaching]. *Prove all things; hold fast that which is good. Abstain from all appearance of evil"* (I Thessalonians 5:19-22).

The more sinful and dark the world becomes, the more Christians should stand out in contrast. Why? Because we are not seeking to just stay an arm's length from the world — we are determined to remain upon the unchanging truths of the Bible, regardless of where the ebb and flow of culture and popular opinion takes society.

As we seek to reach our fellow man, our separation makes the light of Christ radiating through us burn brighter. Philippians 2:15-16 declares, *"That ye may be blameless and harmless, the sons of God, without rebuke, in the midst of a crooked and perverse nation, among whom ye shine as lights in the world; Holding forth the word of life;..."* Our separation should make the distinction clearer — and once they see a clearer distinction, then they can start asking eternal questions. As a result, we can bring them more effectively to Christ.

The modern-day church would have you to think differently — that we must become like the world in order to reach the world. The more we are like the world, the dimmer our light of the Gospel will become. Most non-denominational churches today preach a very watered-down Gospel with no reference to Hell or repentance, resulting in few (if any) getting saved. Sadly, people who have already trusted Christ flock to these mega-centers because it offers them a message and an experience that does not offend their flesh or point out the damaging effect of sin. It gives a two-thumbs-up to the "easy life" and allows people to remain comfortable with no Bible convictions.

The truth is: the less distinction we have, the cloudier the issues will get. It leaves the lost world (who we are *supposed* to be reaching) confused: *"What is Christian, and what is not?"* The 21st century church greatly struggles with this! We need to be separated with a life emitting a wholesome Christ-like fragrance (II Corinthians 2:15). God commands it!

Have we been deceived to simply try to maintain a "safe distance" from the world as it ever changes? If so, we will find ourselves compromising and drifting farther and farther away from the principles of God's Word over time. As we strive to keep this "arm's length" from culture, we will soon be standing in the position the world had only years before. Understand that any one of us can become conditioned and desensitized to seeing, hearing, or participating in sinful and wrong things! God reminds us: *"Wherefore let him that thinketh he standeth take heed lest he fall"* (I Corinthians 10:12). He also challenges us, *"Therefore, my beloved brethren, be ye stedfast, <u>unmoveable,</u> always abounding in the work of the Lord,..."* (I Corinthians 15:58).

Any time Christians praise God and give Him glory, Satan's goal is to destroy that praise and glory any way he can. We believe he is achieving his goal by sneaking his music into our churches and youth departments little by little. Beware! Vance Havner (1901-1986) preached, *"Satan is joining our churches. He does more harm by sowing tares than by pulling up wheat. He accomplishes more by imitation than by outright opposition."*[108] The Devil seeks to offer modern day Christianity a fleshly-comfortable, culturally-appealing counterfeit form of worship. God wants us to come away from the Devil's music and be separated unto Him!

If our music echoes the world instead of God's Word, we dare not presume that it is favored by the Holy Ghost. Yet, carnal Christianity loves worldly-sounding gospel music. Observe the Southern gospel singspirations or the Contemporary Christian music concerts held in churches. They will attract large crowds of people. Churches are packed out for these events, but you will find a sparse audience for special revival services. Something is wrong!

If we may reiterate ourselves again (repetition is the key to learning): God is not interested in our offering of worldly music unto Him. Though many Christians may justify the carnality in their music, it does not suddenly make it "okay" with God. In response to worldly music on the part of Israel, the Lord said through His prophet Amos, *"Take thou away from me the noise of thy songs; for I will not hear the melody of thy viols"* (Amos 5:23). Could it be that God is saying the same thing today regarding various styles of our "Christian" music and worship? Absolutely.

What effects will this acceptance of worldly music or worldly *anything* have on us if we allow it to continue? If worldly influences remain in our lives, we will become lukewarm over time like Revelation 3:16 speaks of: *"So then because thou art lukewarm, and neither cold nor hot, I will spue thee out of my mouth"*. The Bible says in Galatians 5:7, *"Be not deceived; God is not mocked: for whatsoever a man soweth, that shall he also reap."* Jesus declared in Matthew 7:17-18, *"Even so every good tree bringeth forth good fruit; but a corrupt tree bringeth forth evil fruit. A good tree cannot bring forth evil fruit, neither can a corrupt tree bring forth good fruit."* Worldly music will not and cannot produce spiritual fruit or growth. Worldly music will produce **worldly fruit.** Maybe this is part of the reason we do not see genuine revival or why our homes are not as strong as they used to be. Maybe this is why our churches are not reaching their full potential and our young people are drifting so easily out into the world.

In Psalm 81:8-11, we find God's heart is breaking as He pours Himself out to His children: *"Hear, O my people, ...if thou wilt hearken unto me; There shall no strange god be in thee; neither shalt thou worship any strange god. I am the Lord thy God, which brought thee out of the land of Egypt: open thy mouth wide, and I will fill it. But my people would not hearken to my voice; and Israel would none of me."*

God brought them out of Egypt not to bring them back into Egypt. God brought them out of Egypt, but they never allowed Him to take Egypt out of them. As a result, the children of Israel turned away from God. They *"would not hearken"* or pay attention to what He had to say. After all that He had done — delivering them from bondage, leading them through the trials and tribulations of the wilderness, and bringing them great victory in the Promised Land — they took advantage of His grace, mercy, and goodness. They lost their awe and wonder of the Lord and considered all of it a "what's-the-big-deal" sort of thing. They refused to listen to the loving voice of God and returned to the morality, methods, mentors, and music of Egypt.

In the Bible, Egypt is used oftentimes to represent the world. God has brought us out of the world not to bring us back into the world. Could it be we have never allowed Him to take the world out of us? Why exploit the grace of God and go back to the music, morality, methods, and mentors of the world? *"But ye are a chosen generation, a royal priesthood, an holy nation, a peculiar people; that ye should shew forth the praises of him who hath called you out of darkness into his marvellous light:"* (I Peter 2:9).

God wants us to be different. God wants our music to be different. God does not want us to have the same inappropriate music styles and instrumentation that the heathen dance, jive, and foot-tap to. *"Be not ye therefore partakers with them. For ye were sometimes darkness, but now are ye light in the Lord: walk as children of light: (For the fruit of the Spirit is in all goodness and righteousness and truth;) Proving what is acceptable unto the Lord. And have no fellowship with the unfruitful works of darkness, but rather reprove them"* (Ephesians 5:7-11).

Understand that *"**God hath put a difference** between the Egyptians and Israel"* (Exodus 11:7b). We know that we are not Israel; but as His people who have been grafted into the Vine and adopted into the family of God (read Romans 11:17-27), we can clearly see that the Lord wants there to be a difference in our lives from the world as well. He gives us discernment from His Biblical principles on how to be different. There should be a distinction in our music from the world. In Leviticus 10:10, He declared, *"And that ye may **put difference between** <u>holy</u> and <u>unholy</u>, and between <u>unclean</u> and <u>clean</u>."* Are we living according to Biblical distinction? Have we yielded to God and allowed Him to alter our tastes to be different from "Egypt", the "unholy", and the "unclean"?

Consider the following report by journalist Jack Kelley as he describes an Amy Grant music concert: *"Inside the pavilion, 10,000 teens clap and stomp in anticipation. The band begins a fast-paced drumbeat. And then, Grant emerges, dressed in a flashy leopard-print jacket and leg-hugging black tights. The screams are deafening."*[109] This is just one example out of so many other Contemporary Christian music artists that could be used. Let's read on.

Describing Grant's music, author Cliff Jahr writes: *"With her successful blend of gospel and rock, Amy's Christian music could easily pass for secular. Its hard-driving arrangements, featuring guitar riffs, and her impassioned delivery sound exactly like today's mainstream pop."*[110]

Then he turned his attention to the thousands of young people from Christian homes that were there: *"She has* attracted hundreds of thousands of well-scrubbed young fans who know every lyric by heart. Like rock fans everywhere, they clap, cheer, join hands, sway in their seats and boogie in the aisles."[111]

Amy Grant said: "We've got to reach kids where they are right now. We've got to get in there with whatever is communicating musically."[112] The youth of our churches in modern-day America are being destroyed, and it's happening with the permission of pastors and youth leaders who imagine that something good is being accomplished through this. NO!

God was upset with His people and preachers in Ezekiel 22:26: "Her priests have violated my law, and have profaned mine holy things: they have put no difference between the holy and profane, neither have they shewed difference between the unclean and the clean, and have hid their eyes from my sabbaths, and I am profaned among them." God's Word is violated when we refuse to make a separation or a distinction in our lives between what's right and what's wrong — this includes our music. This deeply disturbs Him. Are you okay with that? We certainly aren't! Why would we want to grieve our God Who loves us, has our best interests in mind, and wants to use us for His glory, His good pleasure, and the Gospel's sake? It is utterly disrespectful and completely inappropriate.

The Lord specifically instructs that preachers should teach His people the difference between what's right and what's wrong. This is one of the Biblical reasons for this very book. Ezekiel 44:23-24 states, "And they shall teach my people the difference between the holy and profane, and cause them to discern between the unclean and the clean. And in controversy they shall stand in judgment; and they shall judge it according to my judgments: and they shall keep my laws and my statutes

in all mine assemblies; and they shall hallow my sabbaths."
This is something that God takes very seriously. It's not a
trivial thing. He has given permission for His men to clearly,
carefully, correctly, concisely, and courageously utter forth the
statutes of His Word to educate and empower His people in
how to live with all godliness for His glory.

In these verses, a word has caught our attention time
and again: *"profane."* To be *"profane"* or to *"profane"*
something is to treat sacred and Biblical things with
irreverence or disregard, so as to violate, defile, and pollute
them. Oh, God have mercy on us! Could it be? Is modern day
Christianity guilty of putting no difference between the holy
and profane concerning our music? Have we violated God's
principles concerning how He desires our music to be? Have
we defiled our worship with worldliness? Have we polluted
our praise unto the King of kings with sinful justification of
secular styles? There is a lot to ponder here in our hearts.

The need to distinguish between sacred and secular,
holy and profane, spiritual and worldly, has always been a
ruling principle for believers. Until the 1960's, most Christians
believed that the church and the world represented opposite
standards, lifestyles, and tastes — and so most of the world's
popular music was treated with great suspicion. Our music
and worship should never be confused, mixed with, or even
tainted by the debased styles of culture. One belongs to the
realm of sacred things and the other to the realm of secular
and profane things. There a time when a majority of
Christians were convinced that Almighty God would be
offended if the church adopted its song and sound from the
world. An overwhelming majority believed that to do that was
worse than inappropriate — it was sinful. Oh, how far we have
strayed!

We believe it would be wise to read how Psalm 81 ends. *"So I gave them up unto their own hearts' lust: and they walked in their own counsels. Oh that my people had hearkened unto me, and Israel had walked in my ways! I should soon have subdued their enemies, and turned my hand against their adversaries* [referring to VICTORY]. *Their time should have endured for ever* [referring to LONGEVITY]. *He should have fed them also with the finest of the wheat: and with honey out of the rock should I have satisfied thee* [referring to PROSPERITY]*"* (Psalm 81:12-16).

In a similar way, if we reject the instructions and involvement of God in our lives, we will miss out on the joy of being *"more than conquerors through Him that loved us,"* and of being a testimony for Christ that will leave behind a legacy for the generations to come. We will miss the fullness of His blessings. How sobering!!

As Christ-honoring Christians, we should not try to get as close to the world as possible. God does not want us to live this way. We should strive through the direction of Holy Spirit and the inner work of Jesus Christ to stay as separated from the world as possible. We are to avoid even the appearance of evil (I Thessalonians 5:21). If a piece of music would be comfortable in a bar, nightclub, or rock concert, then we should not be using the same styles in our church, home, or car. As we mentioned before, though it may not always be easy to know exactly where to "draw the line" with Christian music, we truly believe that the best place to the draw the line is as *far* from the world as possible.

In conclusion, please listen to Dr. Frank Garlock as he pours out his heart:

"One of the issues I see today that saddens me most is the ever-growing worldliness in the church. Christians need to

recognize that the standards once held by many have deteriorated dramatically. *This is true especially since 1968 when the Hays Code was abandoned by Hollywood and the whole entertainment industry. I would like to suggest that anyone reading this take a few minutes to read about the Hays Code of 1930 online.* [The Hays Code was the informal name for The Motion Picture Production Code.]

There are 12 pages of standards that were to be followed by the movie industry. Here are just a few:

1. *No picture shall be produced that will lower the moral standards of those who see it.*
2. *The sanctity of the institution of marriage and the home shall be upheld.*
3. *Sex perversion or any inference to it is forbidden.*
4. *Obscenity in word, gesture, reference, song, joke, or by suggestion is forbidden.*
5. *Indecent or undue exposure is forbidden.*
6. *Mankind has always recognized the importance of entertainment and its value in rebuilding the bodies and souls of human beings But it has also recognized that entertainment can be of a character either helpful or harmful to the human race.*
7. *The motion picture, because of its importance as entertainment and because of the trust placed in it by peoples of the world, has special moral obligations.*

"Because men are sinners, the code was not universally enforced and producers pushed the boundaries of risqué behavior. Movie producers nudged the limits so much that Dr. John R. Rice wrote a book in 1938 called 'What's Wrong with the Movies.' Those who hold Biblical standards realize that this

downward trend has greatly affected churches. Many people who call themselves Christians no longer have strict standards regarding morals, dress, or any of the standards in the Hays Code that were actually meant to apply to the non-Christian world. This spiritual decline has affected the music of some Christians. The most graphic illustration of this degradation is exemplified by the producers and followers of what is called Contemporary Christian music.

"We do not apologize for appearing to be 'narrow' when it comes to avoiding sensuality in music, especially sacred music. We are very concerned about the direction in which we see fundamentalism going and this includes both in our schools and in our churches. We face an alarming situation in seeking to be consistent with the Biblical principles that we have always believed and taught.

"We who believe and live by the Bible all have the same God and the same Bible that we preach and follow. Even among Bible believers, however, there is room for disagreement because we are human individuals who are not perfect, and we live in an imperfect world. I am a Baptist on purpose, and I have been one for more than 60 years. I am very much aware, however, that not all Baptists believe the same things today that Baptists believed when I was ordained in 1952.

"When some Baptists say that music is neutral or amoral, they are saying that there are no standards by which music can be judged. They say that there is no line that can be crossed that can make music unacceptable.

"In the final analysis, HE is the One we have to please and not any group, no matter what they might claim to be. May God give the desire to be faithful to the Lord in all decisions, including musical ones. May we be true and unwavering until our Lord returns to take us to be with Him."[113]

May God give us the courage and conviction to live holy! Our churches and nation are in desperate need of a generation who will passionately arise in the power of Christ and say "No" to the world and what is popular.

Jesus said twice, *"No man can serve two masters: for either he will hate the one, and love the other; or else he will hold to the one, and despise the other. Ye cannot serve God and mammon"* (Matthew 6:24 and Luke 16:13). We cannot hold hands with the world and with the Word at the same time. It has to be one or the other! It's time that we determined: *"I have decided to follow Jesus — no turning back, no turning back! Though no one join me, still I will follow with the world behind me and the cross before me. Take the world, but give me Jesus!"*

WHAT MESSAGE DOES MY MUSIC COMMUNICATE WITHOUT THE WORDS?

Some Christians say, *"As long as the words are okay, how can anything be wrong with it?"* Yes, the words might be Biblically sound, but the style communicates a message on its own. Timothy Leary, a New Age activist and an avid promoter of LSD usage, openly believed: *"Don't listen to the words, it's the music that has its own message. I've been stoned on music many times. The music is what will get you going."*[114] The music itself *does* send a message and we see proof of that in the book of Exodus with the children of Israel.

Listen to an account the Word of God gives us: *"And when Joshua heard the noise of the people as they shouted, he said unto Moses, There is a **noise of war** in the camp. And he said, It is not the voice of them that shout for mastery, neither is it the voice of them that cry for being overcome: but the **noise of**

them that sing *do I hear. And it came to pass, as soon as he came nigh unto the camp, that he saw the calf, and the dancing: and Moses' anger waxed hot, and he cast the tables out of his hands, and brake them beneath the mount. And he took the calf which they had made, and burnt it in the fire, and ground it to powder, and strawed it upon the water, and made the children of Israel drink of it"* (Exodus 32:17-20).

Moses and Joshua were far away from the camp of the Israelites, having just received the Ten Commandments from God. As they came within hearing range of the camp, they thought they heard sounds of war. Then they realized it was actually singing! What Moses and Joshua heard the Israelites singing (during their idolatry and wild dancing) was <u>not</u> sounds of contentment, satisfaction, peace, serenity, joyfulness, and worship. Rather, what was communicated was discontentment, rebellion, unrest, confusion, defiance, and a lack of reverence for God. (Interestingly, their first insight to the sensual and carnal worship that was taking place came from the *music!*)

So many excuse away their Contemporary Christian music and other worldly styles of music, saying that the lyrics are Biblical and that's all that matters. But if the words were taken away, what message would the instrumentation be conveying? Is it any different from the music that the world produces? This MUST be considered.

God spoke in Haggai 2:11-12, seeking to reason with His people, *"Ask now the priests concerning the law, saying, If one bear holy flesh in the skirt of his garment, and with his skirt do touch bread, or pottage, or wine, or oil, or any meat, shall it be holy? And the priests answered and said, No."* The principle here is that the clean cannot be combined with the unclean. Thus applied, Christian words should not be combined with a sinful, worldly music style. Music is not made godly by simply adding godly words to it.

If we removed the lyrics from many Contemporary Christian music and Southern Gospel music soundtracks, unfortunately the sound would be no different from the popular trends of mainstream worldly entertainment today in rock, pop, and country music. As we have already discussed in the previous chapter, these industries tend to utilize soft rock rhythms, embrace a "Nashville" tone, and emulate the breathiness of popular commercial music. They imitate the secular sound of the world, ranging from the styles made popular in the 1960's to present day. Alarmingly, their soundtracks and instrumentation can hardly be differentiated from the origins of rock-n-roll. Much of Southern Gospel music can be defined by a prominent backbeat, a strong rolling rhythm, with an electric lead guitar.

Martha Bayles, a notable authority on American soul music, described the beginning of this secular blending (we have already read the first part of this quote in the previous chapter while referencing born-again slaves): *"Historically, these African Americans had drawn the line between particular instruments and practices; they permitted tambourines, for instance, but NOT DRUMS. But this line shifted dramatically in the 1920's, when a black vaudevillian named Thomas A. Dorsey was converted at a Baptist convention and decided to incorporate the sounds he knew best into a new genre called 'gospel songs.' Many people would be surprised to learned that this same man wrote the salty blues classic, 'It's Tight Like That.' Since he incorporated blues into gospel, it has been tricky to say what (apart from some song structure and lyric content) distinguishes gospel from blues and other secular strains."*[115]

Unbiasedly listening to the styles of the Blackwoods, Statesmen, and other Southern Gospel groups of the late 1940's, one can notice a direct link of this music with early rock-n-roll styles. The first Southern Gospel group in history to have a nationally popular best-selling record was the Homeland Harmony Quartet in 1948 for a song called *"Gospel Boogie."* What?

Interestingly, the Southern Gospel genre first had an influence on early rock-n-roll; but then over time, rock-n-roll began to heavily influence Southern Gospel. Elvis Presley (the King of rock-n-roll) grew up admiring Southern Gospel music as a Pentecostal and was fascinated with its blues' sound. He listened closely to groups such as the Blackwoods and the Statesmen, especially lead Statesmen singer Jake Hess. His own personal record collection contained a large portion of gospel records, particularly Southern Gospel quartets. He used gospel groups as his backup singers, and they often toured with him when he gave concerts. When Elvis wanted to relax or when he wanted to warm up for recording sessions he used Southern Gospel music to get him in the mood.[116] In the 1972 documentary film *Elvis on Tour,* Presley said, *"We do two shows a night for five weeks. A lotta times we'll go upstairs and sing until daylight — gospel songs. We grew up with it.... It more or less puts your mind at ease. It does mine."* [117]

In 1950, Rupert Cravens (one of the key men behind the publishing of Southern Gospel music and the promoting of its "singing conventions") was convicted and burdened to call out this style of music with its blues' sound: *"Why should people who love the Lord and clean Christian society have to listen to the music of the 'juke box' to find a medium of expression toward God? Would Wesley have written poems to be set to some of the modern boogy-woogy songs that so many of the so-called better quartets go wild about? Why should men who are supposed to love the Lord make for their most popular phonograph records and 'song hits' a type of songs that is too cheap in the light of God's holy purpose to deserve mention?"*[118]

We believe those same questions should be asked to "fundamentalists" again today.

It baffles us why numerous independent fundamental Baptists pattern their music after culture. It *breaks* our hearts. Do we have your permission to transparently bear our soul to you for a moment? We are in no-wise seeking to be passive aggressive here. We have no ulterior motive. This is an Isaiah 58:1 *"cry aloud, spare not, lift up thy voice like a trumpet"* moment to any and all who will hearken. Please... We are begging you.... Please stop grieving the Holy Ghost, please stop giving place to the Devil, and please stop gratifying the carnality of the flesh. Has American Christianity become ensnared and, as a result, become enslaved? Just like an addict either cannot see or refuses to acknowledge that he has a problem, could it be that we are justifying our carnality and excusing away our compromise? Could it be that we are so calloused that we don't even realize that we have a problem?

Interestingly, a study conducted by Valorie Salimpoor and Robert Zatorre, neuroscientists at McGill University, investigated the ways in which dopamine affects the brain while music is playing (this type of experimentation was referenced in Chapter 3). They also measured body temperature and heart rate along with it.

With their brains under observation via Position Emission Tomography (PET), volunteers listened to their favorite music as scientists observed their dopamine release. The subjects were instructed to press a button during times in the music when they felt chills or excitement. Researchers recorded an increase in dopamine when the subjects were anticipating certain parts of their favorite music. The brain's limbic system, which governs its response to emotion, reacted to the peak moment when subjects pressed their buttons to signify that they were experiencing a music-induced high. Dr. Salimpoor noted, *"the euphoric 'highs' from music are neuro-chemically reinforced by our brain so we keep coming back to them. It's like drugs. It works on the same system as cocaine. It's working on the same systems of addiction, which explain why we're willing to spend so much time and money trying to achieve musical experiences."*[119]

The human response to music is well-documented throughout history as we have already studied in previous chapters. Research into the physical effects of listening to familiar music and the topic of music addiction is fairly new, however. Dopamine release is commonly associated with a human response to the fulfillment of needs. Music has been able to get people "high" whether they were on drugs or not. Music has become the drug, and up to 40% of listeners in America show telltale signs of addiction to it.

"Crack cocaine" isn't specifically named in the Bible, but because of its addictive and damaging qualities, it is considered absolutely harmful and wrong for a person to use. Even a lost world understands this from just a "common sense" point-of-view. But as God's people, we have more than just "common sense" — we have the command of Scripture to not violate our bodies. We are to keep ourselves pure (I Thessalonians 4:1-7) and ought to respect our bodies as God's temple (I Corinthians 6:19-20). Therefore by conviction, we see the Biblical application to avoid cocaine at all costs.

Scientifically proven, music can become just as powerful of an "addiction" as the substance abuse of cocaine. An addict is enslaved to his drug and frequently, vehemently justifies his use of it. He cannot clearly discern how it's inflicting severe damage to his mind and body. Could it be that many Bible-believing Christians are addicted to the wrong styles of music and don't even realize the harm that it's bringing them or the hindrance that it's placing on the Lord from being fully magnified and completely maximized through their lives (Psalm 78:36-41)? Yes, we believe so, and we believe that it is crippling modern-day fundamentalism.

The albums by industry Southern Gospel artists and Contemporary Christian Music artists are a scourge across fundamentalism. They are "killing" us and grieving the Holy Ghost. It has perverted our praise, secularized our singing, and made our worship worldly. We believe it is a modern day form of Balaamism (an intermingling of worldly practices with the church) — and that it is hindering 21st century Christianity from experiencing the full extent of true Heaven-sent revival.

Bruce Lackey, who was the Dean of Tennessee Temple Bible School in the 1970's, had played the piano professionally in bars before he was saved. Years later, he warned that much of the sound tracking from Southern Gospel music and Contemporary Christian music would be right at home in these ungodly environments because the rhythm, beat, and instrumentation was the same. Caleb's parents (who had an extensive musical background in the world before they were saved) also warned him of this as he grew up. A multitude of first-generation Christians has borne record of the same testimony.

Every Christian we have ever met who was saved out of the world and had been heavily involved with music before they came to Christ has emphatically shared this with us as well. They grew up with worldly music blaring over the radios in their homes and cars. They frequented bars/nightclubs before they were saved and they know what kind of music is played there. Now, as believers, many of them want as far away from that kind of music as possible. However, many second-generation Christians have a difficult time accepting the fact that their music actually sounds just like the world's, because they were never fully exposed to those places and atmospheres.

Listen again to what God has to say: *"As obedient children, **not fashioning yourselves according to the former lusts in your ignorance**: But as he which hath called you is holy, so be ye holy in all manner of conversation* [lifestyle]; *Because it is written, Be ye holy; for I am holy"* (I Peter 1:14-16). God reasons with us in Galatians 4:9, *"But now, after that ye have known God, or rather are known of God, **how turn ye again to the weak and beggarly elements, whereunto ye desire again to be in bondage?"***

God is looking for a generation that will arise and stand up for what is right whether it is popular or not and whether they will be ridiculed for it or not: *"**Stand fast therefore** in the liberty wherewith Christ hath made us free, and **be not entangled again** with the yoke of bondage"* (Galatians 5:1). Where are the Christians and young people who will no longer bow in obeisance to culture or go along with the flow of what is being accepted in modern-day Christianity as the new musical "norm"? Though it may not be popular, God still promises, *"Blessed is the man that walketh not in the counsel of the ungodly, nor standeth in the way of sinners, nor sitteth in the seat of the scornful"* (Psalm 1:1). We should stand for and do what is right rather than give in and knowingly do what is wrong. God desires a generation that will proclaim: *"but as for me and my house, we will serve the Lord"*! (Joshua 24:15b).

We would like to encourage you: *"fear* [reverence and respect] *the Lord, and serve him in sincerity and in truth: and put away the gods which your fathers served on the other side of the flood, and in Egypt; and serve ye the Lord"* (Joshua 24:14).

Because music can become such a stronghold in the mind, we must understand that it can be a very real struggle — a very real wrestling with God within our flesh to bring it into subjection (I Corinthians 9:27) and for God's presence and principles to reign supreme. II Corinthians 10:4-5 says that with vigilance we need to be *"pulling down...strong holds; Casting down imaginations, and every high thing that exalteth itself against the knowledge of God, and bringing into captivity every thought to the obedience of Christ."* If we do not do this with our music, it will become an addiction and a vice in our lives. Praise God that: *"I can do all things through Christ which strengtheneth me"* (Philippians 4:13). There is hope! We can have the victory!

We must allow the Lord to transform us by *"the renewing"* of our minds (Romans 12:2). This Greek word for *"transformed"* is the word *"metamorphoo"* (which alludes to metamorphosis). Just as a hungry caterpillar will voraciously eat, then wrap itself within a cocoon, and over a period of time come out as a beautiful butterfly, so ought we to feast upon God's Word, cocoon ourselves in His presence alone, and allow Him to transform our lives completely. We must let God completely re-write and re-wire our thinking and desires so that they may be transformed from the fleshly and earthly to the spiritual and the Heavenly. God desires to do this work, and we must let Him.

This word *"metamorphoo"* is only used four times in the

New Testament Scripture — once here in Romans 12:2, once in II Corinthians 3:18, and twice in the Gospels when the Bible describes how our Lord was *"transfigured"* before Peter, James, and John. When this happened to Christ, He allowed Himself to experience *"metamorphoo"* and *"his face did shine as the sun, and his raiment was white as the light"* (Matthew 17:2). May our music and every other area of our lives be transfigured. May there be a righteous radiance and a godly glow about the music we listen to — music that is above reproach and that unmistakably shines forth the glory and grace of our holy God.

II Corinthians 3:18 teaches us, *"But we all, with open face beholding as in a glass the glory of the Lord, are **changed** [metamorphoo] into the same image from glory to glory, even as by the Spirit of the Lord."* The Holy Spirit of God and the Holy Word of God will perform this transformative work. This is why it is so very important to be sensitive to the Holy Spirit in this area and have a Biblical approach to music.

To those of you who are reading this right now and are unsettled in where you stand, or maybe some of these things that we have discussed have ruffled you a bit — we would like to lovingly challenge you: *"choose you this day whom ye will serve"* (Joshua 24:15a). Please do right. Please *"Give unto the Lord the glory due unto His name; worship the Lord in the beauty of holiness"* (Psalm 29:2) — not with the beat of Hollywood.

John 4:24 reminds us, *"they that worship Him **must** worship Him in spirit and in truth."* Worship is no longer worship when it reflects the culture around us more than the Christ within us. As we had stated at the beginning of this book: may we determine to follow Christ and not follow culture or the control of our own flesh.

Contemporary Christian music sounds identical to today's pop music trends. Sadly, Southern Gospel music has become merely a countrified version of secular-sounding Contemporary Christian music and "Christian" rock.

Many songs within Southern Gospel music are powerful with a strong Biblical and spiritually-motivating message. But, if they have been adulterated with rock-n-roll's backbeat (as a vast majority of the industry's recordings are), they should be "off-limits" to the child of God. The songs (lyrics and melody) themselves are not the issue — it is how they are produced. This is not a cultural preference; this is a Biblical issue of whether or not we are going to associate with an element in music that goes against what Almighty God has established. If we do, this is great pride and rebellion toward Him. Backbeat is rebellion. We have clearly studied this, and there is no way to dismiss this or excuse it away. The Devil has no business being involved in our music or defiling it!

Southern Gospel has deteriorated rapidly in recent decades, but unfortunately many do not see this and indulge in it anyway. The backbeat has become much more prominent, and popular groups have become more secular in their styles and fashions. Some men have even grown their hair out long like women, but God still says: *"Doth not even nature itself teach you, that, if a man have long hair, it is a shame unto him?"* (I Corinthians 11:14). The music has become so similar to pop rock music or country western music — it's easily discernible to hear it if the lyrics are dropped and only the accompaniment is played. One can definitely distinguish an unnatural rhythm emphasized by a heavy backbeat.

There are a number of doctrinally-sound Southern Gospel songs that have been written over the decades. Are we speaking directly against the songs and lyrics themselves?

QUESTIONS TO ASK YOURSELF WHEN ANALYZING YOUR MUSIC

Absolutely not. Their message and melody have inspired countless. Unfortunately however, as we have just observed, there has been a great secularization in how these songs are presented, performed, or played.

Dr. R. G. Lee gave the unique analogy that as Christians, we should not wade through sewage to get just a thimble of truth. Why would any Christian willingly do this with their music when we have been given plenteous godly alternatives for Christ-honoring music? We should listen to Gospel music that has been produced correctly. We should sing and play Gospel songs properly (and there are countless examples of this being done). Remember, rock-styled music cannot be the right kind of accompaniment for godly music or the soundtrack of a Christ-honoring life.

Be careful! Don't accept the wrong kind of Christian music just because *"it's what I've always listened to"* or *"it's what I like"* (this is a flesh problem) or *"my favorite group sings it and it's okay because they are such good guys."* Sure, those Contemporary Christian music and Southern Gospel music artists might be saved (many of them are) and sincere about what they are doing. However, sincerity and a love for Jesus do not instantly and magically make the *music* right. As we observed before, the fact remains: unscriptural music is unscriptural music regardless of our personal preferences, justifications, or opinions.

IS MY MUSIC "SINCERE AND RIGHT" OR "SINCERE AND WRONG"?

As we just stated, simply because we are able to justify something within our own hearts and minds does not automatically make it right before God. T. S. Eliot is attributed for having made this profound statement: *"Most of the evil in this world is done by people with good intentions.*"[120] How true that is! Good intentions or sincerity (even tears or a heart-flooded sensation) cannot make something suddenly good. The Bible says, *"All the ways of a man are clean in his own eyes; but the Lord weigheth the spirits"* (Proverbs 16:2). *"Every way of a man is right in his own eyes: but the Lord pondereth the hearts"* (Proverbs 21:2). The feelings of our heart can scream to us that something feels so right. It MUST be right. Wait a minute. If God says it's wrong, it's wrong. There is no other way around it.

God's Word makes it perfectly clear that separation from the world, non-conformity to the world, is not an optional part of Christianity. The modern-day Christian mindset that you can be *"theologically conservative and culturally liberal,"*[121] as Mark Driscoll describes it, is **heresy**.

Remember, God alone is the Authority — He is the Potter, we are the clay. *"O man, who art thou that repliest against God? Shall the thing formed say to him that formed it, Why hast thou made me thus? Hath not the potter power over the clay?"* (Romans 9:20-21). We are exhorted to become Biblically-sound as Christians, *"transformed"* (Romans 12:2) by the Word of God to live according to the truth that lies therein (James 1:22-25).

The Lord also desires that His children be *sincere*. Oh God, please help us to cease from being so ritualistic and formalistic! We revolt against spiritual hypocrisy, religious stuffiness, and "dead" works! Oh, to see again a revival of authentic tears, hallowed excitement, and an uncontainable joy of the Lord that naturally flows from the hearts of God's people! It is time that modern-day Christianity genuinely rose up and cried out, *"Lord God, set my soul AFIRE!!"*

The Bible admonishes us in Titus 2:7, *"In all things shewing thyself a pattern of good works: in doctrine shewing uncorruptness* [purity], *gravity* [reverential honesty], *sincerity."* In II Corinthians 2:17 we read, *"For we are not as many, which corrupt the word of God: but as of sincerity, but as of God, in the sight of God speak we in Christ."* Our sincerity is to be centered around Christ and the Word, not culture and the world. Also, in Philippians 1:10, God declares that He wants our motives and our message to be Biblically sound: *"That ye may approve things that are excellent; that ye may be sincere and without offence till the day of Christ;"* May our music be above reproach! "Sincere and right" — not "sincere and wrong," "insincere and right," or "insincere and wrong."

In 1974, while he stood firmly against the pervasiveness of rock music that sought to infiltrate our churches, Dr. Frank Garlock wrote: *"Sincerity and motivation have never been a test of real spirituality or even of Christianity for that matter. The Word of God is that which will abide forever, and it is upon His Word that God hinges all spiritual truth. It is not right to ignore the Bible, to become worldly in philosophy and practice, to call things Christian which are not, nor to disobey the Word of God, even to try to win people to Christ."*[122]

Some Christians have used the wrong reasoning, "Well, if I am 'blessed' by the music, it is okay." Wait a moment.... According to whom? Many defend the worldliness in their Christian music because it "moves" them or "the singers are just so sincere" or "I was just so real when I sang that and it came from my heart." But, just because something or someone is sincere does not justify it or make it right. Feelings are not the standard of what is right or what make things right; the "facts" of the Holy Scripture must be our solid foundation. In comparison, if someone robbed a bank with sincere motives and for a worthy cause, it does not suddenly make their actions acceptable. They are still absolutely wrong for what they have done. The ends do NOT justify the means!

The devil is sly and subtle — crafty. He is always seeking to manipulate us and activate the deception of our human hearts. The standard of "I was blessed by the music" is insufficient and dangerous. God requires obedience to His Word and does not accept man's sincere disobedience. His Word has many examples concerning this. God says in Micah 6:6-8, *"Wherewith shall I come before the Lord, and bow myself before the high God? shall I come before him with burnt offerings, with calves of a year old? Will the Lord be pleased with thousands of rams, or with ten thousands of rivers of oil? shall I give my firstborn for my transgression, the fruit of my body for the sin of my soul? He hath shewed thee, O man, what is good; and what doth the Lord require of thee, but to do justly* [to understand the difference between right and wrong according to His Word and determine to do what is right], *and to love mercy, and to walk humbly with thy God?"*

Ecclesiastes 12:13 sums this up very well: *"Let us hear the conclusion of the whole matter: Fear God* [a heart filled with Christ-honoring sincerity], *and keep his commandments* [a life based and built up upon Scripture]: *for this is the whole duty of man."* May God help us not be sincere and Biblically wrong in our music but sincere and Biblically right!

AM I ABUSING GOD'S GRACE THROUGH MY MUSIC?

We don't know; only you can answer that question. Are you? Search your heart as we study together about God's grace, liberty in Christ, legalism, and more!

Romans 6 boldly declares that we should not take

advantage of God's grace for the sake of our sinful desires or fleshly pleasure. *"What shall we say then? Shall we continue in sin, that grace may abound? God forbid. How shall we, that are dead to sin, live any longer therein?"* (Romans 6:1-2). God forbid. Let those two words sink in. If we are saved, we should not live as though we are lost.

We are certainly thankful that through God's grace, we have been eternally released from the bondage of sin — Heaven is our home! *"Amazing Grace, how sweet the sound that saved a wretch like me."* We can enjoy this powerful liberty only through Jesus and have the privilege of showing others how to experience this spiritual freedom also. Daily, we can rejoice in sweet victory with Christ as His grace teaches us that *"denying ungodliness and worldly lusts, we should live soberly, righteously, and godly, in this present world; Looking for that blessed hope, and the glorious appearing of the great God and our Saviour Jesus Christ"* (Colossians 2:12-13).

Our Lord exhorts us: *"Stand fast therefore in the liberty wherewith Christ hath made us free, and be not entangled again with the yoke of bondage"* (Galatians 5:1). He urges us not to give in to the impulses of our flesh and consequentially submit ourselves back under the shackling grip of sin which He saved us from.

Some of you reading this were born and raised in a Christian home just like we were, and you're wondering how this applies to you. We do not "have a past" like some of our parents did. We've never smoked a cigarette, done drugs, been immoral, drunk alcohol, etc. — and by God's grace, this will be our dying testimony (I Corinthians 10:12). Understand that the same grace of God that saved them out of a horrible life of sin is the same grace that has kept us from experiencing that horrible life of sin. Praise God!!

"I've missed out on the heartache
Of living my life in sin.
I've missed out on the sorrow
Of facing the world without Him.

And I have no regrets for things that I've missed,
'Cause deep down in my heart the truth was and is,
Everyday that I live, I thank God for what I've missed!"

Nevertheless, we have all been saved the same way: *"For by grace are ye saved through faith; and that not of yourselves: it is the gift of God: Not of works, lest any man should boast"* (Ephesians 2:8-9). God is no respecter of persons; the ground is level at the foot of the Cross!

Galatians 4:3-9 describes the glorious plan of redemption that was made possible through the love of God. At the end of the passage, it poses a provoking question: *"Even so we, when we were children, were in bondage under the elements of the world: But when the fulness of the time was come, God sent forth his Son, made of a woman, made under the law, To redeem them that were under the law, that we might receive the adoption of sons. And because ye are sons, God hath sent forth the Spirit of his Son into your hearts, crying, Abba, Father. Wherefore thou art no more a servant, but a son; and if a son, then an heir of God through Christ. Howbeit then, when ye knew not God, ye did service unto them which by nature are no gods. But now, after that ye have known God, or rather are known of God, how turn ye again to the weak and beggarly elements, whereunto ye desire again to be in bondage?"*

As Christians, we have liberty in Christ. But, this

wonderful liberty we enjoy is not a blank license or freedom to live like a sinner, but freedom to live like the Saviour! Galatians 5:13 declares, *"For, brethren, ye have been called unto liberty; only use not liberty for an occasion to the flesh,…"* God did not give us His grace to help us appreciate pleasurable sins that the world offers and that our flesh enjoys. It is utterly blasphemous to suggest such a thing. Grace is not a permission to sin or an enabler to enjoy sin. To use God's grace as an excuse for wickedness or worldliness is to *"turn again to the weak and beggarly elements, whereunto ye desire again to be in bondage."* Grace will never take people away from the Word of God but rather will always direct them toward godliness.

Furthermore, grace was not given unto us to exempt us (or as contemporary Christians would claim — "free us") from our personal responsibilities of sanctification ("being set apart for God's use") and separation and to let us live however we want. Grace doesn't call the child of God to sin, but rather it gives a clear call to sanctification. *"For this is <u>the will of God</u>, even your <u>sanctification</u>, that ye should abstain from fornication: That every one of you should <u>know how to possess his vessel in sanctification</u> and honour; Not in the lust of concupiscence, even as the Gentiles which know not God: For God hath not called us unto uncleanness, but unto holiness"* (I Thessalonians 4:3-7).

All Christians believe in a Christian's liberty to do right; but interestingly enough, those who strongly promote Christian liberty as a means to excuse cultural conformity and as "freedom to live however," many times end up being the ones with looser dress, music, and entertainment standards. Again, Jesus says, *"Stand fast* [hold your ground and don't waver from your Biblical conviction] *therefore in the liberty wherewith Christ hath made us free, and be not entangled again with the yoke of bondage"* (Galatians 5:1).

The path of the new "Christian liberty" being advertised today that is supposedly based on "grace" looks more like the wide road that leads toward compromise and carnal licentiousness — and ultimately, to destruction. Sadly, there has been a shifting and a drifting. Over the years, there have been incremental changes in music — and it always has shifted in the direction of the world.

We do live under grace, but this does not give us license to live loosely or without boundaries regarding what we do, see, wear, and hear. God has given us commands and principles about how we are to live as His children. In fact, He is very emphatic about how we should live! Take, for instance, some passages that we have already referenced.

I John 2:15-16 states, *"Love not the world, neither the things that are in the world. If any man love the world, the love of the Father is not in him. For all that is in the world, the lust of the flesh, and the lust of the eyes, and the pride of life, is not of the Father, but is of the world."*

Philippians 4:8-9 commands, *"Finally, brethren, whatsoever things are true, whatsoever things are honest, whatsoever things are just, whatsoever things are pure, whatsoever things are lovely, whatsoever things are of good report; if there be any virtue, and if there be any praise, think on these things. Those things...do: and the God of peace shall be with you."*

I Peter 2:11-12 challenges, *"Dearly beloved, I beseech you as strangers and pilgrims, abstain from fleshly lusts, which war against the soul; Having your conversation honest."*

God saved us out of sin; He saved us out of the world! He saved us out of it not so we could turn around and go right back into it or abuse His grace to justify our worldly practices and even music preferences. Could it be that many in modern-day Christianity are ignoring God's call to *"come out from among them, and be ye separate"* (II Corinthians 6:17)?

Let's face it: it seems that many Christians in this generation have let themselves begin to cuddle close to various worldly philosophies or practices — especially in their music. As they "pet" it and "caress" it (just as a child would with a stray cat, not realizing it is diseased and will soon infect them), they critically eye other Bible-believers and quickly, arrogantly lash out, *"We live under grace. Show me in the Bible, chapter and verse, where it's wrong!"*

Scripture does not specifically condemn any particular style of music by name, but God does instruct and warn us about the works of the flesh. God tells us, *"Walk in the Spirit, and ye shall not fulfill the lust of the flesh"* (Galatians 5:16).

God then proceeds to describe the works of the flesh: *"Now the works of the flesh are manifest, which are these; Adultery, fornication, uncleanness, lasciviousness, Idolatry, witchcraft, hatred, variance, emulations, wrath, strife, seditions, heresies, Envyings, murders, drunkenness, revellings, and such like:"* (Galatians 5:19-21). This list given in Scripture (it is just one of many) is not comprehensive; because if you noticed, it ends with *"and such like."*

Instead of listing all the works of the flesh, God gives us Biblical principles by which we can make applications to guide our hearts, minds, behavior, emotions, and choices. God has given us brains to help us discern as we follow His Word and the guidance of the Holy Spirit. Each of us are responsible for searching out and living according to what God has said and the unwavering, unchanging principles He has etched in the pages of the Bible. We have no reason or excuse to justify worldly practices or sinful actions.

We have frequently heard the term *"grace living"* from those who see themselves having been unfettered from all the "rules" in Scripture. They mislabel those who have high Bible standards to be "legalists." What? That doesn't make any sense. Are they suggesting then that they wish to be "illegalists" and practice "illegalism"?

Honestly, when Christians argue about legalism, most of the time it's because they have lowered their standards and are trying to quiet those Biblical principles that are challenging their compromise. It's simple — Biblical legalism that Paul fought against was about adding works to salvation NOT removing works because of salvation!

Whenever people use the terms "legalism" or "legalist" in the wrong way, it is a telltale sign to us that they have been reading the wrong books, hanging out with the wrong type of "religious" crowd, listening to compromising preachers, or letting contemporary music influence them. We are not being judgmental, just flat out honest. We have never heard anyone who truly loves God and has an absolutely openness to the whole counsel of the Bible ever use those terms inappropriately or out of context.

Sadly, they have the definition of "legalism" completely wrong. Holiness is not legalism. Godly separation is not legalism. Having standards is not legalism. Nonconformity to the world is not legalism. Those things are all BIBLICAL — it has nothing to do with legalism. However, making works a prerequisite for salvation *IS* legalism. Trying to add anything to God's grace for salvation *IS* legalism (Titus 3:5, Ephesians 2:8-9, and other passages).

We are living in a generation that has sought to REDEFINE the word (this is a liberal philosophy). Don't let anybody tell you that you are a legalist for having standards. Grace doesn't give us permission to be wicked or evil. *"What then? shall we sin, because we are not under the law, but under grace?* **God forbid.** *Know ye not, that to whom ye yield yourselves servants to obey, his servants ye are to whom ye obey; whether of sin unto death, or of obedience unto righteousness?"* (Romans 6:15-16).

Grace doesn't eliminate standards. In fact, under grace, Jesus raised standards and stressed a greater need of holiness. Understand this: **God will never condone in grace what His holiness condemns.** *"As obedient children, not fashioning yourselves according to the former lusts in your ignorance: But as he which hath called you is holy, so be ye holy in all manner of conversation* [this is referring to our lifestyle — including our music!]; *Because it is written, Be ye holy; for I am holy"* (I Peter 1:14-16).

As we live for Christ and pursue His holiness, we are not subjecting ourselves to rules; but rather, we are willing and joyfully submitting to the Ruler Himself, as we draw out application from His pure Word for our lives. Please don't let people criticize or confuse you about what we do and how we do it according to the Bible!

Again, the wonderful liberty we enjoy in Christ is not freedom to live like a sinner, but freedom to live like the Saviour. Those who take advantage of God's grace for their own carnality are abusing it. It is telling God, *"I don't care what You think. This is what I like, and this is how I want to live my life."* But, the Bible — our sole authority for faith and practice — exhorts in I Peter 2:16 that we should live *"As free, and not using your liberty for a cloke of maliciousness, but as the servants of God."* God admonishes us to not use our position in His grace for *malicious intent* as an excuse for sin.

It should be used as any opportunity to *magnify Christ* and *glorify* His name for the furtherance of His Gospel through our lives.

We were not saved and set free from sin to live according to the world and what we think is right but to live according to God's Word and what His righteousness is. The Lord says eight verses later in I Peter 2:24, *"Who His own self bare our sins in His own body on the tree, that we, being dead to sins, should live unto righteousness:"*

Another passage says it this way — *"For the love of Christ constraineth us.... He died for all, that they which live should not henceforth live unto themselves, but unto Him which died for them, and rose again"* (II Corinthians 5:15). As born-again Christian, we should not be passionately living for ourselves but be passionately living for Jesus. We believe that the basis for everything we do should always come back to our love for God and truly being overwhelmed with His love for us.

Ponder what the Bible testifies in I John 3:1-3: *"Behold, what manner of love the Father hath bestowed upon us, that we should be called the sons of God: therefore the world knoweth us not, because it knew him not. Beloved, now are we the sons of God, and it doth not yet appear what we shall be: but we know that, when he shall appear, we shall be like him; for we shall see him as he is* [One day we will be with Jesus in Heaven. The best is yet to come!]. *And every man that hath this hope* [excitement and anticipation] *in him purifieth himself, even as he is pure."*

The overwhelming sense of the love of God should motivate us, move us, compel us, and constrain us to purify our lives — not because we "have to" but because we "get to." If we love Jesus the way we should, our hearts will naturally ask, *"What shall I render unto the Lord for all his benefits toward me?"* (Psalm 116:12).

I John 5:2-3 declares, *"By this we know that we love the children of God, when we love God, and keep his commandments. For this is the love of God, that we keep his commandments: and his commandments are not grievous* [burdensome or causing one to roll his eyes in drudgery]."

If we are not careful, what begins as a desire to serve God and live for Jesus can quickly turn into a duty. We are concerned that too many Christians in fundamental Baptist churches are driven by the letter of the law, rather than by a love for the Lord. Duty will deteriorate into a display — and being a hypocrite and a Pharisee is *dangerous*. It greatly grieves the Lord. We shouldn't have standards so that God will love us more; no, we should have standards because we love Him more. There is nothing legalistic about this, in fact, that's what grace and liberty are for — to conform us to the image of His Son as He gives us the power to become more like Jesus in all we say and do.

Our passion for Christ should be an affectionate zeal — a love that rejoices and warms the heart! We need another generation that will fall back in love with Jesus! *"We love Him, because He first loved us"* (I John 4:19). Oh, that we would have the same intensity for Jesus as He has for us. Oh, how our love for Christ should inspire our every motive!

God's love should stir and strengthen our commitment for Christ in pursuing His holiness. A genuine love for Him will not send us toward secularism and sin. The person that falls back in love with the world had to first fall out of love with Christ. Love Him, and this world and the allurement of it will fade to nothing in the back of your mind.

As we meditate upon the love of God and the great joy

we receive in walking and talking with Him throughout the day, our commitment should be: *"I refuse to lower myself and fulfill the lusts of my flesh… because I love Jesus TOO MUCH!!"*

In Psalm 113:5-8, the Bible beautifully describes the demonstration of His great love for us: *"Who is like unto the Lord our God, who dwelleth on high, Who humbleth himself to behold the things that are in heaven, and in the earth! He raiseth up the poor out of the dust, and lifteth the needy out of the dunghill; That he may set him with princes, even with the princes of his people."* There is absolutely no reason to live in the gutter when Jesus has exalted us to live with the King! Could it be that we are talking and walking like we are STILL living in a sewer hole? God saved us from that!

Sin should not have control of us if we are risen and living with Christ. We must choose to *"die daily"* (I Corinthians 15:31), surrender our wills and our wants over to our loving God (Romans 12:1-2), and allow our carnal man to be mortified (Colossians 3:5). *"[R]eckon ye also yourselves to be dead indeed unto sin, but alive unto God through Jesus Christ our Lord. Let not sin therefore reign in your mortal body, that ye should obey it in the lusts thereof. Neither yield ye your members as instruments of unrighteousness unto sin: but yield yourselves unto God"* (Romans 6:11-13).

As we yield ourselves to the Lord — that is when we truly start to **LIVE**. *"I am crucified with Christ: nevertheless I live; yet not I, but Christ liveth in me: and the life which I now live in the flesh I live by the faith of the Son of God, who loved me, and gave himself for me.* ***I do not frustrate the grace of God"*** (Galatians 2:20-21).

Are you frustrating the grace of God by misusing it? God's love and holiness should permeate every area of our lives. As we die to self and allow His holiness and love to consume us, worldliness and the taste for it should disappear. We love that old hymn of the faith, *"Turn your eyes upon Jesus.... Look full in His wonderful face! And the things of this world will grow strangely dim in the light of His glory and grace."* We all need the grace of God in order to grow! But no one should use grace as an excuse to promote sinful living or encourage others to continue in a sinful lifestyle.

The world should be unfamiliar with our music — since it should not be borrowed from theirs but should come from Christ and reflect of His holiness. We do live under grace, but this does not give us license to live loosely or without boundaries. God has given us commands and principles about how we are to live as His children. That is what we are studying throughout this book!

Are you abusing and "frustrating" the grace of God in your music? Are you using it to justify carnality and to excuse away worldly instrumentation or styles? Join with us in praying: *"Search me, O God, and know my heart: try me, and know my thoughts: And see if there be any wicked way in me, and lead me in the way everlasting."* (Psalm 139:23-24).

WOULD MY MUSIC CAUSE OTHER BROTHERS AND SISTERS IN CHRIST TO STUMBLE?

To address this question, we must first give Biblical context. There has been much confusion in recent years over the principles the Bible seeks to convey in Romans 14. God's Word places a great emphasis here about a Christian carefully and graciously conducting his life in such a way that it will honor the Lord and not hinder anyone around him to live for Christ.

God specifically uses two examples in Romans 14:2-6 —
a person who doesn't see a problem with eating meat while
another one will only be a vegetarian, and an individual who
places a great importance upon a certain day while someone
else sees that day to be no different than the rest. He then
concludes, *"Let not him that eateth despise him that eateth not;
and let not him which eateth not judge him that eateth: for God
hath received him"* (Romans 14:3). Regardless of where your
personal preference might be on a subject, God's Word
exhorts us that we should not criticize other brothers and
sisters in Christ, rather that we should be careful about our
spirit toward them and how we influence them (we should
help, not hinder). Romans 12:10 declares, *"Be kindly
affectioned one to another with brotherly love; in honour
preferring one another."*

God, of course, is the only true Judge of people's
motives (not those who feel like they have been given the "gift
of discernment"), because He alone can see *"the thoughts and
intents of the heart"* (Hebrews 4:12). Being in that ultimate
position of authority, He asks us then in Romans 14:10: *"But
why dost thou judge thy brother? or why dost thou set at nought
thy brother?"* We are not the Authority — He is. He will
accurately judge us according to the standards and statutes of
His Word. Therefore, we must consistently tether ourselves to
the principles of Bible truth.

Because we are *"the temple of the living God;"*
(II Corinthians 6:16), we are instructed to be *"proving
[demonstrating truth through evidence and explanation] what
is acceptable to the Lord"* (Ephesians 5:10). Scripture warns us
about and instructs us against the works of the flesh. God tells
us, *"Walk in the Spirit, and ye shall not fulfill the lust of the
flesh"* (Galatians 5:16). When any Christian, however,

admonishes others regarding the works of the *"lusts of the flesh,"* some respond vindictively with Matthew 7:1, *"Judge not, that ye be not judged."* (The context of Matthew 7 doesn't teach us not to judge at all, but rather not to judge others based on appearances. He says to *"judge righteous judgment"* (John 7:24). When we have a beam in our own eye, we are first to cast it out so that we can see clearly to cast out the mote from our brother's eye.) The Bible encourages us: *"And let us consider one another to provoke unto love and to good works: ...exhorting one another: and so much the more, as ye see the day approaching"* (Hebrews 10:24-25). However, we are not to criticize each other with an opinionated self-righteousness — any statement that we make must be grounded upon *"Thus saith the LORD."* We must allow His Authority to speak through us. We must speak *"the truth in love"* (Ephesians 4:15) and with gentleness and meekness (II Timothy 2:24-26; Titus 3:2).

Although Matthew 7 warns against making wrong judgments and being unjustly critical, Jesus is not saying that we should ignore Biblical discernment as mature Christians (Hebrews 5:14) or fail to weigh the spirits (I John 4:1). Nor is He teaching that we are supposed to sit idly by while others are flaunting their error and leading people astray. In fact, Romans 16:17 tells us: *"Now I beseech you, brethren, mark them which cause divisions and offences contrary to the doctrine which ye have learned; and avoid them."* Jesus is teaching us that we are to help others who have gone astray and instruct them in the context of righteousness found within the Scriptures, not based on personal opinion (John 7:24). Our thinking and our view of things might be flawed, but the Bible is infallible. Let's point people to the Bible!

We are commanded to *"judge righteous judgment"* (John 7:24). As we discussed earlier, judgment in its most basic definition is *"to form a conclusion about something."* We are commanded to passionately pursue His Word and evaluate (i.e. "judge") His positions against ours and allow Him to transform our preferences and positions unto His own.

Again, may it be our heart's desire unto the Lord: *"Teach me good judgment and knowledge: for I have believed thy commandments"* (Psalm 119:66). And, *"Hear my voice according unto thy lovingkindness: O Lord, quicken me according to thy judgment"* (Psalm 119:149). We need God's wisdom in order to come to the correct conclusion of what we should do in our lives that will glorify and magnify Him!

Back in Romans 14, the Bible continues by stating something peculiar: *"I know, and am persuaded by the Lord Jesus, that there is nothing unclean of itself: but to him that esteemeth any thing to be unclean, to him it is unclean"* (Romans 14:14). No one should ever violate his/her own conscience. And obviously, God's Word is not radically going "off the reservation" here saying that sinful things are actually okay except to those who believe they are wrong. It is not advocating that all things are neutral and nothing is sinful. No. Sin is sin. Sensual is sensual. Wrong is wrong. Right is right. Truth is truth. Those things have been set forth in His Word, and they are not up for debate.

What God *is* teaching here is that there are inanimate, neutral things in our lives — such as a car, a television, a computer, a cell phone, and so on — that are not bad things in and of themselves. But, if they are not handled with the proper spirit, the right attitude, and a pure heart, they can certainly be used for evil. We should never take something and use it inappropriately to hurt other people (Romans 14:14-15). Rather, we should press toward the mark of spiritual values — righteousness, peace, and joy in the Holy Ghost (Romans 14:17).

"For he that in these things serveth Christ is acceptable to God, and approved of men" (Romans 14:18).

Then, a sobering truth is put forth in Romans 14:10-12, *"...for we shall all stand before the judgment seat of Christ. For it is written, As I live, saith the Lord, every knee shall bow to me, and every tongue shall confess to God. So then every one of us shall give account of himself to God."* Eventually, each of us are going to have to give an account for the things done in our lives — what we do, where we go, the choices we make, and even the music that we listen to. One day *"we must all appear before the judgment seat of Christ; that every one may receive the things done in his body, according to that he hath done, whether it be good or bad"* (II Corinthians 5:10). We will not be responsible for decisions other people make but will be held accountable for our own actions and our influence on others.

Now specifically notice what Romans 14:13 & 21 says: *"Let us not therefore judge one another any more* [because one day we *will* stand and give an account]*: but judge this rather, that no man put a stumblingblock or an occasion to fall in his brother's way.... It is good neither to eat flesh, nor to drink wine, nor **any thing*** [this includes our music] *whereby thy brother stumbleth, or is offended, or is made weak."* We should refrain and abstain from doing something that will tear down, weaken even more, or wreck the life of another Christian.

We also need to remember that there are baby Christians around us, still young in the faith. Perhaps they are believers who got saved later in life and have a lot of baggage from their past without Jesus. We must be careful to disciple them and raise them up with spiritual nurturing and Biblical holiness — not direct them away from that.

The last thing they need is to hear us or our churches playing/singing music that — while it may be labeled

"Christian" — might remind them of their former days in sin and bondage. This is confusing to young believers. How can a "called out assembly" use the same styles and even a "rock beat" which they were supposed to be called out from? This is a stumblingblock and an occasion for them to falter in their faith. This could perhaps even tempt them to return to that sensual style of music from their past again.

In the context of our music, if it is carnal or worldly, it will hinder us and those around us from flourishing for Christ. *"Thus saith God, Why transgress ye the commandments of the Lord, that ye cannot prosper?"* (II Chronicles 24:20).

"I recently listened to a seminary student try to explain why he thought CCM [Contemporary Christian music] *was okay for the Christian. He used Romans 14 as his text, which was no surprise because many CCM advocates use this passage to justify their music choices. Romans 14 speaks of the law of love concerning doubtful things. The more this seminary student went around the barn using complicated theological rhetoric in explaining how the text defended CCM, the more confused I became. When he was asked, 'So you think those with stricter standards are the weaker brothers?' the student replied, 'Yes.'*

"To make eating meat or regarding one day over another as mentioned in Romans 14 parallel to doing something sensual is not accurate. If rock music is sensual and God tells me to put away all uncleanness — how by my not listening to Christian rock am I the weaker brother? How can you equate holiness with weakness and a sensual lifestyle with being strong? How could the same God who tells you to put away deceitful lust also say that by doing so you are weaker? It just doesn't make sense.

"The weaker brother in Romans 14 is less mature spiritually and less informed Scripturally. The larger point of

the chapter is that mature Christians are kind and respectful toward those who are less informed and less mature and vice versa — the less informed and less mature are kind and respectful to those who are more mature and better informed Scripturally.

"Paul's intent in Romans 14 is to teach the importance of not developing a sinfully judgmental attitude and behavior toward those who differ with us in matters that are not inherently moral or matters not specifically commanded or prohibited in Scripture. To use Romans 14 as an argument that a believer with strong convictions against the use of music in the rock genre for Christian devotional listening and worship is a weaker brother misapplies the passage in two ways — especially since Scripture teaches that greater spiritual maturity is demonstrated by discernment between good and evil (Hebrews 5:13-14).*

"First, the view that only weaker brothers object to the Christian use of rock does not account for the moral and spiritual content of rock music, both through the lyrics and through the association of its sound with the current corrupt American entertainment culture. Second, the view that only weaker brothers object to the Christian use of rock music does not account for the nearly universally held view by both religious and secular authorities that music is capable of causing profound moral effects in the listener. Most important, this is the view of Scripture that states that music is a powerful medium for spiritual growth in holiness and love for the glory of Christ (Colossians 3:16). *Certainly the opposite is truth as well, so believers are not to be conformed to the world* (Romans 12:1-2) *and are to embrace the truth that evil communications corrupt good morals* (I Corinthians 15:33). *"*[123]

The Bible commands, *"Let not then your good be evil*

spoken of:" (Romans 14:16). Our testimonies for Christ should be above reproach and our integrity should be upstanding and outstanding — always pointing others to Jesus and His holiness, not to the world and its wickedness. Our music should be saturated with our Saviour, not filled with the ways of this world.

The opposite of causing others to stumble is to help build them up spiritually. In Romans 14:19, the Bible says we should do everything in our power to be engaged in edifying others, not tearing them down. *"Let us therefore follow after the things which make for peace, and things wherewith one may edify another."* And in Romans 15:2, we read, *"Let every one of us please his neighbor for his good to edification."* Concerning music, by listening, enjoying, singing, and promoting the kind that doesn't resemble the world's style and has a Christ-honoring message, we can help others go forward instead of causing them to stumble. Let us actively help one another grow spiritually!

WHAT PHYSICAL RESPONSE DOES MY MUSIC PRODUCE?

As we have addressed before, beware of music with a backbeat or singing style (sensual and breathy) that produces the physical urge to dance or behave in a worldly inappropriate way. *"Glorify God in your body, and in your spirit, which are God's"* (I Corinthians 6:20).

Notice what God says in Psalm 149:1-5: *"Praise ye the Lord. Sing unto the Lord a new song, and his praise in the congregation of saints. Let Israel rejoice in him that made him: let the children of Zion be joyful in their King. Let them praise his name in the dance: let them sing praises unto him with the timbrel and harp. For the Lord taketh pleasure in his people: he* will beautify the meek with salvation. Let the saints be joyful in glory: let them sing aloud upon their beds."

Unfortunately, when Christians see the word "dancing" in the Bible, they immediately justify the sensual movement of the world and what the flesh desires to do with the music. However, Psalm 149:3 is not teaching us to praise God with dancing. Yes, you read that last sentence right. Psalm 149:3 is not teaching us to praise God with dancing. Notice the specific wording God used, because after all — every word in the Bible is there for a purpose, and we must pay attention to how God worded it in a particular way. God said, "Let them praise his name in the dance." It did not say "with dancing" but "in the dance", which are two very different things.

"With dancing" implies and advocates that we should praise Him by dancing with our bodies (which an overwhelming majority of the time is a sensual or inappropriate movement, accentuating certain parts that should always be maintained with dignity). But God would never suddenly change His mind and approve of sensual or fleshly gyrating and moving. He does not contradict Himself.

God was teaching His people that if you are "in the dance" (which directly refers to the ceremonial dance of Jewish custom, not our modern interpretation of dancing), be sure that it is done in such a way that it glorifies the Lord. **He is firmly exhorting His people to <u>not</u> let it become fleshly or sensual!**

God desires all of His people to engage solely in those things which are physically, mentally, emotionally, and spiritually wholesome. Galatians 4:18 says, "But it is good to be zealously affected always in a good thing." God also commands us: "Finally, brethren, whatsoever things are...pure, ...lovely, ...if there be any virtue, ...think on these things. Those *things...do: and the God of peace shall be with you."* Think on these things alone! Engage in these sorts of activities only! As a result, we will enjoy the fullness of God's presence and peace upon our lives.

Now, let us move forward and talk about the "elephant in the room" when it comes to this topic — David. Unfortunately, the story of David dancing before the Lord is also sometimes used to justify all sorts of fleshly behavior with music. It's important that we look closely at what the Scripture actually says. In order to understand why King David and the people of Israel were so exhilarated and excited, we need to recognize the importance of what was happening in II Samuel 6. David *did,* in fact, *dance* before the Lord! Let's read from the chapter to become familiar with the context of what is happening.

> *"David gathered together all the chosen men of Israel, thirty thousand. And David arose, and went with all the people that were with him from Baale of Judah, to bring up from thence the ark of God, whose name is called by the name of the Lord of hosts that dwelleth between the cherubims. And they set the ark of God upon a new cart, and brought it out of the house of Abinadab that was in Gibeah: and Uzzah and Ahio, the sons of Abinadab, drave the new cart. And they brought it out of the house of Abinadab which was at Gibeah, accompanying the ark of God: and Ahio went before the ark. And David and all the house of Israel played before the Lord on all manner of instruments made of fir wood, even on harps, and on psalteries, and on timbrels, and on cornets, and*

on cymbals.

"And when they came to Nachon's threshingfloor, Uzzah put forth his hand to the ark of God, and took hold of it; for the oxen shook it. And the anger of the Lord was kindled against Uzzah; and God smote him there for his error; and there he died by the ark of God. And David was displeased, because the Lord had made a breach upon Uzzah: and he called the name of the place Perezuzzah to this day. And David was afraid of the Lord that day, and said, How shall the ark of the Lord come to me? So David would not remove the ark of the Lord unto him into the city of David: but David carried it aside into the house of Obededom the Gittite. And the ark of the Lord continued in the house of Obededom the Gittite three months: and the Lord blessed Obededom, and all his household.

"And it was told king David, saying, The Lord hath blessed the house of Obededom, and all that pertaineth unto him, because of the ark of God. So David went and brought up the ark of God from the house of Obededom into the city of David with gladness. And it was so, that when they that bare the ark of the Lord had gone six paces, he sacrificed oxen and fatlings. And David danced before the Lord with all his might; and David was girded with a linen ephod. So David and all the house of Israel brought up the ark of the Lord with shouting, and with the sound of the trumpet. And as the ark of the Lord came into the city of David, Michal Saul's daughter looked through a window, and saw king

David leaping and dancing before the Lord; and she despised him in her heart.

"And they brought in the ark of the Lord, and set it in his place, in the midst of the tabernacle that David had pitched for it: and David offered burnt offerings and peace offerings before the Lord. And as soon as David had made an end of offering burnt offerings and peace offerings, he blessed the people in the name of the Lord of hosts."

The nation of Israel was beginning a new era as a people. The Ark of the Covenant (the seat of God's presence) was coming home to Jerusalem! The Ark had not been a focal point for worship in Israel or in the Tabernacle since before Saul became king. The tabernacle had remained at Shiloh for 369 years until the Ark was taken into the battle (I Samuel 4:3-5 & 10-11) and captured by the Philistines. The Philistines brought the Ark with them to their capital city, Ashdod and put it in the temple of their idol god Dagon. However, on the next day, the statue of Dagon had fallen to the ground. The same thing happened again the following day with the idol's head and hands cut off (I Samuel 5:1-4). Soon after, the city of Ashdod suffered from plague after plague. The Ark was moved to the city of Gath and then Ekron, but the plague continued (I Samuel 5:1-12).

After keeping the Ark for seven months, the Philistines decided to return it to the Israelites together with offerings of expensive gifts upon the advice of their diviners and priests. The Ark was brought back to Bethshemesh and then transported to Kirjathjearim, where it stayed in the home of Abinadab for twenty years (I Samuel 6:1-18, 21; 7:1-2).

When David became Israel's king, he determined that

one of the first things he would do was bring the Ark of the Covenant to Jerusalem. He believed this would unify the people of Israel around the Lord and would reignite their hearts to once again worship Him in the new capital city of Jerusalem.

In II Samuel 6, David gathered 30,000 people, priests, and musicians to journey with him to Kirjathjearim and bring back the Ark. David was a talented musician and desired for the Ark's return to be a reverential musical celebration like never before. Verse 5 tells us, *"And David and all the house of Israel played before the Lord on all manner of instruments made of fir wood, even on harps, and on psalteries, and on timbrels, and on cornets, and on cymbals."* Nevertheless, as we read earlier, they did not treat the Ark as they were supposed to Biblically. When Abinadab's son Uzzah reached out to steady the Ark on the ox cart it was being transported on, he was instantly struck dead.

David's parade came to a halt. The Ark of God stayed with Obededom and his home for three months before David gathered as much of Israel as possible to join him a second time to bring the Ark to Jerusalem. Only this time it was going to be done right! Despite David's previous genuine motives, he learned that God must be worshiped according to God's way, and not his own way.

The parallel passage in I Chronicles 15 tells us that instead of putting the Ark on an ox cart, David follows God's prescribed method of transportation as laid out in the Old Testament (I Chronicles 15:13-15). The Levites purified themselves and carried the Ark on their shoulders the entire way. The long-awaited procession began. The anticipation among the throngs built. Harpists, psaltery players, cymbalists, and trumpeters played their instruments loudly yet skillfully and singers lifted up their voices in song with joy (I Chronicles 15:16). After every six steps, David stopped and offered to God a sacrifice. The Ark was finally and successfully brought to its rightful place with the presence of God in the midst of the nation!

It was in the midst of all of this wonderful excitement and the worshipful exhilaration of the moment that David *"danced before the Lord."* We must understand that Jewish religious dancing at the time of David was not like the jiving, bopping, or swaying of today. It was not men with women, not movement in a sexual manner, and not done in such a way that sensually accentuated certain parts of the body. It was a triumphant, joyful, rhythmic marching and skipping! We can't picture 21st century dancing when we read the word "dancing" in the Bible.

David was not found wiggling his hips or stepping loosely so his body would shake with the timing of the music the priests and musicians were playing. No! David was leaping and skipping about in joy, stamping his feet down with might occasionally, just happily beside himself — his heart was overflowing with Biblical delight and joy-filled praise for what God was doing and allowing them to do.

In conclusion, a fascinating aspect about this account is that David did not lead this procession as a king in fancy robes or in a flashy chariot, but he walked like everyone else. There was nothing to distinguish him as king. The Bible says that he *"was girded with a linen ephod"* (II Samuel 6:14) — a special garment that was common attire for the priests. His focus was on God, not on himself. After all, this wasn't a celebration honoring David; it was a worshipful ceremony honoring Jehovah — and David wasn't about to detract from that.

Sadly, his wife Michal decided to not be a part of this

glorious day in Israel's history. She was a haughty king's daughter who was used to the attention being placed upon the position of royalty. But David understood that God was no respecter of persons and that we are all the same — precious and loved — in His sight.

As she looked out her palace window and saw David and what he was doing, *"she despised him in her heart"* (II Samuel 6:16). This was not because he was immodestly dressed and dancing provocatively in front of the young ladies (II Samuel 6:20), but because she thought he looked foolish for not wearing his royal garb. Michal was upset that David willingly choose to look so "common" and became embarrassed over his zeal and exuberance for God. She thought his love for God was much too extreme.

After the Ark of God was set correctly *"in the midst of the tabernacle that David had pitched for it"* (II Samuel 6:17a), David lead the multitude in *"burnt offerings and peace offerings before the Lord"* (II Samuel 6:17b). Following this sacred time of worship, he typified the humble spirit of Christ by personally serving the people and handing out food and drink to those who had come to take part in this momentous spiritual occasion.

When David returned home, Michal bitterly lashed out with her tongue and accused him of sinful things he was not guilty of. David simply responded back, *"I...will be base in mine own sight"* (II Samuel 6:22). He wanted all the focus to be on the Lord and not him.

May God be thoroughly glorified and have the absolute preeminence in every aspect of our music. *Are you completely yielded to Him?* May the things we listen to lead us to generate a wholesome, spiritual, and godly response physically. When godly music is playing, many times as Christians we might shout out "Amen!" because we agree with the truths in the song. Or we may make some exclamation of praise because we cannot contain the joy that has flooded over us. It is something that suddenly hits you and warms your heart with exaltation that you find your soul and spirit with a "spring of joy" as David experienced. We can become so spiritually stirred by the message in song, we might raise our hand(s) in the air in genuine worship to the Lord while seated, or even stand up to render praise. This is not a sensual, fleshy gyration. It is not wiggling the hips or swaying with the timing of the music. It is a hallowed moment overcome with Biblical delight and spiritual ecstasy.

For several years in our church's annual *Live Animal Christmas Show,* we have portrayed Mary and Joseph. We sing several songs in character with beautiful lighting, special effects, and orchestra scores. Our singing is frequently described as being filled with majestic-flowing movements, exuberant motions, joyful facial expressions, and worshipful hand gestures unto God. Again, this is not a sensual, fleshy gyration or inappropriate body movements. In a sense, it is somewhat similar to the way David *"danced before the Lord."* It is a sincere and wholesome expression of triumphant, passionate praise born out of an overwhelming sense of God that renders holy reverence to our King of kings.

Music often will produce a physical response. Make sure your music is the right kind of music, initiating the right kind of responses. If good music causes one to respond with the right heart and the right motives, this wholesome behavior is not wrong because it does not seek to draw attention to self but to Jesus. It does not cause our bodies to move in a way that is unholy. We must be careful that our music produces physical responses that glorify and exalt Him!

CHAPTER VIII

YOUTHFUL WARNINGS AGAINST WORLDLY "CHRISTIAN" MUSIC

You are about to read some sobering accounts concerning the dangers of worldly "Christian" music. We beg of you, please listen carefully to these powerful testimonies that have been accumulated from young people across the country who were affected by it.

Some use the term "Christian rock" which is synonymous with Contemporary Christian music and its abbreviation "CCM". On multiple secular websites, *Casting Crowns* is ranked as the #4 "Christian Rock" group in the world; *Newsboys* as #6; *MercyMe* as #10; *Tobymac* as #15; *Jars of Clay* as #28; Michael W. Smith as #36; and the list goes on.

Now, many modern Southern Gospel groups have a very similar sound (though more "countrified") to Contemporary Christian music artists, and the two music movements have had more of a blending together than ever before. In fact, in 2015, National Quartet Convention president Les Beasley was a board member of the *"Gospel Music Trust Fund"* that sponsored the *"We Will Stand"* concert. A main emphasis of this concert was to encourage more ecumenical unity among Christians (that we should join forces with numerous denominations and even Catholicism for the sake of the Gospel).[124] Many well-known Contemporary Christian music artists participated, such as Michael W. Smith, Steven Curtis Chapman, Sandi Patti, Amy Grant, the Newsboys, and 4Him. The concert also promoted the secular philosophy that *"music is neutral"* and that *any* music can be used to glorify God. It began with a piano and orchestra piece, but then throughout the concert, numerous "rock music" styles were performed.[125]

Consider the gravity from the following personal testimonies that we have decided to include:

"Rock-styled Christian music has probably been the biggest hindrance to my spiritual growth. When I first heard this kind of music, it really bothered my spirit. But then this music was brought into my church. The more I heard it, the less it bothered me. The less it bothered me, the more I listened to it. It wasn't long before I was involved in secular music because I didn't see any difference. This music caused me to resist the Lord and hold parts of my life back from Him. I was not able to have a freedom to truly serve Him and be totally dedicated to Him until I was willing to give up this music." — Age 16 from Florida

"When I got started listening to contemporary Christian music, I started out on 'mild' music, but it grew to harder music. It grew to the point where the music took the place of Bible reading. It was addictive. This music, which is supposed to promote Christianity, caused me to violate

God's commandments about idolatry." — Age 17 from Missouri

"*My father told me that if I listened to CCM it would open the door for Satan. I just laughed, and listened anyway. It totally deadened my Christian growth and led to terrible immorality, rebellion, and rejection of God. It then developed into secular music. I still have a scar in my life that will never be removed.*" — Age 16 from Oklahoma

"*I personally don't like CCM but at the cafe where I work as a waitress, they have been playing it. Since I have been working there I have had no desire to pray or read the Bible or to even get to know the Lord.... It has subconsciously affected my spiritual growth, but I found that I desire to read my Bible and to pray when I left that job and have been away from that rock-styled Christian music.*" — Age 23 from Wisconsin

"*I believe God designed the world to conform to Christianity, not Christianity to the world. Please, please, don't pollute your minds or your spiritual life with this awful music.*" — Age 18 from Indiana

"*CCM at one time really messed up my view of Christianity. I would listen to it and think, 'Look how Christianity is trying to blend in with the world.'*" — Age 19 from Ohio

"'*Christian rock' music has divided my youth group. It has kept me in bondage spiritually. Whenever I walk into*

YOUTHFUL WARNINGS AGAINST WORLDLY "CHRISTIAN" MUSIC

my youth group, rock is being played. I feel Satan's control start to tighten. I find it almost impossible to have beneficial, reverent quiet times when the sensual beat pops into my mind." — Age 17 from Georgia

"Christian Contemporary Music has, in my life, been a stepping stone. Not up — but down. Just a few months of listening to CCM led to a life of being controlled by secular rock. This quickly led to and encouraged rebellion, greed, moral impurity, and trying to hide from my parents." — Age 17 from Pennsylvania

"The music I started with was soft, slow, and contemporary, but it took over my life. I became dependent upon it rather than upon God. I did not realize it, but I was a lukewarm Christian, no matter how many times I sought God at the altar. Eventually, God gave me the conviction to not listen to CCM. This made me free in my soul!" — Age 16 from Illinois

"When I started listening to CCM I slowly started to listen to 'soft rock.' Then I was listening to something harder and harder. It not only led me into worldly rock, but I was getting rebellious toward my parents, and I was having sensual and lustful thoughts. I also could not memorize or read God's Word and understand it or retain it." — Age 15 from Nebraska

"'Christian rock' had made me a shallow, rebellious young Christian. It made it easy for me to get into regular rock music.... I finally submitted to God and got all of *this music out of my life, and I praise God for His help in releasing me from it!"* — Age 18 from Indiana

"I began with a high standard of music in my life. Through my youth group, that became watered down. I gradually began to build a collection of contemporary artists who professed to be Christians. As I collected more songs and the music's beat became stronger, I became more rebellious. The so-called 'Christian music' led me straight into rebellion." — Age 19 from Texas

"Now my church plays 'Christian rock' and I see it ruining many kids in our youth group. It is so sad. It has ruined kids that were so sweet." — Age 16 from Texas

"I began listening to 'Christian rock,' and shortly thereafter I began a fast, steady pace downhill. This eventually led me into a totally backslidden state.... I remember the specific day and the song I listened to first. I remember feeling rebellious.... Within weeks, maybe months, a very apparent breakdown of my conscience, morality, and appearance was evident. I had completely fallen away from the Lord. I appeal to Church leaders today — I plead with you to purge your churches, youth groups, and homes of rock-n-roll. I pray that the devastating results of rock music will be realized in the Church before it steals anymore of the souls of our youth." — Age 19 from California

"We as Christians do not take drugs to witness to drug users, and we do not convert to worldly habits to identify with the world. So I saw no reason to use worldly music

with Christian words so that I could minister to the world!" — Age 17 from California

May our hearts take heed and be warned of the slippery slope of worldly Christian music. In many of these testimonies, you will find a similar pattern — a progression downward away from God and not progression upward closer to Christ. The Bible says, *"Therefore we ought to give the more earnest heed to the things which we have heard, lest at any time we should let them slip"* (Hebrews 2:1).

Each one of us are capable of this downward spiral. If we are not careful and if we do not remain vigilant, we will become more lax and weak in our Biblical conviction. *"Wherefore let him that thinketh he standeth take heed lest he fall."* (I Corinthians 10:12). God gives us an urgent exhortation in Deuteronomy 4:9: *"Only take heed to thyself, and keep thy soul diligently, lest thou forget the things which thine eyes have seen, and lest they depart from thy heart all the days of thy life: but teach them thy sons, and thy sons' sons."*

We have been given a Biblical mandate to instruct truth to our children and grandchildren. Deuteronomy 6:7 shows us how frequently we should be engaged in teaching them: *"And thou shalt teach them diligently unto thy children, and shalt talk of them when thou sittest in thine house, and when thou walkest by the way, and when thou liest down, and when thou risest up."* Yet, how can we effectively guide our youth if we ourselves are not rooted and grounded in the faith? We must be *"a workman that needeth not to be ashamed, rightly dividing the word of truth"* (II Timothy 2:15).

As Bible-believing Christians, when we embrace worldliness, it will cost us. It will cost us dearly. It will not only cost us our closeness with God *(Let's not deceive ourselves that an emotional experience is always a spiritual experience. It is very possible that it is simply a fleshly experience that we wish to justify in our hearts as a spiritual one.)*; but, it potentially will cost us our children and the subsequent generations.

If we are not tethered to principles and convictions from God's Word, we will drift from what is right. May God strengthen us to remain steadfast and unmovable in our music — that we would remain Scriptural in our approach and Christ-honoring in our worship and praise.

CHAPTER IX:

CONGREGATIONAL SINGING AND THE CHURCH HYMNAL

In 1927, John Gillman wrote in his historical work, *The Evolution of the English Hymn:* "*A hymnbook is a transcript for real life, a poetical accompaniment to real events and real experiences. Like all literature that counts, it rises directly out of life. The heart of a nation is written in its songs. Even so the heart of the Christian Church is revealed in its hymns.*"[126]

Gillman then proceeded to describe how the widespread revival under John and Charles Wesley "*saved the souls of England,*" both in the country as a whole and in the churches. He closed the above quote with this comment, "*At the heart of it all was a hymnbook.*"[127]

Later in his work, he adds: "*The great hymns of the past that are still found in our hymnals have survived because of their intrinsic power to help successive generations of men and women. There is an air of 'everlastingness' about them. They deal with themes that never grow old; the majesty and love of God, the mysteries of the incarnation and redemption, the need of pardon and grace, the warfare and ultimate triumph of those who follow Christ. Thus, one generation after another is bound together by a golden chain of praise."*[128]

Hymns are not old songs in dusty old books just used to "fill up time" in a church service; rather, they ought to be exciting offerings of genuine worship and heart-filled praise directed to our Lord and Saviour, Jesus Christ. Congregational hymn singing should also never become a ritualistic part of a church service. (Although, looking at the faces of people in most church congregations today, you might think that!) It should be a time to magnify and exalt Almighty God, preparing hearts for the message from His Word to come. It should be done with the mind engaged, the heart attentive, and the face reflecting the joy of the songs being sung. Sing together as a congregation, and sing from the heart unto the Lord! We have discussed much already through this book on congregational singing.

Hymns were written, born out of sincere spirituality, with the intent of drawing us closer to God. The lyrics are so profound and full of Biblical truth that one cannot help but be broken when they stop and meditate upon its deep meanings.

Unfortunately, we are living in a time when so many Christians of this generation are pursuing worldly contemporary music and have no knowledge of what hymns truly are. Nor are they familiar with the authors such as John Newton, Fanny Crosby, Charles Wesley, Ira Sankey, Dwight Whittle, Robert Lowry, George Stebbins, James McGranahan, Daniel Towner, and Philip P. Bliss.

Today, the tragedy is that we do not prize what our hymnals contain, and we do not even use it well. Let's face it: hymns are becoming more and more non-existent in most American churches and are being replaced with praise choruses. Other churches sing the same few — 30-40 different songs or so — over and over again with little variation. (We totally understand that this could be as a result of what a pianist is limited to play.) Many Christians don't appreciate and meditate upon the poetic and imagery-driving lyrics of hymns, and frequently young people associate the word "hymn" with "boring." Moreover, a large number of all the Christians who *do* sing hymns in church have never heard of the powerful stories behind these precious songs we sing; nor are they aware of how abundantly God has used them in the past. God *still* has a great use for them and the hymnal today!

We are so thankful for our many fundamental friends who are still excited to genuinely use the timeless hymns that have been now entrusted unto us. There is still a generation that has not bent their knee to blend in with status quo Laodicean Christianity. We seek to encourage you. Keep standing!

We enjoy using the hymnal, now especially as parents. As our kids grow older, we are able to teach them how musical structure works with notes, measures, stanzas, and parts. If there were no hymnal, there would be no repetitious opportunity to give the next generation a glimpse into the order of "music theory" at an early age. We are delighted to watch them trace their little fingers along the words as they seek to follow the movement of each song and sing the tune.

This is also true for new believers in Christ who might be unfamiliar with these hymns. Instead of blankly looking at a screen with no foreseeable direction of what is going to happen with the melody of the song, if they have some sort of background in music (as many do, having played in band in junior high or high school), they will be able to comfortably follow along, seeing the melody in their hymnals.

Furthermore, those who have difficulty in seeing can customize where they wish their hymnal to be held in their hands so they can read the words clearly and comfortably, instead of having to strain their eyes toward the stage and see words on a screen.

There is a dynamic power at work that God created when congregations sing together — corporate singing fosters unity among people in a fascinating way. Researchers of the Sahlgrenska Academy at the University of Gothenburg in Sweden studied the heart rates of choir members as they joined together their voices. The findings, published in *Frontiers in Neuroscience,* confirmed that by using pulse monitors attached to the singers' ears, they were able to measure the changes in the members' heart rates as they navigated the melody and harmonies of a hymn. They were amazed at what they discovered. When the singing began, something unique took place.

"When you sing the phrases, it is a form of guided breathing," said project leader and musicologist, Bjorn Vickhoff, of Sahlgrenska Academy. *"You exhale on the phrases and breathe in between the phrases, and when you exhale, the heart slows down."*[129]

Vickhoff furthered stated that it took almost no time at all for the singers' heart rates to become synchronized. The read-out from the pulse monitors started out as a jumble of jagged lines, but quickly became a series of uniform peaks. The heart rates fell into a shared rhythm guided by the song's tempo. How powerful! This is something that the Lord designed for His people to experience as we sing together unto Him as a congregation — hearts physically and spiritually beating in unity!

In conclusion, below is an excerpt written by Dr. Frank Garlock in regards to the hymnal, its purpose and usage. The following segment has been used by permission and adapted from Mrs. Shelly Hamilton's *Why I Don't Listen to Contemporary Christian Music*. Something for us to consider!

The Bible is the Word of God, inspired by Him and unique; however, many church leaders down through the centuries, as well as the Bible itself, have acknowledged the importance of Christians lifting their voices in praise to the Lord.

But there is a current trend in churches drifting away from the hymnbook, with congregations singing while following lyrics on PowerPoint instead. This practice appears to include several benefits:

- *The congregation is looking up while singing, not having their heads buried in a book*
- *Unison singing is louder than singing in parts*
- *By not concentrating on singing in four-part harmony, the congregation can better concentrate on the spiritual message of the text*
- *The congregation can flow at predetermined times from one hymn to another in a segue without the interruption of having to turn to different hymnbook pages.*

Although benefits exist from PowerPoint singing, I believe congregational singing from a hymnbook has numerous advantages that cannot be ignored. Singing from a hymnbook allows:

- *The beauty and power of four-part singing, especially in an a cappella setting*
- *The musical edifications of the congregation in learning to sing four-part harmony*
- *The inclusion of many traditional sacred songs, some of which only work well sung in four parts — such as Luther's "A Mighty Fortress Is Our God", Bliss's "Man of Sorrows", "And Can It Be?", and "All Hail the Power of Jesus' Name", as well as Gospel songs such as "Wonderful Grace of Jesus."*

Dan Lucarini, former worship leader, realizes the dangers of disregarding the hymnbook by what he calls the "twenty-five years of the experiment." In his book "It's Not About the Music", Dan warns: "When we throw out the hymnals, we also throw out God-given protections against doctrinal drift, heresy, and shocking musical worldliness. We turn over the musical catechism of our children to an ecumenical music industry driven by the worst fashions and lusts of this present age. It is past time to end the experiment and invest again in a good hymnal Buy one for every home too!"

We believe the hymnbook should never be thrown out of the church, but be utilized as the tool for which it is designed — a wealth of sacred song text for the enrichment of the believer musically and doctrinally.

There is one use of the PowerPoint that is especially effective in church services — the displaying of song lyrics for [choir and] instrumental specials, such as offertories. This practice enables the congregation to more easily meditate on the message of the music.

So, what is the purpose of the hymnbook? Congregational singing should be the center of any church music program because every believer is commanded to sing praises to the Lord (Ephesians 5:18-20; Colossians 3:16-17). God has given the gift of music to every Christian to help us fulfill our chief purpose in life — to glorify God. The hymnbook has a wealth of Biblically solid music that benefits the church member as well as the church body as a whole. Part of our responsibility as music ministers is to educate our congregation concerning what it means to worship the Lord together. God is our audience; and we, both the music leaders and the people, are accountable to Him for the quality of our singing as a congregation. The hymnbook is the foundation upon which good congregational singing is built and is the vehicle for accomplishing this purpose.[130]

CHAPTER X

THE POWER OF SACRED SONG

George F. Pentecost (1842-1920) was a well-renowned pastor and evangelist of his day. When D. L. Moody was not able to preach at certain meetings in his campaigns in the northeast, it was common belief that Dr. Pentecost was the only man who could best fill his shoes. Furthermore, when it was time for Moody and Sankey to leave and conduct a revival crusade in a different city, George Pentecost was frequently asked to stay behind and continue the meetings that were still running strong. Thousands flocked to his services, and multitudes trusted Christ as their personal Saviour through his evangelistic work. He was an active soulwinner, dynamic preacher, and prolific author.

He was a dear friend to many of the hymn writers of the 19th century — including Ira Sankey, George C. Stebbins, P. P. Bliss, James MacGranahan, and Fanny Crosby. He witnessed first-hand the godly effect that the timeless hymns penned in that period had upon people.

The reason this chapter (and the next) has been included in this book is to cultivate a greater love and appreciation for the classic hymns that we use today in the musical worship and congregational singing portion of our church services. Also, it is wonderful to behold how he shares with us the great value of what godly music can do for the believer and in church meetings.

We are not advocating that we should *only* use the old and avoid anything that is new and Biblically sound. Remember, the Bible teaches us to sing *"psalms, hymns, and spiritual songs"* — we should sing Bible passages, older songs of the faith, and modern ones too. There should be a healthy balance in our song services. There are numerous hymnals produced in recent years that maintain and promote this Biblical balance — such as *"Majesty Hymns"* by Majesty Music, Inc., and *"Songs and Hymns of Revival"* by North Valley Publications.

Many churches today, however, are seeking to move away from the old to use only the new. Others have compromised completely and are striving to replace the old-fashioned hymns with modern, trendy choruses and Contemporary Christian music. **This is tragic.**

There is a great need for God's people to be writing hymns NOW! When Dr. Pentecost wrote about the great hymns, they weren't old — they were written by his peers. Of course, something is *not* bad because it's new — it just has to line up with Biblical principles. We should sing old hymns from our hymnal and also sing newer ones.

If you are musically gifted, would you please pray about how the Lord could use you in this area? Who will be the modern day "Ira Sankey," "P. P. Bliss," and "Fanny Crosby"?

Now, join with us as we step back into time over a hundred years ago and catch the heart of this "golden era" in hymn history. The following exposé was written in 1877 when

Dr. Pentecost was only 35 years old. We own a first edition of the book *"Song Victories"* from whence it was taken. This is an extremely insightful read from a passionate preacher in the annals of yesteryear!

My dear brother, you ask me to give you (from my own personal experience and observation) any facts in relation to the use and power of sacred song in connection with the work of the Holy Spirit for the conversion and sanctification of sinners — and I most gladly bear my testimony. I presume my experience is not different in kind from that of all other Christians who have submitted themselves to God under this wonderful instrument of the Spirit.

THE POWER OF SONGS UPON CHILDHOOD

Some of my earliest religious awakenings were in connection with the hymns for children that were just beginning to be sung in the Sunday schools when I was yet a little boy. I mention one *"how He called little children like lambs to His fold."* Those little hymns would always quiet me and beget within my heart seriousness and longing.

When as a child, I used to hear or sing them, I would wonder if there was any blessing that I might have from Jesus that would correspond to His calling little children to Himself, and laying His gentle, loving hands on their heads and blessing them.

In after years, when I had grown to be a young man, away from home, and far from God by wicked works, those little hymns of my childhood would often come to my memory; and more than once I sang them with choking voice and tearful eyes, and with motions of real penitence in my heart. It is true that these effects were transient, but they were real and mighty; and I doubt not that God used those child hymns and the sweet echoes of many others to keep my heart from becoming completely hardened against His gentle voice.

THE POWER OF SONGS IN YOUNG MANHOOD

Today, on looking back over the fourteen years that have passed since I gave my life to Jesus, among the precious recollections of those happy days, I recall a few dear old hymns that taught me truths of God in my heart that otherwise I might not have learned, and led me to the sources of joy and delight which otherwise I might not have found.

I can hear those voices now, that used to lead the singing in that blessed revival time. Some of them, it is true, were poor and cracked and discordant — it was a congregation of "common people"; but, they sung in those hours of the Spirit's presence and power, with hearts making melody to the Lord.

I think it was the singing of those simple old hymns that awakened in me the desire to be a Christian, by setting before me its promise of "sweetest pleasure" and "solid comfort" in strong contrast with the unsatisfying portions I was getting from worldly pleasures, and the fear and dread of death that was so constantly before me. Eternity only will reveal the power those hymns had over me, both in bringing me to God, and in strengthening and encouraging me in the first days of trial and temptation that came to me as a young Christian.

Time would fail to speak at length of my relations to

those old classics — *"There is a fountain filled with blood"*, *"Rock of ages, cleft for me"*, and *"Jesus, lover of my soul."*

SONGS AS A DELIVERER

I am profoundly sure that among the divinely ordained instruments for the conversion of the soul, God has not given a greater (beside the preaching of the Gospel) than the singing of the *"psalms and hymns and spiritual songs."* I have known a hymn to do God's work in a soul when every other thing has failed. I cannot begin to recount the times God has refreshed my heart from discouragement and weariness by the singing of a hymn, generally by bringing one to my own heart and causing me to sing it to myself.

A year or two after I entered the ministry, I passed through a dark time that lead me to believe I had been mistaken in supposing that God had called me to the work of the ministry. Oh! The blackness and darkness of those hours! Having almost yielded up to despair, I was returning to my home from a neighboring town where I had been supposedly assisting a ministering brother in a "meeting."

I got aboard the train, flung myself into a seat next to a window of the car, and made another desperate effort to recover myself, my faith, my hope, and my confidence in God. I prayed in the Spirit, I even called aloud on God, unmindful of the people around me; I went over the promises, and searched my memory through for some word of the Lord that would bring me help. But God's Word was a silent and sealed book for me, and my heart seemed to be turning into stone.

In the midst of this wretchedness, I was looking out of the car window up into the star-lit heavens, as a man might feel who knows he is freezing to death without power to help himself, and, indeed, not caring to any longer because it seems easier to die. It was in this moment that I heard a faint voice of singing in my heart, *I say I heard the voice of singing within me,* and harkening I caught to words of it, and with my own lips in low, tremulous tones began to sing:

> *"Jesus, I my cross have taken,*
> *All to leave and follow Thee:*
> *Naked, poor, despised, forsaken,*
> *Thou from hence my all shall be."*

I wondered at myself and at the song; I found my heart softening. I know that tears were in my eyes; I felt them running down my cheeks. I was away back with Jesus on the cross — I heard His cry, *"My God! My God! Why hast thou forsaken me?"* And in that same moment, the Holy Ghost gave me fellowship with my Saviour, and I knew that cry from Him was not for Himself alone, but for *me.* I sang on through the hymn with still melting heart, with returning faith, hope, and confidence, until in a perfect ecstasy of peace I reached the lines:

> *"Man may trouble and distress me,*
> *'Twill but drive me to Thy breast;*
> *Life with trials hard may press me,*
> *Christ will bring me sweeter rest.*
> *Oh, 'tis not in griefs to harm me,*
> *While Thy love is left on me;*
> *Oh! 'twere not in joy to charm me,*
> *Were that joy unmixed with Thee."*

And then, like a comforted child, I fairly laid my weary

heart against His dear loving heart on that train, knowing in my soul that He loved me, that He died and rose again for me, that He lived for me and that as never before we were united to each other. I recalled, *"he died for all, that they which live should not henceforth live unto themselves, but unto him which died for them, and rose again"* (II Corinthians 5:15).

Thus that precious hymn was God's hand reaching out to help me when I was sinking. Thus, He was pleased to manifest Himself to me in a sweeter, surer, and stronger way than I had yet known Him. He had chosen to do this by and in a hymn, rather than by a prayer, mediation, or promise. I have not turned back since that very day; I am still even now walking.

SONGS AS A HELP TO CONSECRATION

Years after when I was passing through consecration into deeper fellowship with the Lord, it pleased Him to use that same hymn again; this time not so much for immediate comfort as for searching. By inward teaching, the Spirit was making me to know something of the meaning of the Master when He said, *"If any man will come after me, let him deny himself, and take up his cross daily and follow me"* (Luke 9:23). Whilst I was learning somewhat painfully this lesson, I was one day suddenly checked in the singing of this (now one of my favorite hymns) with the distinct question, *"Can you truly sing —*

> *'Jesus, I my cross have taken,*
> *All to leave and follow Thee?'"*

I say I found myself checked in the singing of it for a

long time; until, in my deepest heart and purpose, I had truly denied myself into His hands, to be *"armed with the same mind."* But now, *"thanks be to God, which giveth us the victory,"* after having been searched by it (as I had been never searched before) I can joyfully and honestly sing that dear old hymn in the Spirit and with understanding also. And as a response to that hymn, now, always come those lines of Charles Wesley's great song:

> *"Thou, O Christ, art all I want,*
> *More than all in Thee I find."*

I magnify the grace of God ministered to me. He has made use of hymns in dealing with my soul, and in a similar manner, the power of song affected others coming under my own pastoral care.

SONGS AS A MEANS OF CONVERSION

I have known a hymn to be used of God for the saving of a soul where every other means had failed to bring light into the darkened and troubled heart. Once I was detained after prayer-meeting with a few others, to converse and pray with a young woman who was under deep conviction and refused to go away from the place of prayer until she had found Jesus.

It seemed to be all in vain that I talked with her, explaining the atonement, quoting the strongest promises of the Gospel, and urging her to an immediate and simple faith. It seemed all in vain that I pray with her and for her. At last, because (as it seemed) I could do nothing else, I began to sing that little hymn (written by William Bradbury who also penned *"Jesus Loves Me"*), the last verse of which goes:

"Oh! Bear my longing heart to Him
Who bled and died for me;
Whose blood now cleanses from all sin,
And gives me victory."

The others with me had joined in. During the singing of that last stanza, our friend had lifted her weeping face toward mine, and was looking intently and eagerly at me, drinking in the words and power of the song. We had sung the whole hymn through and were quieted into a silence by the Spirit. Now in the hush that was upon us, reaching out both her hands to me, she said in a plaintive kind of whisper, *"Please sing that last verse again."* And we sang those sweet words softly and tenderly.

As the words and melody died away, the expression of her face changed; the darkness was overpast, and the light and gladness of His peace had come in the place of it. With a cry of joy she turned and flung herself into the arms of her sister, exclaiming, *"I am saved! I am saved!! Oh! Blessed Jesus!"* And she continued to rejoice, as we all.

HYMNS IN PUBLIC WORSHIP

It would be easy to fill many pages with interesting facts in connection with the use of hymns in the public worship of the house of God. I have seen vast audiences melted and swayed by a simple hymn when they have been unmoved by a powerful sermon from the pulpit.

From close and repeated observation, I am persuaded that Mr. Spurgeon, the great metropolitan preacher of England, places great reliance on the use of hymns in public worship. By them, he prepares his vast audiences for the service that is to follow; and fastens his discourse with a hymn, which he always reads with great power, and which is sung by that vast choir of 7,500 people with an effect that is indescribable.

Indeed, the use of hymns in the service of the sanctuary, when in the hands of a pastor or leader who understands and feels the inspiration of them, cannot be too highly estimated. It is a great pity that the power of *"psalms and hymns and spiritual songs"* has been so sadly weakened, if not utterly destroyed by the introduction of "fancy quartettes."

May the Lord hasten the day when the service of song shall be restored to the people!

IN THE PRAYER MEETING

Hymns are simply indispensable. A pastor skilled in the use of them holds the prayer-meeting almost absolutely in his power. An unfortunate or ill-timed address or exhortation may be covered by a hymn, and the people's hearts and minds brought back to the Lord.

A pungent address, a ringing testimony, or a prevailing prayer may be strongly supplemented and reinforced by a well chosen hymn promptly and sweetly sung. Without giving out page or number, it should spring spontaneously from the lips of the pastor or any brother or sister in the congregation who has spiritual discernment.

For myself, I should feel utterly lost, and without "sword" or "trowel" for the building and defense of the walls of Zion, if I were without the "armory" and "kit" of hymns which God has given the church to profit withal.

SONGS IN REVIVAL WORK

I shall close this letter by giving a brief account of the triumph of song as seen in connection with the great revival of the last few years on both sides of the Atlantic. All know the story of the two simple-hearted and "unlearned" men — Moody and Sankey — who went only a few years ago, led of the Spirit, to the British Isles, to preach and sing the Gospel. Moody with his open Bible. Sankey with his stirring hymns and his sweet, God-given, sanctified voice.

Whether the most is to be ascribed to Moody's preaching or Sankey's singing — one with the simple words of truth the other with sweetest song — represent a two-edged instrument which the Holy Spirit has been pleased to use in the accomplishment of His mighty work. But certain it is that whoever visited Scotland for years knew that Sankey had been there, for he has sung a hundred songs into the hearts and spiritual lives of more than 20,000 converts to Jesus. God used him to fill the whole land, Highlands and Lowlands, with their sacred echoes.

Eminent Scotch preachers told me, while in conversation with them on this subject, that it was Sankey's singing that melted the hearts of the people and made an open door for Moody with his Bible lessons, for such they were rather than sermons. Of course, this is not mentioned to disparage the preaching of the Gospel — God forbid — but only to show the relation of song to the spoken word. **This service of song was not a passing gift but a permanent legacy.** For you see, none can reproduce Moody's matchless Bible expositions, but all of Scotland for years has sung Sankey's songs.

It was in the Barkley church in Edinburgh where these men began their work, having been invited thither by the Pastor James Wilson, who was a bold advocate of *"hymns and spiritual songs"*. I was in that church, the guest of the pastor, during a crowded Thursday evening prayer-meeting. One of our little American hymns was announced. In a twinkling everyone present whipped out of pocket a little penny copy of *"Sankey's Hymns"*. Every face was radiant, and every voice was vocal. The house seemed filled with the Spirit, and every heart seemed to be pouring out its faith and hope to God.

I witnessed the same effect in Dr. Wallace's great congregation in Glasgow, the same in Dr. Bonar's church, the same in the great noonday meetings in Assembly Hall, and in other places that I visited. Indeed, Scotland was ringing with songs and gladness.

Riding once from Ayr to Glasgow on a third-class train crowded with the "common people", who had been off on some excursion, my ears were filled all the way with the melody of those revival hymns. They rose ever and anon above the noise of the rushing train and rang out clear and beautiful when we stopped for a few moments at the stations along the line. It seemed as though we were on board the very car of salvation, being speeded along by bands of singing angels comes to convoy us.

Again, one Sunday evening, I left my hotel in Glasgow to go to Dr. Andrew Bonar's church some two miles distant. On my way I was treated to a novel spectacle, and one which was repeated every few hundred yards until I reached the church. I had gone but a little way from the hotel when my ears were greeted with the familiar strains:

"Safe in the arms of Jesus,
Safe on His gentle breast,
Then by His love o'ershaded,
Sweetly my soul shall rest."

Looking ahead of me I saw a crowd, from whence came the singing. Pressing up I joined the multitude of men, women, and children gathered about a little band of brothers and sisters in the Lord, who were holding a service of song on the street corner. This little company could not *preach*, in the technical sense of that word, but they could *sing* the glad gospel out on the evening air, and thus say to all, "Come!"

I was very deeply impressed with their simple service, for they were evidently engaging in it as a matter that was to be done unto the Lord. As they passed from the singing of one hymn to another, sometimes slipping in a brief prayer between, I noted the effect upon the crowd. Though made up mostly of the street rabble, such as is seen only in the large cities of Great Britain, it was hushed into quiet, and even eager attention to the singing.

My attention was called to some faces grown serious and thoughtful as they harkened to words of love and hope, and more than once I saw the tears stealing down the grim cheek of some sinner unused to weep. Thus was God at work in those neglected hearts, and His dear love crept into many a soul through those songs.

As I have already said, these singing bands with their attendant crowds were stationed all the way down the long street to the church, at intervals of a few hundred yards, and other of the principal streets of the city were similarly occupied. In no other way, it seems to me, could the gospel have been so effectually "preached" to that class of people.

At Dr. Bonar's church, the whole mighty congregation worshipped God, filling the church with the sound of their song:

> *"I hear the Saviour say,*
> *Thy strength indeed is small*
> *Child of weakness, watch and pray,*
> *Find in Me thine all in all."*
> *Jesus paid it all,*
> *All to Him I owe;*
> *Sin had left a crimson stain,*
> *He washed it white as snow."*

In conclusion, is it out of place to express the hope and venture the prediction that this revival of sacred song is the forerunner and first fruits of a general revival of religion in the church of God? I believe it, and hail it as one who, watching for the morning, hails the gray dawn and roseate light in the East. *"Even so, come, Lord Jesus."* Come quickly!

REV. GEORGE F. PENTECOST.

CHAPTER XI

GOSPEL SONGS AND THEIR MINISTRY

This closing chapter is a brief glimpse into the exciting life of Charles M. Alexander, who was considered to be the *"Prince of Gospel Singers"* at the turn of the twentieth century. As a young man, he tirelessly worked alongside many of those who wrote and arranged the hymns that we now enjoy today.

Alexander, originally from East Tennessee, was a popular 19th century gospel musician, who was acknowledged as the successor of Ira D. Sankey. His early Christian influence came from his mother, who was in the habit of reading D. L. Moody sermons to the family every night around the fireplace.

After Moody died in 1899, R. A. Torrey took up Moody's mantle of evangelism and engaged in campaigns in major American cities and around the world in Australia, New Zealand, India, Great Britain, and other countries. He took great interest in this young man, and the two of them teamed up together and conducted evangelistic meetings for several years.

Over the course of his ministry, Alexander traveled around the world twice with R. A. Torrey and J. Wilbur Chapman on their revival crusades, enthusiastically leading the singing and the choirs. At the Royal Albert Hall, in London, he conducted for two months the largest evangelistic choir ever organized, 4,000 persons joining daily in the great services. Alexander led the congregations like a great choir — he exhorted and he jested, and the great audiences of thousands enjoyed it. They sang with ease, fire, and exultation as he waved his arms vigorously with a radiant face and fine voice. His music fulfilled its highest function of preparing the crowd for the preaching and his message.

But more than his music, Alexander was characteristically known for his *"deep yearning to bring souls to Christ."* His wife said of him that every person with whom he came in contact was someone he sought to lead to Jesus. Alexander would often declare: *"You claim you are following Jesus. Are you fishing for men? If you are not fishing, you are not following."* Hundreds of thousands were saved through their endeavors in Australia, the Philippines, Hong Kong, China, Korea, Japan, and Africa. With his wife Helen, he organized the *Pocket Testament League* that distributed more than one million New Testaments to the soldiers in the trenches of World War I.

The following excerpt is taken from his biography written by his loving wife Helen Cadbury Alexander after he died at age of 52 in 1920. We have the first edition of this soul-stirring book — the very copy that was given to Leonard C. Voke (pianist for the evangelistic campaigns) and signed by Mrs. Alexander. We also own an original rare record of Alexander's singing *"The Glory Song"* in 1905, along with old photographs of him, R. A. Torrey, their meetings, and their evangelistic team. In addition to this, we have a hymnal from Alexander's personal library that contains notes and comments penned by his own hand.

Dr. Frank Garlock shared with us over the phone recently that when he went into the ministry in the 1950's as a young preacher and musician, he was greatly influenced by the testimony and musical philosophy of Charles Alexander. Dr. Garlock gleaned from and followed many of Alexander's teachings and insight on choir leading and congregation singing, among other principles. In part, Charles Alexander is a spiritual grandfather to the Christ-honoring ministry of Majesty Music and Patch the Pirate. *Incredible!*

Brother Alexander was a pivotal man that God used in the development of our hymns and music in fundamental Christianity. May his love and passion for joyful, godly music rejoice your heart and reinforce the truths that we have made evident in our study. Truth is timeless, and it is wonderful to see that what he believed and exhorted others to believe over a century ago is the exact same truth today!

No one ever asks why the birds sing, because we know that they burst into song as naturally and as easily as they breathe or fly. And no one who ever heard Charles Alexander sing, or who watched him as he lifted a great crowd, on the wings of music, into the heavens, needed to be told that he, like the birds, sang because there was within him a holy impulse which he could not resist.

It was not his profession to sing; it was his very life. Long before the dawn of those great opportunities which drew him around the globe, inspiring Christians everywhere to the joyful service of praise and of zeal for souls, Charles Alexander had learned the power and the value of sacred song.

In the home of his boyhood in Tennessee he had seen the influence of it upon the lives of the community in which he lived. He had seen it at work in the scattered villages of the beautiful Tennessee and North Carolina mountains. In his first evangelistic work with John Kittrell, he had seen its power to melt sin-hardened hearts. Through his days of training at the Moody Bible Institute, he had been a keen student of religious movements.

In an article on Gospel hymns, he says: *"I do not recall any religious awakening without Gospel singing. Music was a vital part of the revival under the Wesley's. The revival of 1859 was a time of hymn-singing. Gospel songs were fully half the power of the Moody and Sankey meetings, and we all know what a prominent part music played in the Welsh Revival. I have yet to see the first church that remained empty for long, where each person entered heartily into the singing of hymns. When singing is delegated to the few, with no responsibility upon the rest of the audience, the interest dies, the numbers dwindle, and all kinds of expedients must be resorted to in order to draw the people. This method crowds out music from its proper place, which should be co-ordinate with preaching. In order to maintain this equality, every individual must be made to feel his responsibility in the singing part of the worship. This is as true in a church service, as in an evangelistic meeting."*

More, perhaps, than any man of this or any other generation, Charles Alexander revealed and demonstrated the great resources and possibilities of sacred song. From the time when he first realized that this was to be his God-given calling, he set himself to make people sing and to give them something worth singing. To the end, he was never satisfied with past achievements, and would constantly test one theory after another, working out his results with scientific care and exactness.

On first acquaintance, his methods seemed to be full of spontaneous simplicity, but, behind the seeming ease of his work, lay the careful preparation into which the calculating brain and glowing heart had poured their best efforts. He realized, to an unusual degree, the rivalry of Satan in the matter of music, which God has ordained for praise of Himself, and which, when perverted to other uses, may ruin, rather than upbuild, human character.

Charles Alexander loved to trace the holy use of joyful music through all God's dealings with those who have trusted Him in every age of the world's history. He loved to read and tell how David appointed *"singers with instruments of music"* under the leadership of Chenaniah, who *"instructed about the song because he was skilful"*; of how they *"lifted up the voice with joy,"* as they, with all Israel, accompanied the Ark of God homewards from the house of Obed-edom.

He loved to picture the dedication of the new Temple by Solomon, when *"the trumpeters and singers were as one, to make one sound to be heard in praising and thanking the Lord"*; the re-dedication under Josiah, when *"the singers, the sons of Asaph, were in their place"*; *"the dedication of the wall of Jerusalem,"* rebuilt by the faithful efforts of Nehemiah and Ezra, which was celebrated *"with gladness, both with thanksgivings and with singing,"* when the singers sang so loudly, and the rejoicing of men, women and children was so exuberant, that *"the joy of Jerusalem was heard even afar off."*

In the New Testament, he read with delight of the songs of the angels at Bethlehem, announcing the arrival of the Son of God on the earth; of the *"psalms and hymns and spiritual songs*" which rose from the gatherings of the first believers, from the time they knew that their Lord was risen from the dead; of the songs of unconquerable faith which echoed through the old prison at Philippi in the darkness of midnight; of the revelation of that *"new song"* which will make the vaults of Heaven ring throughout eternity.

But, most of all, he loved to read of the close of that long, tender conversation between our Lord and His disciples on the eve of the crucifixion, when, before descending the stairs from the upper room in Jerusalem, and making their way in the moonlight to the garden of Gethsemane on the slopes of Olivet, they sang a hymn together: *"How I would have loved to hear His voice singing a hymn!"* Alexander would often say.

Whenever he met with any objection to his fondness for interesting people in freshly-written songs and hymns, his rejoinder was, "Well, I love the good old standard hymns as much as you do, but don't forget that we are told in the Psalms to *'sing unto the Lord a new song.'*"

Praise and prayer were parts of a whole to him. He rarely began even a preliminary practice with a choir, without saying, *"Let us have a word of prayer first, and then the singing will go better."* He never for a moment permitted his choir to think that the beauty of a song was an end in itself. Always, the purpose for which it was sung was held up before them. This is why he insisted constantly upon clear enunciation of the words, and upon the intelligent interest of every member of the choir. He would often pray, *"Help them to sing with the heart, and with the heart, and with the understanding also."*

At the beginning of the evangelistic meeting in Bangor, Ireland, in the Spring of 1911, an incident occurred, illustrating his concern for the spiritual responsibility of the singers. Charles Alexander met the choir the day before Dr. Chapman arrived. Eager and expectant, the singers gathered. The first thing he asked them to sing was the chorus, *"O Lord, send a revival, and let it begin in me!"*

As soon as they had learned the melody, he told them the story of the young Welsh girl who had first uttered the words in a small meeting, and had started the blaze of revival which spread all over Wales in 1905. Over and over again the Bangor choir sang, until the hall rang with the melody. Lifting his hand, Alexander suddenly hushed them into silence.

"Now you know the tune," he said, *"but what do the words mean to you? Have you thought that, before Dr. Chapman ever preaches a word, you have a chance to sing the message? We want a revival here. Why should it not begin in the choir? Let us sing it softly now, and make it a prayer."* The earnest appeal that followed brought great results, for the Holy Spirit was working, and nine members of the choir who had never before taken a stand for Christ, rose to acknowledge Him openly as their Saviour.

The wonderful effects gained by Charles Alexander through his skillful use of song aroused curiosity everywhere. Over and over again, people tried to explain his power as personal magnetism, and spoke of him as hypnotizing the crowds into singing. But these things were generally said by those who had little experience of the power of the Holy Spirit, when the instrument of an entirely consecrated life is placed at His service.

To explain how it was that some of the simple songs he used could produce such wonderful spiritual results, Charles Alexander was constantly asked to write articles for newspapers and magazines. In one of these, he told the people of Boston: *"There is a wonderful influence in song, and that influence spreads with great rapidity when once it gets started. To become quickly popular, songs must be easy to learn; there must be a simple, easy, flowing melody, and a small range, not much over an octave, and a picture in every line of every verse. The words must be simple, but full of faith, hope and promise. I never make up any final list of songs before I go to a meeting. As soon as I come on the platform I begin to study my audience, and then select my first song in accordance with my impression of what the people desire, or of what may reach them. If the first verse does not go well, I go no further with it, and sing something else. It is not my method to sing new songs exclusively; I frequently have a new one first, in order to get the people interested, and then follow with an old one which has appropriate relation to the other. For instance, what can be more effective than to begin with 'He Will Hold Me Fast' and follow with 'Safe in the Arms of Jesus'; or, after the solo, 'Is He yours?' with 'Blessed Assurance'?"*

An incident which occurred in a men's meeting in the Sydney Town Hall one night in August, 1912, illustrates the influence of this way of using the hymns. The choir and congregation had been singing *"Where is My Wandering Boy To-night?"* The second verse was sung by the men of the congregation, standing. A wave of the hand brought the whole of the vast company to its feet, as if in earnest entreaty, when they began the last verse. The voicing of the line *"Bring him to me with all his blight"* spoke of a yearning desire to make the words tell. Without a break, the chorus, *"Lord, I'm Coming Home,"* followed on, making the answer very personal to those who sang it:

"Coming Home, coming Home,
Never more to roam;

By Thy grace I will be Thine,
Lord, I'm coming Home."

It welled up from the floor, and floated down from the galleries. Dr. Chapman gave a word of invitation in his tenderest tones for decisions to be made. He was about to ask those who desired it to rise for prayer, when from the centre of the hall, a dozen seats back, there rose an old man, bent with age, grasping his hat and stick to make his way, as it seemed, out of the building.

It was a palpable interruption to the appeal, but the old man, instead of turning to leave, went straight up to the reporters' table, near the platform, and knelt there for prayer. *"God bless you,"* was the fervent prayer uttered by the preacher, echoed in hushed tones through all the audience, as the aged wanderer *"came Home,"* to the Lord.

It was a great discovery for Charles Alexander, when he realized that busy men who thought they could not sing, or take time for singing, were like a crowd of boys, when they came together in a meeting, and sang just as heartily. He found that down in every man's heart there is a love of song, and that even the men who had no sympathy with Christianity as they knew it, liked the Gospel hymns, and would come to hear them. Many and many a time these songs clung to a man day and night, and eventually led him to Jesus.

Alexander never sang, or set others singing, without feeling sure that some one would be laid hold of, and be transformed into a new being. This expectancy, and its constant fulfillment, so revived him, that he could go to a crowded song service, and after three or four hours' work, feel fresher than at the start.

In London, during the never-to-be-forgotten Albert Hall

Mission, it was an almost everyday experience, throughout the two months, for people to stay from two o'clock till six. *"Dr. Torrey,"* to quote Alexander's account of those marvellous days, *"would take up three-quarters-of-an-hour preaching, and all the rest of the time, before and after the sermon, men and women in the galleries and boxes would be calling for some simple Gospel song. After a hasty meal, we would go back and sing again till nearly eleven. I have never seen any other kind of music that would get hold of people like this."*

The contrast between the effect of an ordinary song and that of a Gospel hymn was always pressed home by the great leader. *"Long ago,"* he said, *"I found that when I got people worked up by a concert or something of that kind, it stopped there. I would be all exhausted, and to no purpose. I would ask myself: 'Where did I take those people? Where did I land them, anyway? There must be something more in the world than this.' Now, when I am at work from ten o'clock in the morning until nearly midnight, I go home feeling satisfied that I have been doing the best work in the world. But I believe in taking pains to use hymns that really help and save people, and not wasting time on others."*

"You fellows know," he said once to a business men's club in Toronto, at which he was the principal guest, *"that if you try a thing and it doesn't do the business, you quit it. I get the songs that do the business, and if I find one that won't, I cut it right out.*

"I hesitated a long time before I would use the song, 'Tell Mother I'll Be There.' I have been criticized all over the world for using it, but you would not criticize if you knew what it has done, and what letters and testimonies I have received about it.

"The song had an interesting origin. When President McKinley was in office, his mother lay dying in Canton, Ohio,

several hundred miles away. She sent word that she wanted to see her boy once more before she died. President McKinley chartered a special train, and telegraphed, 'Tell mother I'll be there.' A Gospel-song writer caught up the idea and wrote the song. A friend of mine cut it out of a magazine, and sent it to me with a suggestion that I try it in my work. I pasted it in my scrap-book, more for my friend's sake than because I saw any merit in it, and carried it around for a year before I ever used it.

"One night in Newton, Kansas, I was called on to sing a solo. I saw in the audience a great crowd of railway men, and said to myself: 'I wonder what would reach those men.' With some doubt, I finally decided to try this touching song, and was surprised at the extraordinary result. Many of the men confessed Christ immediately.

"When the meeting was over, one big, burly engineer came up to me and said, 'Mr. Alexander, I promised my mother on her death-bed that I would become a Christian; but, instead of that, I have been going to the devil faster than ever. Preaching never touched me, but this song did. If you will sing it to-morrow night, I will bring the men.'

*"He did bring them for many nights. I used the song every night, and I have been using it ever since. **I have seen as many as one hundred and fifty men at a single meeting rise and confess Christ, during the singing of that hymn, before the sermon was begun.** Everywhere it has been the same. It reaches all classes, because everybody has a mother. It has been criticized from a musical, and from a literary, standpoint, but no song has ever been written that can take the place of it. Those who criticize are unable to replace it with a better."*

Of all the songs with which the name of Charles M. Alexander is linked, perhaps the *"Glory Song"* stands first. Both the words and music of it were written in Chicago by

Charles H. Gabriel, one of the most popular Gospel-hymn writers of America.

"I remember quite well," Alexander once wrote, *"the first time I ever saw this song. In looking over a new song-book, I just glanced at it, and said, 'That man has wasted a page, for I do not believe that song will be sung much.' Some months later, however, I stepped into a large Sunday-school convention, and heard an audience singing it. It took such a hold of me that I could think of nothing else for days thereafter. I got all my friends to sing it. I dreamed about it, and awoke to the rhythm of it. Then I began to teach it to large audiences, and soon whole towns were ringing with the refrain."*

The *"Glory Song"* captured Melbourne in a single night, and from there swept through the whole of Australia.

"At the close of our first revival campaign in Melbourne," wrote Charles, *"it seemed to me that everybody in the city was singing the 'Glory Song.' People going away on the suburban trains were singing it. Brass bands played it, and it was sung and played in all sorts of out- of-the-way places. The last day I was in Melbourne, I had to rise early to catch a train for Warrnambool. As I came out of my room, the maid was scrubbing the floor of the hall outside my door, and softly crooning: 'When by His grace, I shall look on His face, That will be glory for me.'*

"I went down to the hotel office, and took the receiver off the telephone, wishing to ring up to a friend across the city. As I placed the receiver to my ear, I heard the girl at the telephone exchange singing, as she clicked the pegs into their places: 'Oh, that will be glory for me.'"

As the train passed through Terang, a couple whom Alexander had met in Melbourne came down to the station to meet him, and they had a few words together. The lady said,

"Mr. Alexander, I am sure you will be interested to know anything about the 'Glory Song.' I learned it at the meetings in Melbourne. I have been over today to see a friend on her deathbed. I sang one verse of the 'Glory Song,' and she said, 'Oh, that is glorious; please sing another.' I sang another, and while I was singing the chorus, 'When by His grace I shall look on His face,' she passed to see the King in His beauty."

"I suppose few songs have spread all over the world as the 'Glory Song' has done," Charles Alexander was frequently heard to say. *"I have received translations in Chinese, Dutch, German, Italian, Danish, Welsh, Zulu, and other languages, and have received letters from places all over the globe, where it has become a favorite. Some people try to analyze it, and say that it has no power, but people keep right on calling for it, and singing it."*

Charles also shared a touching story by the influence of this song. *"When Dr. Torrey and I were conducting our campaign in the great Town Hall, Sydney, Australia, we distributed leaflets with the 'Glory Song,' words and music, and an invitation to the meetings printed at the bottom. We would ask the people, if they already possessed a copy of the song-book, to post the leaflets to friends in the country who never get new songs, or to put them in parcels as they sent them away.*

"One day, after I had asked them to do this, a lady, when she reached home, was sending some shoes to be mended. She happened to think about her 'Glory Song' leaflet, and put it into the bundle with the shoes. The next day she went down to the shoemaker's to get them, and found the old fellow pegging away, with the tears rolling down his cheeks.

"She asked, 'What is the matter?'

"And he answered, 'Do you remember the 'Glory Song' that you put into the bundle? Last night I got my little family

round the organ, and we sang it. I noticed the invitation to come to the Town Hall and hear Torrey and Alexander, so I went last night. I heard that man preach, and I gave my heart to God. I have sent my wife and children up to this afternoon's meeting, and I am just here praying that God will save them.'

"And God did save them. The next night the whole family publicly confessed their acceptance of Jesus Christ."

Many books could be written about the songs Alexander used. A number of them were composed under the direct inspiration of his influence. Robert Harkness [**Robert Harkness was one of Alexander's personal assistants and the pianist who popularized the evangelistic style of hymn playing that we use today.**] tells how he was led to write the music to one of his early hymns, *"Never Lose Sight of Jesus"*:

"Mr. Alexander came upon the words in Glasgow, and said to me: 'I want you to put a new tune to them.' I looked at the words for a long time, and began to write settings. I suppose I wrote a dozen, submitting them to him, but somehow or other he could not be pleased. In desperation, I put the hymn aside.

"At last, in Aberdeen, a month later, he said: 'You really must write a tune for that hymn.' I sat down in the drawing-room at the piano, and he went up to pray that I might get the right tune. At once I struck upon the chorus, and began to play softly. He rushed out of his room, with his coat off, and said, 'That's the tune! Hold on to that!' So the tune came quite naturally at last, and has since become popular everywhere."

Occasionally, the hymns came to Alexander from unexpected sources, and they would never have been known, but for that intuition of his, which made him so keenly sensitive to the true value of a hymn. *"He Lifted Me," "I Surrender All,"* and numerous other hymns from Alexander's wonderful collection are surrounded by an ever-growing romance of blessing and uplifting influence upon the lives of people. How many quarrels have been made right, and how much coldness melted, by the repetition of [these melodies]!

With regard to the children, he always insisted that, to a very large extent, children get their theology from the hymns which they sing. As this again is true of adults as well, Alexander felt that no pains should be spared to ensure that the teaching of the hymns was strictly in accordance with that of the Word of God; and he preferred, wherever possible, the actual words of Scripture. This was the reason why he loved so dearly the hymns written by his old friend Major D. W. Whittle (*"I Know Whom I Have Believed"* and others), so often set to music by his co-worker James McGranahan (*"All Hail the Power of Jesus' Name"* and others).

Never did Charles Alexander tire of the ministry of song, which to him was an ever-fresh delight. When asked to account for this, he was once heard to reply, *"It is the work the Lord has given me to do, and I guess He will tell me when it is time to stop."* Without doubt, many a soul greets him today in Heaven because of the Gospel songs he taught the people of many lands [and generations] to sing!

CHAPTER XII

A BIBLE CONCORDANCE OF MUSIC

The verses you are about to read are those found in the Bible with only a specific reference to music, musical instruments, or musical terms. We have decided to not include the multitude of Scripture verses that can be drawn from by way of application to the topic of music (as we have already gleaned from these throughout our studies). Also, we did not incorporate the texts of the many songs in Scripture from Psalms (several chapters), the children of Israel's song as led by Moses and Miriam in Exodus 15, Deborah's and Barak's duet written in Judges 5, or Zacharias' and Mary's solos recorded in Luke 1. Again, since these are just lyrics and are not *direct* references to music, they have not been included in this concordance. Katie and I have been delighted to conduct this painstaking research in compiling this wonderful selection about music in the Bible. We believe that it will deepen your love and understanding for God's passion of it.

This concordance begins in Genesis and goes in order verse by verse throughout the Bible, ending in Revelation. It is a product of tireless hours of Bible study and is comprised of over 250 passages. After these selections below, there is a final section about the word *"praise"* when it directly means *"a song of praise or thanksgiving"* in Scripture.

Genesis 4:21 — *"And his brother's name was Jubal: he was the father of all such as handle **the harp** and **organ**."*

Genesis 31:27 — *"Wherefore didst thou flee away secretly, and steal away from me; and didst not tell me, that I might have sent thee away with mirth, and with **songs**, with **tabret**, and with **harp**?"*

Exodus 15:1-2 — *"Then **sang** Moses and the children of Israel **this song** unto the Lord, and spake, saying, I will **sing** unto the Lord, for he hath triumphed gloriously: the horse and his rider hath he thrown into the sea. The Lord is my strength and **song**, and he is become my salvation: he is my God, and I will prepare him an habitation; my father's God, and I will exalt him."*

Exodus 15:20-21 — *"And Miriam the prophetess, the sister of Aaron, took a **timbrel** in her hand; and all the women went out after her with **timbrels** and with **dances**. And Miriam answered them, **Sing** ye to the Lord, for he hath triumphed gloriously; the horse and his rider hath he thrown into the sea."*

Exodus 19:19 — *"And when the voice of **the trumpet** sounded long, and waxed louder and louder, Moses spake, and God answered him by a voice."*

Exodus 32:18 — *"And he said, It is not the voice of them that shout for mastery, neither is it the voice of them that cry for being overcome: but **the noise** of them that **sing** do I* *hear."*

Leviticus 25:9 — *"Then shalt thou cause **the trumpet** of the jubile to sound on the tenth day of the seventh month, in the day of atonement shall ye make **the trumpet sound** throughout all your land."*

Numbers 21:17 — *"Then Israel **sang** this **song**, Spring up, O well; **sing** ye unto it:"*

Numbers 29:1 — *"And in the seventh month, on the first day of the month, ye shall have an holy convocation; ye shall do no servile work: it is a day of **blowing the trumpets** unto you."*

Numbers 31:6 — *"And Moses sent them to the war, a thousand of every tribe, them and Phinehas the son of Eleazar the priest, to the war, with the holy instruments, and **the trumpets** to blow in his hand."*

Deuteronomy 31:19 — *"Now therefore write ye **this song** for you, and teach it the children of Israel: put it in their mouths, that **this song** may be a witness for me against the children of Israel."*

Deuteronomy 31:21-22 — *"And it shall come to pass, when many evils and troubles are befallen them, that **this song** shall testify against them as a witness; for it shall not be forgotten out of the mouths of their seed: for I know their imagination which they go about, even now, before I have brought them into the land which I sware. Moses therefore wrote **this song** the same day, and taught it the children of Israel."*

Deuteronomy 31:30 — *"And Moses spake in the ears of all the congregation of Israel the words of **this song**, until they were ended."*

Deuteronomy 32:44 — *"And Moses came and spake all the*

words of **this song** in the ears of the people, he, and Hoshea the son of Nun."

Joshua 6:4-6 — *"And seven priests shall bear before the ark seven **trumpets** of rams' horns: and the seventh day ye shall compass the city seven times, and the priests shall **blow with the trumpets**. And it shall come to pass, that when they make **a long blast** with the ram's horn, and when ye hear **the sound of the trumpet**, all the people shall shout with a great shout; and the wall of the city shall fall down flat, and the people shall ascend up every man straight before him. And Joshua the son of Nun called the priests, and said unto them, Take up the ark of the covenant, and let seven priests bear seven **trumpets** of rams' horns before the ark of the Lord."*

Joshua 6:8-9 — *"And it came to pass, when Joshua had spoken unto the people, that the seven priests bearing the seven **trumpets** of rams' horns passed on before the Lord, and **blew with the trumpets**: and the ark of the covenant of the Lord followed them. And the armed men went before the priests that **blew with the trumpets**, and the rereward came after the ark, the priests going on, and **blowing with the trumpets**."*

Joshua 6:13 — *"And seven priests bearing seven **trumpets** of rams' horns before the ark of the Lord went on continually, and **blew with the trumpets**: and the armed men went before them; but the rereward came after the ark of the Lord, the priests going on, and **blowing with the trumpets**."*

Joshua 6:16 — *"And it came to pass at the seventh time, when the priests **blew with the trumpets**, Joshua said unto the people, Shout; for the Lord hath given you the city."*

Joshua 6:20 — *"So the people shouted when the priests **blew with the trumpets**: and it came to pass, when the people heard **the sound of the trumpet**, and the people shouted with a great shout, that the wall fell down flat, so that the people went up into the city, every man straight before him, and* *they took the city."*

Judges 5:1-3 — *"Then **sang** Deborah and Barak the son of Abinoam on that day, saying, Praise ye the Lord for the avenging of Israel, when the people willingly offered themselves. Hear, O ye kings; give ear, O ye princes; I, even I, will **sing** unto the Lord; I will **sing praise** to the Lord God of Israel."*

Judges 5:12 — *"Awake, awake, Deborah: awake, awake, utter **a song**: arise, Barak, and lead thy captivity captive, thou son of Abinoam."*

Judges 7:16-22 — *"And he divided the three hundred men into three companies, and he put a **trumpet** in every man's hand, with empty pitchers, and lamps within the pitchers. And he said unto them, Look on me, and do likewise: and, behold, when I come to the outside of the camp, it shall be that, as I do, so shall ye do. When I **blow with a trumpet**, I and all that are with me, then **blow ye the trumpets** also on every side of all the camp, and say, The sword of the Lord, and of Gideon. So Gideon, and the hundred men that were with him, came unto the outside of the camp in the beginning of the middle watch; and they had but newly set the watch: and they **blew the trumpets**, and brake the pitchers that were in their hands. And the three companies **blew the trumpets**, and brake the pitchers, and held the lamps in their left hands, and **the trumpets** in their right hands to **blow** withal: and they cried, The sword of the Lord, and of Gideon. And they stood every man in his place round about the camp: and all the host ran, and cried, and fled. And the three hundred **blew the trumpets**, and the Lord set every man's sword against his fellow, even throughout all the host: and the host fled to Bethshittah in Zererath, and to the border of Abelmeholah, unto Tabbath."*

Judges 11:34 — *"And Jephthah came to Mizpeh unto his house, and, behold, his daughter came out to meet him with **timbrels** and with dances: and she was his only child; beside* *her he had neither son nor daughter."*

I Samuel 10:5 — *"After that thou shalt come to the hill of God, where is the garrison of the Philistines: and it shall come to pass, when thou art come thither to the city, that thou shalt meet a company of prophets coming down from the high place with a **psaltery**, and a **tabret**, and a **pipe**, and a **harp**, before them; and they shall prophesy:"*

I Samuel 16:16-18 — *"Let our lord now command thy servants, which are before thee, to seek out a man, who is a **cunning player** on an **harp**: and it shall come to pass, when the evil spirit from God is upon thee, that he shall **play with his hand**, and thou shalt be well. And Saul said unto his servants, Provide me now a man that can **play well**, and bring him to me. Then answered one of the servants, and said, Behold, I have seen a son of Jesse the Bethlehemite, that is **cunning in playing**, and a mighty valiant man, and a man of war, and prudent in matters, and a comely person, and the Lord is with him."*

I Samuel 16:23 — *"And it came to pass, when the evil spirit from God was upon Saul, that David took an **harp**, and **played with his hand**: so Saul was refreshed, and was well, and the evil spirit departed from him."*

I Samuel 18:6-7 — *"And it came to pass as they came, when David was returned from the slaughter of the Philistine, that the women came out of all cities of Israel, **singing** and dancing, to meet king Saul, with **tabrets**, with joy, and with **instruments of musick**. And the women answered one another as they **played**, and said, Saul hath slain his thousands, and David his ten thousands."*

I Samuel 18:10 — *"And it came to pass on the morrow, that the evil spirit from God came upon Saul, and he prophesied in the midst of the house: and David **played with his hand**, as at other times: and there was a javelin in Saul's hand."*
[refers to I Samuel 16:23]

I Samuel 19:9 — *"And the evil spirit from the Lord was upon Saul, as he sat in his house with his javelin in his hand: and David **played with his hand**."* [refers to I Samuel 16:23]

II Samuel 6:5 — *"And David and all the house of Israel **played** before the Lord on **all manner of instruments** made of fir **wood**, even on **harps**, and on **psalteries**, and on **timbrels**, and on **cornets**, and on **cymbals**."*

II Samuel 6:15 — *"So David and all the house of Israel brought up the ark of the Lord with shouting, and with **the sound of the trumpet**."*

II Samuel 22:1 — *"And David spake unto the Lord the words of **this song** in the day that the Lord had delivered him out of the hand of all his enemies, and out of the hand of Saul:"*

II Samuel 22:50 — *"Therefore I will give thanks unto thee, O Lord, among the heathen, and I will **sing praises** unto thy name."*

I Kings 4:32 — *"And he [Solomon] spake three thousand proverbs: and his **songs** were a thousand and five."*

I Kings 10:12 — *"And the king made of the almug trees pillars for the house of the Lord, and for the king's house, **harps** also and **psalteries** for **singers**: there came no such almug trees, nor were seen unto this day."*

II Kings 3:14-16 — *"And Elisha said, As the Lord of hosts liveth, before whom I stand, surely, were it not that I regard the presence of Jehoshaphat the king of Judah, I would not look toward thee, nor see thee. But now bring me **a minstrel**. And it came to pass, when **the minstrel played**, that the hand of the Lord came upon him. And he said, Thus saith the Lord, Make this valley full of ditches."*

II Kings 12:13 — *"Howbeit there were not made for the house of the Lord bowls of silver, snuffers, basons, **trumpets**, any vessels of gold, or vessels of silver, of the money that was brought into the house of the Lord:"*

I Chronicles 6:31-33 — *"And these are they whom David set over **the service of song** in the house of the Lord, after that the ark had rest. And they **ministered** before the dwelling place of the tabernacle of the congregation **with singing**, until Solomon had built the house of the Lord in Jerusalem: and then they waited on **their office** according to their order. And these are they that waited with their children. Of the sons of the Kohathites: Heman a **singer**, the son of Joel, the son of Shemuel,"*

I Chronicles 9:33 — *"And these are the **singers**, chief of the fathers of the Levites, who remaining in the chambers were free: for they were employed in that work day and night."*

I Chronicles 13:8 — *"And David and all Israel **played** before God with all their might, and with **singing**, and with **harps**, and with **psalteries**, and with **timbrels**, and with **cymbals**, and with **trumpets**."*

I Chronicles 15:16-28 — *"And David spake to the chief of the Levites to appoint their brethren to be **the singers with instruments of musick, psalteries** and **harps** and **cymbals, sounding**, by **lifting up the voice with joy**. So the Levites appointed Heman the son of Joel; and of his brethren, Asaph the son of Berechiah; and of the sons of Merari their brethren, Ethan the son of Kushaiah; And with them their brethren of the second degree, Zechariah, Ben, and Jaaziel, and Shemiramoth, and Jehiel, and Unni, Eliab, and Benaiah, and Maaseiah, and Mattithiah, and Elipheleh, and Mikneiah, and Obededom, and Jeiel, the porters. So **the singers**, Heman, Asaph, and Ethan, were appointed to **sound with cymbals of brass**; And Zechariah, and Aziel, and Shemiramoth, and Jehiel, and Unni, and Eliab, and Maaseiah, and Benaiah, **with psalteries** on Alamoth; And*

Mattithiah, and Elipheleh, and Mikneiah, and Obededom, and Jeiel, and Azaziah, **with harps** *on the Sheminith to excel. And Chenaniah, chief of the Levites, was* **for song***: he instructed about* **the song***, because he was* **skilful***. And Berechiah and Elkanah were doorkeepers for the ark. And Shebaniah, and Jehoshaphat, and Nethaneel, and Amasai, and Zechariah, and Benaiah, and Eliezer, the priests, did* **blow with the trumpets** *before the ark of God: and Obededom and Jehiah were doorkeepers for the ark. So David, and the elders of Israel, and the captains over thousands, went to bring up the ark of the covenant of the Lord out of the house of Obededom with joy. And it came to pass, when God helped the Levites that bare the ark of the covenant of the Lord, that they offered seven bullocks and seven rams. And David was clothed with a robe of fine linen, and all the Levites that bare the ark, and* **the singers***, and Chenaniah* **the master of the song with the singers***: David also had upon him an ephod of linen. Thus all Israel brought up the ark of the covenant of the Lord with shouting, and* **with sound** *of the* **cornet***, and with* **trumpets***, and with* **cymbals***, making a noise with* **psalteries** *and* **harps***."*

I Chronicles 16:5-9 — *"Asaph the chief, and next to him Zechariah, Jeiel, and Shemiramoth, and Jehiel, and Mattithiah, and Eliab, and Benaiah, and Obededom: and Jeiel with* **psalteries** *and with* **harps***; but Asaph made* **a sound with cymbals***; Benaiah also and Jahaziel the priests with* **trumpets continually** *before the ark of the covenant of God. Then on that day David delivered first* **this psalm** *to thank the Lord into the hand of Asaph and his brethren. Give thanks unto the Lord, call upon his name, make known his deeds among the people.* **Sing** *unto him,* **sing psalms** *unto him, talk ye of all his wondrous works."*

I Chronicles 16:23 — *"***Sing** *unto the Lord, all the earth; shew forth from day to day his salvation."*

I Chronicles 16:31-33 — *"Let the heavens be glad, and let the earth rejoice: and let men say among the nations, The*

Lord reigneth. Let the sea roar, and the fulness thereof: let the fields rejoice, and all that is therein. Then shall the trees of the wood **sing** out at the presence of the Lord, because he cometh to judge the earth."

I Chronicles 16:42 — *"And with them Heman and Jeduthun with **trumpets** and **cymbals** for those that should **make a sound**, and **with musical instruments of God**. And the sons of Jeduthun were porters."*

I Chronicles 23:5-6 — *"Moreover four thousand were porters; and four thousand **praised the Lord with the instruments** which I made, said David, to praise therewith. And David divided them into courses among the sons of Levi, namely, Gershon, Kohath, and Merari."*

I Chronicles 25:1-7 — *"Moreover David and the captains of the host separated to the service of the sons of Asaph, and of Heman, and of Jeduthun, who should prophesy with **harps**, with **psalteries**, and with **cymbals**: and the number of the workmen according to their service was: Of the sons of Asaph; Zaccur, and Joseph, and Nethaniah, and Asarelah, the sons of Asaph under the hands of Asaph, which prophesied according to the order of the king. Of Jeduthun: the sons of Jeduthun; Gedaliah, and Zeri, and Jeshaiah, Hashabiah, and Mattithiah, six, under the hands of their father Jeduthun, who prophesied with **a harp**, to give thanks and to praise the Lord. Of Heman: the sons of Heman; Bukkiah, Mattaniah, Uzziel, Shebuel, and Jerimoth, Hananiah, Hanani, Eliathah, Giddalti, and Romamtiezer, Joshbekashah, Mallothi, Hothir, and Mahazioth: All these were the sons of Heman the king's seer in the words of God, to lift up **the horn**. And God gave to Heman fourteen sons and three daughters. All these were under the hands of their father **for song in the house of the Lord**, with **cymbals**, **psalteries**, and **harps**, for the service of the house of God, according to the king's order to Asaph, Jeduthun, and Heman. So the number of them, with their brethren that were **instructed in the songs of the Lord**, even all that were* *cunning,* was two hundred fourscore and eight."

II Chronicles 5:12-13 — *"Also the Levites which were **the singers,** all of them of Asaph, of Heman, of Jeduthun, with their sons and their brethren, being arrayed in white linen, having **cymbals** and **psalteries** and **harps,** stood at the east end of the altar, and with them an hundred and twenty priests sounding with **trumpets:**) It came even to pass, as **the trumpeters** and **singers were as one,** to **make one sound** to be heard in praising and thanking the Lord; and when they lifted up their voice with **the trumpets** and **cymbals** and **instruments of musick,** and praised the Lord, saying, For he is good; for his mercy endureth for ever: that then the house was filled with a cloud, even the house of the Lord;"*

II Chronicles 7:6 — *"And the priests waited on their offices: the Levites also with **instruments of musick** of the Lord, which David the king had made to praise the Lord, because his mercy endureth for ever, when David **praised by their ministry;** and the priests **sounded trumpets** before them, and all Israel stood."*

II Chronicles 9:11 — *"And the king made of the algum trees terraces to the house of the Lord, and to the king's palace, and **harps** and **psalteries for singers:** and there were none such seen before in the land of Judah."*

II Chronicles 15:14 — *"And they sware unto the Lord with a loud voice, and with shouting, and with **trumpets,** and with **cornets.**"*

II Chronicles 20:21-22 — *"And when he had consulted with the people, he appointed **singers unto the Lord,** and that should **praise the beauty of holiness,** as they went out before the army, and to say, Praise the Lord; for his mercy endureth for ever. And when they **began to sing and to praise,** the Lord set ambushments against the children of Ammon, Moab, and mount Seir, which were come against Judah; and they were smitten."*

II Chronicles 20:28 — *"And they came to Jerusalem with* **psalteries** *and* **harps** *and* **trumpets** *unto the house of the Lord."*

II Chronicles 23:18 — *"Also Jehoiada appointed the offices of the house of the Lord by the hand of the priests the Levites, whom David had distributed in the house of the Lord, to offer the burnt offerings of the Lord, as it is written in the law of Moses, with rejoicing and with* **singing**, *as it was ordained by David."*

II Chronicles 29:25-30 — *"And he set the Levites in the house of the Lord with* **cymbals**, *with* **psalteries**, *and with* **harps**, *according to the commandment of David, and of Gad the king's seer, and Nathan the prophet: for so was the commandment of the Lord by his prophets. And the Levites stood with* **the instruments** *of David, and the priests with* **the trumpets**. *And Hezekiah commanded to offer the burnt offering upon the altar. And when the burnt offering began,* **the song of the Lord began also** *with* **the trumpets**, *and with* **the instruments** *ordained by David king of Israel. And all the congregation worshipped, and* **the singers sang**, *and* **the trumpeters sounded**: *and all this continued until the burnt offering was finished. And when they had made an end of offering, the king and all that were present with him bowed themselves, and worshipped. Moreover Hezekiah the king and the princes commanded the Levites to* **sing praise** *unto the Lord with the words of David, and of Asaph the seer. And they* **sang praises** *with gladness, and they bowed their heads and worshipped."*

II Chronicles 30:21 — *"And the children of Israel that were present at Jerusalem kept the feast of unleavened bread seven days with great gladness: and the Levites and the priests praised the Lord day by day,* **singing with loud instruments** *unto the Lord."*

II Chronicles 34:12 — *"And the men did the work*

*faithfully: and the overseers of them were Jahath and Obadiah, the Levites, of the sons of Merari; and Zechariah and Meshullam, of the sons of the Kohathites, to set it forward; and other of the Levites, all that could **skill of instruments of musick.***"

II Chronicles 35:15 — *"And **the singers** the sons of Asaph were in their place, according to the commandment of David, and Asaph, and Heman, and Jeduthun the king's seer; and the porters waited at every gate; they might not depart from their service; for their brethren the Levites prepared for them."*

II Chronicles 35:25 — *"And Jeremiah lamented for Josiah: and **all the singing men and the singing women** spake of Josiah in their lamentations to this day, and made them an ordinance in Israel: and, behold, they are written in the lamentations."*

Ezra 2:41 — *"**The singers**: the children of Asaph, an hundred twenty and eight."*

Ezra 2:65 — *"Beside their servants and their maids, of whom there were seven thousand three hundred thirty and seven: and there were among them two hundred **singing men and singing women.**"*

Ezra 3:10-11 — *"And when the builders laid the foundation of the temple of the Lord, they set the priests in their apparel with **trumpets**, and the Levites the sons of Asaph with **cymbals**, to praise the Lord, after the ordinance of David king of Israel. And they **sang together** by course in praising and giving thanks unto the Lord; because he is good, for his mercy endureth for ever toward Israel. And all the people shouted with a great shout, when they praised the Lord, because the foundation of the house of the Lord was laid."*

Ezra 7:24 — *"Also we certify you, that touching any of the priests and Levites, **singers**, porters, Nethinims, or ministers* *of this house of God, it shall not be lawful to impose toll, tribute, or custom, upon them."*

Ezra 10:24 — *"Of the singers also; Eliashib: and of the porters; Shallum, and Telem, and Uri."*

Nehemiah 7:1 — *"Now it came to pass, when the wall was built, and I had set up the doors, and the porters and the singers and the Levites were appointed,"*

Nehemiah 7:44 — *"The singers: the children of Asaph, an hundred forty and eight."*

Nehemiah 7:67 — *"Beside their manservants and their maidservants, of whom there were seven thousand three hundred thirty and seven: and they had two hundred forty and five singing men and singing women."*

Nehemiah 7:73 — *"So the priests, and the Levites, and the porters, and the singers, and some of the people, and the Nethinims, and all Israel, dwelt in their cities; and when the seventh month came, the children of Israel were in their cities."*

Nehemiah 10:28-29 — *"And the rest of the people, the priests, the Levites, the porters, the singers, the Nethinims, and all they that had separated themselves from the people of the lands unto the law of God, their wives, their sons, and their daughters, every one having knowledge, and having understanding; They clave to their brethren, their nobles, and entered into a curse, and into an oath, to walk in God's law, which was given by Moses the servant of God, and to observe and do all the commandments of the Lord our Lord, and his judgments and his statutes;"*

Nehemiah 10:39 — *"For the children of Israel and the children of Levi shall bring the offering of the corn, of the new wine, and the oil, unto the chambers, where are the vessels of the sanctuary, and the priests that minister, and the* *porters, and **the singers**: and we will not forsake the house of our God."*

Nehemiah 11:22-23 — *"The overseer also of the Levites at Jerusalem was Uzzi the son of Bani, the son of Hashabiah, the son of Mattaniah, the son of Micha. Of the sons of Asaph, **the singers were over the business of the house of God**. For it was the king's commandment concerning them, that a certain portion should be for **the singers**, due for every day."*

Nehemiah 12:27-29 — *"And at the dedication of the wall of Jerusalem they sought the Levites out of all their places, to bring them to Jerusalem, to keep the dedication with gladness, both with thanksgivings, and with **singing**, with **cymbals**, **psalteries**, and with **harps**. And the sons of the singers gathered themselves together, both out of the plain country round about Jerusalem, and from the villages of Netophathi; Also from the house of Gilgal, and out of the fields of Geba and Azmaveth: for the singers had builded them villages round about Jerusalem."*

Nehemiah 12:35-36 — *"And certain of the priests' sons with **trumpets**; namely, Zechariah the son of Jonathan, the son of Shemaiah, the son of Mattaniah, the son of Michaiah, the son of Zaccur, the son of Asaph: And his brethren, Shemaiah, and Azarael, Milalai, Gilalai, Maai, Nethaneel, and Judah, Hanani, with **the musical instruments** of David the man of God, and Ezra the scribe before them."*

Nehemiah 12:41-42 — *"And the priests; Eliakim, Maaseiah, Miniamin, Michaiah, Elioenai, Zechariah, and Hananiah, with **trumpets**; And Maaseiah, and Shemaiah, and Eleazar, and Uzzi, and Jehohanan, and Malchijah, and Elam, and Ezer. And **the singers sang loud**, with Jezrahiah their overseer."*

Nehemiah 12:45-47 — *"And both the **singers** and the porters kept the ward of their God, and the ward of the purification, according to the commandment of David, and* *of Solomon his son. For in the days of David and Asaph of old there were chief of the **singers**, and **songs of praise and thanksgiving unto God**. And all Israel in the days of Zerubbabel, and in the days of Nehemiah, gave the portions of the **singers** and the porters, every day his portion: and they sanctified holy things unto the Levites; and the Levites sanctified them unto the children of Aaron."*

Nehemiah 13:5 — *"And he had prepared for him a great chamber, where aforetime they laid the meat offerings, the frankincense, and the vessels, and the tithes of the corn, the new wine, and the oil, which was commanded to be given to the Levites, and the **singers**, and the porters; and the offerings of the priests."*

Job 21:12 — *"They take the **timbrel** and **harp**, and rejoice at the sound of the **organ**."*

Job 29:13 — *"The blessing of him that was ready to perish came upon me: and I caused the widow's heart to **sing** for joy."*

Job 30:31 — *"My **harp** also is turned to mourning, and my **organ** into the voice of them that weep."*

Job 35:10 — *"But none saith, Where is God my maker, who giveth **songs** in the night;"*

Job 38:7 — *"When the morning stars **sang** together, and all the sons of God shouted for joy?"*

Psalm 7:17 — *"I will praise the Lord according to his righteousness: and will **sing praise** to the name of the Lord most high."*

Psalm 9:2 — *"I will be glad and rejoice in thee: I will **sing praise** to thy name, O thou most High."*

Psalm 9:11 — *"**Sing praises** to the Lord, which dwelleth in*

Zion: declare among the people his doings."

Psalm 13:6 — *"I will **sing** unto the Lord, because he hath dealt bountifully with me."*

Psalm 18:49 — *"Therefore will I give thanks unto thee, O Lord, among the heathen, and **sing praises** unto thy name."*

Psalm 21:13 — *"Be thou exalted, Lord, in thine own strength: so will we **sing and praise** thy power."*

Psalm 27:6 — *"And now shall mine head be lifted up above mine enemies round about me: therefore will I offer in his tabernacle sacrifices of joy; I will **sing**, yea, I will **sing praises** unto the Lord."*

Psalm 28:7 — *"The Lord is my strength and my shield; my heart trusted in him, and I am helped: therefore my heart greatly rejoiceth; and with **my song** will I praise him."*

Psalm 30:4 — *"**Sing** unto the Lord, O ye saints of his, and give thanks at the remembrance of his holiness."*

Psalm 30:12 — *"To the end that my glory may **sing praise** to thee, and not be silent. O Lord my God, I will give thanks unto thee for ever."*

Psalm 32:7 — *"Thou art my hiding place; thou shalt preserve me from trouble; thou shalt compass me about with **songs of deliverance**. Selah."*

Psalm 33:2-3 — *"Praise the Lord with **harp**: **sing** unto him with **the psaltery** and **an instrument of ten strings**. **Sing** unto him a new song; **play skilfully** with a **loud noise**."*

Psalm 40:3 — *"And he hath put **a new song** in my mouth, even praise unto our God: many shall see it, and fear, and shall trust in the Lord."*

Psalm 42:8 — *"Yet the Lord will command his lovingkindness in the daytime, and in the night **his song** shall be with me, and my prayer unto the God of my life."*

Psalm 43:4 — *"Then will I go unto the altar of God, unto God my exceeding joy: yea, upon **the harp** will I praise thee, O God my God."*

Psalm 47:5-7 — *"God is gone up with a shout, the Lord with **the sound of a trumpet. Sing praises** to God, **sing praises**: **sing praises** unto our King, **sing praises**. For God is the King of all the earth: **sing ye praises** with understanding."*

Psalm 49:4 — *"I will incline mine ear to a parable: I will open my dark saying upon **the harp**."*

Psalm 51:14 — *"Deliver me from bloodguiltiness, O God, thou God of my salvation: and my tongue shall **sing aloud** of thy righteousness."*

Psalm 57:7-9 — *"My heart is fixed, O God, my heart is fixed: I will **sing** and give praise. Awake up, my glory; awake, **psaltery** and **harp**: I myself will awake early. I will praise thee, O Lord, among the people: I will **sing** unto thee among the nations."*

Psalm 59:16-17 — *"But I will **sing** of thy power; yea, I will **sing aloud** of thy mercy in the morning: for thou hast been my defence and refuge in the day of my trouble. Unto thee, O my strength, will I **sing**: for God is my defence, and the God of my mercy."*

Psalm 61:8 — *"So will I **sing praise** unto thy name for ever, that I may daily perform my vows."*

Psalm 65:13 — *"The pastures are clothed with flocks; the valleys also are covered over with corn; they shout for joy, they also **sing**."*

Psalm 66:1-4 — *"Make a joyful noise unto God, all ye lands: Sing forth the honour of his name: make his praise glorious. Say unto God, How terrible art thou in thy works! through the greatness of thy power shall thine enemies submit themselves unto thee. All the earth shall worship thee, and shall sing unto thee; they shall sing to thy name. Selah."* [Joyful noise refers to singing.]

Psalm 67:4 — *"O let the nations be glad and sing for joy: for thou shalt judge the people righteously, and govern the nations upon earth. Selah."*

Psalm 68:4 — *"Sing unto God, sing praises to his name: extol him that rideth upon the heavens by his name Jah, and rejoice before him."*

Psalm 68:24-25 — *"They have seen thy goings, O God; even the goings of my God, my King, in the sanctuary. The singers went before, the players on instruments followed after; among them were the damsels playing with timbrels."*

Psalm 68:32 — *"Sing unto God, ye kingdoms of the earth; O sing praises unto the Lord; Selah:"*

Psalm 69:30-31 — *"I will praise the name of God with a song, and will magnify him with thanksgiving. This also shall please the Lord better than an ox or bullock that hath horns and hoofs."*

Psalm 71:22-23 — *"I will also praise thee with the psaltery, even thy truth, O my God: unto thee will I sing with the harp, O thou Holy One of Israel. My lips shall greatly rejoice when I sing unto thee; and my soul, which thou hast redeemed."*

Psalm 75:9 — *"But I will declare for ever; I will sing praises to the God of Jacob."*

Psalm 77:6 — *"I call to remembrance my song in the night: I commune with mine own heart: and my spirit made diligent* *search.*"

Psalm 81:1-3 — *"**Sing aloud** unto God our strength: make **a joyful noise** unto the God of Jacob. Take **a psalm**, and bring hither **the timbrel, the pleasant harp** with **the psaltery. Blow up the trumpet** in the new moon, in the time appointed, on our solemn feast day.*" [Joyful noise refers to singing.]

Psalm 87:7 — *"As well **the singers** as **the players on instruments** shall be there: all my springs are in thee.*"

Psalm 89:1 — *"I will **sing** of the mercies of the Lord for ever: with my mouth will I make known thy faithfulness to all generations.*"

Psalm 89:15 — *"Blessed is the people that know **the joyful sound**: they shall walk, O Lord, in the light of thy countenance.*"

Psalm 92:1-3 — *"It is a good thing to give thanks unto the Lord, and to **sing praises** unto thy name, O most High: To shew forth thy lovingkindness in the morning, and thy faithfulness every night, Upon **an instrument of ten strings**, and upon **the psaltery**; upon **the harp** with **a solemn sound**.*"

Psalm 95:1-2 — *"O come, let us **sing** unto the Lord: let us make **a joyful noise** to the rock of our salvation. Let us come before his presence with thanksgiving, and make **a joyful noise** unto him with **psalms**.*" [Joyful noise refers to singing.]

Psalm 96:1-2 — *"O **sing** unto the Lord **a new song: sing** unto the Lord, all the earth. **Sing** unto the Lord, bless his name; shew forth his salvation from day to day.*"

Psalm 98:1-6 — *"O **sing** unto the Lord **a new song**; for he hath done marvellous things: his right hand, and his holy* *arm, hath gotten him the victory. The Lord hath made known his salvation: his righteousness hath he openly shewed in the sight of the heathen. He hath remembered his mercy and his truth toward the house of Israel: all the ends of the earth have seen the salvation of our God. Make **a joyful noise** unto the Lord, all the earth: **make a loud noise**, and rejoice, and **sing praise**. **Sing** unto the Lord with **the harp**; with **the harp**, and **the voice of a psalm**. With **trumpets** and sound of **cornet** make **a joyful noise** before the Lord, the King."* [Joyful noise refers to singing.]

Psalm 100:2 — *"Serve the Lord with gladness: come before his presence with **singing**."*

Psalm 101:1 — *"I will **sing** of mercy and judgment: unto thee, O Lord, will I **sing**."*

Psalm 104:12 — *"By them shall the fowls of the heaven have their habitation, which **sing** among the branches."*

Psalm 104:33 — *"I will **sing** unto the Lord as long as I live: I will **sing praise** to my God while I have my being."*

Psalm 105:2 — *"**Sing** unto him, **sing psalms** unto him: talk ye of all his wondrous works."*

Psalm 106:12 — *"Then believed they his words; they **sang** his praise."*

Psalm 108:1-3 — *"O God, my heart is fixed; I will **sing** and **give praise**, even with my glory. Awake, **psaltery** and **harp**: I myself will awake early. I will praise thee, O Lord, among the people: and I will **sing praises** unto thee among the nations."*

Psalm 118:14 — *"The Lord is my strength and **song**, and is become my salvation."*

Psalm 119:54 — *"Thy statutes have been **my songs** in the house of my pilgrimage."*

Psalm 126:2 — *"Then was our mouth filled with laughter, and our tongue with **singing**: then said they among the heathen, The Lord hath done great things for them."*

Psalm 135:3 — *"Praise the Lord; for the Lord is good: **sing praises** unto his name; for it is pleasant."*

Psalm 137:1-4 — *"By the rivers of Babylon, there we sat down, yea, we wept, when we remembered Zion. We hanged **our harps** upon the willows in the midst thereof. For there they that carried us away captive required of us **a song**; and they that wasted us required of us mirth, saying, **Sing** us one of the songs of Zion. How shall we **sing the Lord's song** in a strange land?"*

Psalm 138:1-5 — *"I will praise thee with my whole heart: before the gods will I sing praise unto thee. I will worship toward thy holy temple, and praise thy name for thy lovingkindness and for thy truth: for thou hast magnified thy word above all thy name. In the day when I cried thou answeredst me, and strengthenedst me with strength in my soul. All the kings of the earth shall praise thee, O Lord, when they hear the words of thy mouth. Yea, they shall **sing** in the ways of the Lord: for great is the glory of the Lord."*

Psalm 144:9 — *"I will **sing a new song** unto thee, O God: upon **a psaltery** and **an instrument of ten strings** will I **sing praises** unto thee."*

Psalm 145:7 — *"They shall abundantly utter the memory of thy great goodness, and shall **sing** of thy righteousness."*

Psalm 146:2 — *"While I live will I praise the Lord: I will **sing praises** unto my God while I have any being."*

Psalm 147:1 — *"Praise ye the Lord: for it is good to **sing praises** unto our God; for it is pleasant; and praise is comely."*

Psalm 147:7 — *"**Sing** unto the Lord with thanksgiving; **sing praise** upon **the harp** unto our God:"*

Psalm 149:1-5 — *"Praise ye the Lord. **Sing** unto the Lord a **new song**, and his praise in the congregation of saints. Let Israel rejoice in him that made him: let the children of Zion be joyful in their King. Let them praise his name in the dance: let them **sing praises** unto him with **the timbrel** and **harp**. For the Lord taketh pleasure in his people: he will beautify the meek with salvation. Let the saints be joyful in glory: let them **sing aloud** upon their beds."*

Psalm 150:1-6 — *"Praise ye the Lord. Praise God in his sanctuary: praise him in the firmament of his power. Praise him for his mighty acts: praise him according to his excellent greatness. Praise him with **the sound of the trumpet**: praise him with **the psaltery** and **harp**. Praise him with **the timbrel** and dance: praise him with **stringed instruments** and **organs**. Praise him upon **the loud cymbals**: praise him upon **the high sounding cymbals**. Let every thing that hath breath praise the Lord. Praise ye the Lord."*

Proverbs 25:20 — *"As he that taketh away a garment in cold weather, and as vinegar upon nitre, so is he that **singeth songs** to an heavy heart."*

Proverbs 29:6 — *"In the transgression of an evil man there is a snare: but the righteous doth **sing** and rejoice."*

Ecclesiastes 2:8 — *"I gathered me also silver and gold, and the peculiar treasure of kings and of the provinces: I gat me **men singers** and **women singers**, and the delights of the sons of men, as **musical instruments**, and that of all sorts."*

Ecclesiastes 7:5 — *"It is better to hear the rebuke of the wise, than for a man to hear **the song** of fools."*

Song of Solomon 1:1 — *"**The song of songs**, which is*

Solomon's."

Song of Solomon 2:12 — *"The flowers appear on the earth; the time of **the singing of birds** is come, and the voice of the turtle is heard in our land;"*

Isaiah 5:1 — *"Now will I sing to my wellbeloved **a song** of my beloved touching his vineyard. My wellbeloved hath a vineyard in a very fruitful hill:"*

Isaiah 5:12 — *"And **the harp**, and **the viol, the tabret**, and **pipe**, and wine, are in their feasts: but they regard not the work of the Lord, neither consider the operation of his hands."*

Isaiah 12:2 — *"Behold, God is my salvation; I will trust, and not be afraid: for the Lord Jehovah is my strength and **my song**; he also is become my salvation."*

Isaiah 12:5 — *"**Sing** unto the Lord; for he hath done excellent things: this is known in all the earth."*

Isaiah 14:7 — *"The whole earth is at rest, and is quiet: they **break forth** into **singing**."*

Isaiah 16:10-11 — *"And gladness is taken away, and joy out of the plentiful field; and in the vineyards there shall be no **singing**, neither shall there be shouting: the treaders shall tread out no wine in their presses; I have made their vintage shouting to cease. Wherefore my bowels shall sound like **an harp** for Moab, and mine inward parts for Kirharesh."*

Isaiah 23:15-16 — *"And it shall come to pass in that day, that Tyre shall be forgotten seventy years, according to the days of one king: after the end of seventy years shall Tyre **sing** as an harlot. Take **an harp**, go about the city, thou harlot that hast been forgotten; make **sweet melody, sing many songs**, that thou mayest be remembered."*

Isaiah 24:8-9 — *"The mirth of **tabrets** ceaseth, the noise of them that rejoice endeth, the joy of **the harp** ceaseth. They shall not drink wine with **a song**; strong drink shall be bitter to them that drink it."*

Isaiah 24:14-16 — *"They shall lift up their voice, they shall **sing** for the majesty of the Lord, they shall cry aloud from the sea. Wherefore glorify ye the Lord in the fires, even the name of the Lord God of Israel in the isles of the sea. From the uttermost part of the earth have we heard **songs**, even glory to the righteous."*

Isaiah 26:1 — *"In that day shall this **song** be **sung** in the land of Judah; We have a strong city; salvation will God appoint for walls and bulwarks."*

Isaiah 30:29 — *"Ye shall have **a song**, as in the night when a holy solemnity is kept; and gladness of heart, as when one goeth with **a pipe** to come into the mountain of the Lord, to the mighty One of Israel."*

Isaiah 35:2 — *"It shall blossom abundantly, and rejoice even with joy and **singing**: the glory of Lebanon shall be given unto it, the excellency of Carmel and Sharon, they shall see the glory of the Lord, and the excellency of our God."*

Isaiah 35:6 — *"Then shall the lame man leap as an hart, and the tongue of the dumb **sing**: for in the wilderness shall waters break out, and streams in the desert."*

Isaiah 35:10 — *"And the ransomed of the Lord shall return, and come to Zion with **songs** and everlasting joy upon their heads: they shall obtain joy and gladness, and sorrow and sighing shall flee away."*

Isaiah 38:20 — *"The Lord was ready to save me: therefore we will **sing my songs** to **the stringed instruments** all the days of our life in the house of the Lord."*

Isaiah 42:10-12 — *"**Sing** unto the Lord **a new song**, and his praise from the end of the earth, ye that go down to the sea, and all that is therein; the isles, and the inhabitants thereof. Let the wilderness and the cities thereof lift up their voice, the villages that Kedar doth inhabit: let the inhabitants of the rock **sing**, let them shout from the top of the mountains. Let them give glory unto the Lord, and declare his praise in the islands."*

Isaiah 44:23 — *"**Sing**, O ye heavens; for the Lord hath done it: shout, ye lower parts of the earth: break forth into **singing**, ye mountains, O forest, and every tree therein: for the Lord hath redeemed Jacob, and glorified himself in Israel."*

Isaiah 48:20 — *"Go ye forth of Babylon, flee ye from the Chaldeans, with a voice of **singing** declare ye, tell this, utter it even to the end of the earth; say ye, The Lord hath redeemed his servant Jacob."*

Isaiah 49:13 — *"**Sing**, O heavens; and be joyful, O earth; and break forth into **singing**, O mountains: for the Lord hath comforted his people, and will have mercy upon his afflicted."*

Isaiah 51:3 — *"For the Lord shall comfort Zion: he will comfort all her waste places; and he will make her wilderness like Eden, and her desert like the garden of the Lord; joy and gladness shall be found therein, thanksgiving, and **the voice of melody**."*

Isaiah 51:11 — *"Therefore the redeemed of the Lord shall return, and come with **singing** unto Zion; and everlasting joy shall be upon their head: they shall obtain gladness and joy; and sorrow and mourning shall flee away."*

Isaiah 52:8-10 — *"Thy watchmen shall lift up the voice; with the voice together shall they **sing**: for they shall see eye to eye, when the Lord shall bring again Zion. Break forth into joy, **sing together**, ye waste places of Jerusalem: for the Lord hath comforted his people, he hath redeemed Jerusalem. The Lord* hath made bare his holy arm in the eyes of all the nations; and all the ends of the earth shall see the salvation of our God."

Isaiah 55:11-12 — "So shall my word be that goeth forth out of my mouth: it shall not return unto me void, but it shall accomplish that which I please, and it shall prosper in the thing whereto I sent it. For ye shall go out with joy, and be led forth with peace: the mountains and the hills shall break forth before you into **singing**, and all the trees of the field shall clap their hands."

Isaiah 65:14 — "Behold, my servants shall **sing** for joy of heart, but ye shall cry for sorrow of heart, and shall howl for vexation of spirit."

Jeremiah 20:13 — "**Sing** unto the Lord, praise ye the Lord: for he hath delivered the soul of the poor from the hand of evildoers."

Jeremiah 31:4 — "Again I will build thee, and thou shalt be built, O virgin of Israel: thou shalt again be adorned with **thy tabrets**, and shalt go forth in the dances of them that make merry."

Jeremiah 31:7 — "For thus saith the Lord; **Sing** with gladness for Jacob, and shout among the chief of the nations: publish ye, praise ye, and say, O Lord, save thy people, the remnant of Israel."

Jeremiah 31:12 — "Therefore they shall come and **sing** in the height of Zion, and shall flow together to the goodness of the Lord, for wheat, and for wine, and for oil, and for the young of the flock and of the herd: and their soul shall be as a watered garden; and they shall not sorrow any more at all."

Lamentations 3:14 — "I was a derision to all my people; and **their song** all the day."

Lamentations 3:63 — *"Behold their sitting down, and their rising up; I am **their musick**."*

Lamentations 5:14 — *"The elders have ceased from the gate, the young men from **their musick**."*

Ezekiel 26:13 — *"And I will cause the noise of **thy songs** to cease; and the sound of **thy harps** shall be no more heard."*

Ezekiel 27:25 — *"The ships of Tarshish did **sing** of thee in thy market: and thou wast replenished, and made very glorious in the midst of the seas."*

Ezekiel 28:13 — *"Thou hast been in Eden the garden of God; every precious stone was thy covering, the sardius, topaz, and the diamond, the beryl, the onyx, and the jasper, the sapphire, the emerald, and the carbuncle, and gold: the workmanship of **thy tabrets** and of **thy pipes** was prepared in thee in the day that thou wast created."* [speaking of Lucifer]

Ezekiel 33:32 — *"And, lo, thou art unto them as **a very lovely song** of one that hath **a pleasant voice**, and can play well on **an instrument**: for they hear thy words, but they do them not."*

Ezekiel 40:44 — *"And without the inner gate were the chambers of **the singers** in the inner court, which was at the side of the north gate; and their prospect was toward the south: one at the side of the east gate having the prospect toward the north."*

Daniel 3:5 — *"That at what time ye hear the sound of **the cornet, flute, harp, sackbut, psaltery, dulcimer**, and **all kinds of musick**, ye fall down and worship the golden image that Nebuchadnezzar the king hath set up:"*

Daniel 3:7 — *"Therefore at that time, when all the people heard the sound of **the cornet, flute, harp, sackbut, psaltery**,* and **all kinds of musick**, all the people, the nations, and the languages, fell down and worshipped the golden image that Nebuchadnezzar the king had set up."

Daniel 3:10 — "Thou, O king, hast made a decree, that every man that shall hear the sound of **the cornet, flute, harp, sackbut, psaltery,** and **dulcimer,** and **all kinds of musick,** shall fall down and worship the golden image:"

Daniel 3:15 — "Now if ye be ready that at what time ye hear the sound of **the cornet, flute, harp, sackbut, psaltery,** and **dulcimer,** and **all kinds of musick,** ye fall down and worship the image which I have made; well: but if ye worship not, ye shall be cast the same hour into the midst of a burning fiery furnace; and who is that God that shall deliver you out of my hands?"

Daniel 6:18 — "Then the king went to his palace, and passed the night fasting: neither were **instruments of musick** brought before him: and his sleep went from him."

Hosea 2:15 — "And I will give her her vineyards from thence, and the valley of Achor for a door of hope: and she shall **sing** there, as in the days of her youth, and as in the day when she came up out of the land of Egypt."

Hosea 8:1 — "Set **the trumpet** to thy mouth."

Joel 2:15 — "Blow **the trumpet** in Zion, sanctify a fast, call a solemn assembly:"

Amos 5:23 — "Take thou away from me **the noise of thy songs;** for I will not hear **the melody of thy viols.**"

Amos 6:1, 5-6 — "Woe to them that are at ease in Zion,... That chant to **the sound of the viol,** and invent to themselves **instruments of musick,** like David; ...but they are not grieved for the affliction of Joseph."

Amos 8:3 — *"And **the songs** of the temple shall be howlings in that day, saith the Lord God: there shall be many dead bodies in every place; they shall cast them forth with silence."*

Amos 8:10 — *"And I will turn your feasts into mourning, and all **your songs** into lamentation; and I will bring up sackcloth upon all loins, and baldness upon every head; and I will make it as the mourning of an only son, and the end thereof as a bitter day."*

Habakkuk 3:17-19 — *"Although the fig tree shall not blossom, neither shall fruit be in the vines; the labour of the olive shall fail, and the fields shall yield no meat; the flock shall be cut off from the fold, and there shall be no herd in the stalls: Yet I will rejoice in the Lord, I will joy in the God of my salvation. The Lord God is my strength, and he will make my feet like hinds' feet, and he will make me to walk upon mine high places. To the chief **singer** on **my stringed instruments.**"*

Zephaniah 3:14 — *"**Sing**, O daughter of Zion; shout, O Israel; be glad and rejoice with all the heart, O daughter of Jerusalem."*

Zephaniah 3:17 — *"The Lord thy God in the midst of thee is mighty; he will save, he will rejoice over thee with joy; he will rest in his love, he will joy over thee with **singing.**"*

Zechariah 2:10 — *"**Sing** and rejoice, O daughter of Zion: for, lo, I come, and I will dwell in the midst of thee, saith the Lord."*

Matthew 6:2 — *"Therefore when thou doest thine alms, do not sound **a trumpet** before thee, as the hypocrites do in the synagogues and in the streets, that they may have glory of men. Verily I say unto you, They have their reward."*

Matthew 9:23-24 — *"And when Jesus came into the ruler's house, and saw **the minstrels** and the people making a noise,*

He said unto them, Give place: for the maid is not dead, but sleepeth. And they laughed him to scorn."

Matthew 11:17 — *"And saying, We have **piped** unto you, and ye have not danced; we have mourned unto you, and ye have not lamented."*

Matthew 26:30 — *"And when they had **sung an hymn**, they went out into the mount of Olives."*

Mark 14:26 — *"And when they had **sung an hymn**, they went out into the mount of Olives."*

Luke 7:32 — *"They are like unto children sitting in the marketplace, and calling one to another, and saying, We have **piped** unto you, and ye have not danced; we have mourned to you, and ye have not wept."*

Luke 15:25 — *"Now his elder son was in the field: and as he came and drew nigh to the house, he heard **musick** and dancing."*

Acts 16:25 — *"And at midnight Paul and Silas prayed, and **sang praises** unto God: and the prisoners heard them."*

Romans 15:9 — *"And that the Gentiles might glorify God for his mercy; as it is written, For this cause I will confess to thee among the Gentiles, and **sing** unto thy name."*

I Corinthians 13:1 — *"Though I speak with the tongues of men and of angels, and have not charity, I am become as **sounding brass**, or **a tinkling cymbal**."*

I Corinthians 14:7-8 — *"And even things without life giving sound, whether **pipe** or **harp**, except they give a distinction in the sounds, how shall it be known what is **piped** or **harped**? For if **the trumpet** give an uncertain sound, who shall prepare himself to the battle?"*

I Corinthians 14:15 — *"What is it then? I will pray with the spirit, and I will pray with the understanding also: I will **sing** with the spirit, and I will **sing** with the understanding also."*

I Corinthians 14:26 — *"How is it then, brethren? when ye come together, every one of you hath **a psalm**, hath a doctrine, hath a tongue, hath a revelation, hath an interpretation. Let all things be done unto edifying."*

I Corinthians 15:52 — *"In a moment, in the twinkling of an eye, at the last trump: for **the trumpet** shall sound, and the dead shall be raised incorruptible, and we shall be changed."*

Ephesians 5:19 — *"Speaking to yourselves in **psalms** and **hymns** and **spiritual songs**, **singing** and **making melody** in your heart to the Lord;"*

Colossians 3:16 — *"Let the word of Christ dwell in you richly in all wisdom; teaching and admonishing one another in **psalms** and **hymns** and **spiritual songs**, **singing** with grace in your hearts to the Lord."*

I Thessalonians 4:16 — *"For the Lord himself shall descend from heaven with a shout, with the voice of the archangel, and with **the trump** of God: and the dead in Christ shall rise first:"*

Hebrews 2:12 — *"Saying, I will declare thy name unto my brethren, in the midst of the church will I **sing praise** unto thee."*

James 5:13 — *"Is any among you afflicted? let him pray. Is any merry? let him **sing psalms**."*

Revelation 5:8-10 — *"And when he had taken the book, the four beasts and four and twenty elders fell down before the Lamb, having every one of them **harps**, and golden vials full of odours, which are the prayers of saints. And they **sung a new song**, saying, Thou art worthy to take the book, and to* open the seals thereof: for thou wast slain, and hast redeemed us to God by thy blood out of every kindred, and tongue, and people, and nation; And hast made us unto our God kings and priests: and we shall reign on the earth."

Revelation 14:2-3 — "And I heard a voice from heaven, as the voice of many waters, and as the voice of a great thunder: and I heard the voice of **harpers harping** with **their harps**: And they **sung** as it were **a new song** before the throne, and before the four beasts, and the elders: and no man could learn that **song** but the hundred and forty and four thousand, which were redeemed from the earth."

Revelation 15:2-4 — "And I saw as it were a sea of glass mingled with fire: and them that had gotten the victory over the beast, and over his image, and over his mark, and over the number of his name, stand on the sea of glass, having **the harps** of God. And they **sing the song** of Moses the servant of God, and **the song** of the Lamb, saying, Great and marvellous are thy works, Lord God Almighty; just and true are thy ways, thou King of saints. Who shall not fear thee, O Lord, and glorify thy name? for thou only art holy: for all nations shall come and worship before thee; for thy judgments are made manifest."

The word "praise" in the following verses is translated from the Old Testament Hebrew word "t͏ᵉhillâh". It directly refers to "a song of praise or hymn of thanksgiving" that is rendered in a spirit of reverence and worship unto Almighty God. Notice below:

Exodus 15:11 — "Who is like unto thee, O LORD, among the gods? who is like thee, glorious in holiness, fearful [to stand in awe of with reverence] in **praises**, doing wonders?"

Deuteronomy 10:21 — *"He is thy **praise**, and he is thy God, that hath done for thee these great and terrible things, which thine eyes have seen."*

Deuteronomy 26:19 — *"And to make thee high above all nations which he hath made, in **praise**, and in name, and in honour; and that thou mayest be an holy people unto the LORD thy God, as he hath spoken."*

I Chronicles 16:34-35 — *"O give thanks unto the LORD; for He is good; for His mercy endureth for ever. And say ye, Save us, O God of our salvation, and gather us together, and deliver us from the heathen, that we may give thanks to thy holy name, and glory in thy **praise**."*

II Chronicles 20:22 — *"And when they began to sing and to **praise**, the LORD set ambushments against the children of Ammon, Moab, and mount Seir, which were come against Judah; and they were smitten."*

Nehemiah 9:5 — *"Then the Levites, Jeshua, and Kadmiel, Bani, Hashabniah, Sherebiah, Hodijah, Shebaniah, and Pethahiah, said, Stand up and bless the LORD your God for ever and ever: and blessed be thy glorious name, which is exalted above all blessing and **praise**."*

Nehemiah 12:46 — *"For in the days of David and Asaph of old there were chief of the singers, and songs of **praise** and thanksgiving unto God."*

Psalm 9:13-14 — *"Have mercy upon me, O LORD; consider my trouble which I suffer of them that hate me, thou that liftest me up from the gates of death: That I may shew forth all thy **praise** in the gates of the daughter of Zion: I will rejoice in thy salvation."*

Psalm 22:3-4 — *"But thou art holy, O thou that inhabitest the **praises** of Israel. Our fathers trusted in thee: they trusted,* *and thou didst deliver them."*

Psalm 22:25 — *"My **praise** shall be of thee in the great congregation: I will pay my vows before them that fear him."*

Psalm 33:1-4 — *"Rejoice in the Lord, O ye righteous: for **praise** is comely for the upright. Praise the Lord with harp: sing unto him with the psaltery and an instrument of ten strings. Sing unto him a new song; play skilfully with a loud noise. For the word of the Lord is right; and all his works are done in truth."*

Psalm 34:1-3 — *"I will bless the Lord at all times: his **praise** shall continually be in my mouth. My soul shall make her boast in the Lord: the humble shall hear thereof, and be glad. O magnify the Lord with me, and let us exalt his name together."*

Psalm 35:28 — *"And my tongue shall speak of thy righteousness and of thy **praise** all the day long."*

Psalm 40:3 — *"And he hath put a new song in my mouth, even **praise** unto our God: many shall see it, and fear, and shall trust in the LORD."*

Psalm 48:10 — *"According to thy name, O God, so is thy **praise** unto the ends of the earth: thy right hand is full of righteousness."*

Psalm 51:15 — *"O Lord, open thou my lips; and my mouth shall shew forth thy **praise**."*

Psalm 65:1 — *"**Praise** waiteth for thee, O God, in Sion: and unto thee shall the vow be performed."*

Psalm 66:1-4 — *"Make a joyful noise unto God, all ye lands: Sing forth the honour of his name: make his **praise** glorious. Say unto God, How terrible art thou in thy works! through the greatness of thy power shall thine enemies submit* *themselves unto thee. All the earth shall worship thee, and shall sing unto thee; they shall sing to thy name. Selah."* [Joyful noise refers to singing.]

Psalm 66:8 — *"O bless our God, ye people, and make the voice of his **praise** to be heard:"*

Psalm 71:6-8 — *"By thee have I been holden up from the womb: thou art he that took me out of my mother's bowels: my **praise** shall be continually of thee. O God, thou hast taught me from my youth: and hitherto have I declared thy wondrous works. Let my mouth be filled with thy **praise** and with thy honour all the day."*

Psalm 71:14-16 — *"I will hope continually, and will yet **praise** thee more and more. My mouth shall shew forth thy righteousness and thy salvation all the day; for I know not the numbers thereof. I will go in the strength of the Lord God: I will make mention of thy righteousness, even of thine only."*

Psalm 78:4 — *"We will not hide them from their children, shewing to the generation to come the **praises** of the LORD, and his strength, and his wonderful works that he hath done."*

Psalm 79:13 — *"So we thy people and sheep of thy pasture will give thee thanks for ever: we will shew forth thy **praise** to all generations."*

Psalm 100:4 — *"Enter into his gates with thanksgiving, and into his courts with **praise**: be thankful unto him, and bless his name."*

Psalm 102:21 — *"To declare the name of the LORD in Zion, and his **praise** in Jerusalem;"*

Psalm 106:2 — *"Who can utter the mighty acts of the LORD? who can shew forth all his **praise**?"*

Psalm 106:12 — *"Then believed they his words; they sang his **praise**."*

Psalm 106:47 — *"Save us, O LORD our God, and gather us from among the heathen, to give thanks unto thy holy name, and to triumph in thy **praise**."*

Psalm 109:1 — *"Hold not thy peace, O God of my **praise**;"*

Psalm 111:10 — *"The fear of the LORD is the beginning of wisdom: a good understanding have all they that do his commandments: his **praise** endureth for ever."*

Psalm 119:171 — *"My lips shall utter **praise**, when thou hast taught me thy statutes."*

Psalm 145:21 — *"My mouth shall speak the **praise** of the LORD: and let all flesh bless his holy name for ever and ever."*

Psalm 147:1 — *"Praise ye the LORD: for it is good to sing praises unto our God; for it is pleasant; and **praise** is comely."*

Psalm 148:14 — *"He also exalteth the horn of his people, the **praise** of all his saints; even of the children of Israel, a people near unto him. Praise ye the LORD."*

Psalm 149:1 — *"Praise ye the LORD. Sing unto the LORD a new song, and his **praise** in the congregation of saints."*

Isaiah 42:8 — *"I am the LORD: that is my name: and my glory will I not give to another, neither my **praise** to graven images."*

Isaiah 42:10-12 — *"Sing unto the LORD a new song, and his **praise** from the end of the earth, ye that go down to the sea, and all that is therein; the isles, and the inhabitants thereof. Let the wilderness and the cities thereof lift up their voice, the* *villages that Kedar doth inhabit: let the inhabitants of the rock sing, let them shout from the top of the mountains. Let them give glory unto the LORD, and declare his **praise** in the islands."*

Isaiah 43:21 — *"This people have I formed for myself; they shall shew forth my **praise**."*

Isaiah 48:9 — *"For my name's sake will I defer mine anger, and for my **praise** will I refrain for thee, that I cut thee not off."*

Isaiah 60:6 — *"The multitude of camels shall cover thee, the dromedaries of Midian and Ephah; all they from Sheba shall come: they shall bring gold and incense; and they shall shew forth the **praises** of the LORD."*

Isaiah 60:18 — *"Violence shall no more be heard in thy land, wasting nor destruction within thy borders; but thou shalt call thy walls Salvation, and thy gates **Praise**."*

Isaiah 61:1-3 — *"The Spirit of the Lord God is upon me; because the Lord hath anointed me to preach good tidings unto the meek; he hath sent me to bind up the brokenhearted, to proclaim liberty to the captives, and the opening of the prison to them that are bound; To proclaim the acceptable year of the Lord, and the day of vengeance of our God; to comfort all that mourn; To appoint unto them that mourn in Zion, to give unto them beauty for ashes, the oil of joy for mourning, the garment of **praise** for the spirit of heaviness; that they might be called trees of righteousness, the planting of the LORD, that he might be glorified."*

Isaiah 61:11 — *"For as the earth bringeth forth her bud, and as the garden causeth the things that are sown in it to spring forth; so the Lord GOD will cause righteousness and **praise** to spring forth before all the nations."*

Isaiah 63:7 — *"I will mention the lovingkindnesses of the*

LORD, and the **praises** of the LORD, according to all that
the LORD hath bestowed on us, and the great goodness
toward the house of Israel, which he hath bestowed on them
according to his mercies, and according to the multitude of
his lovingkindnesses."

Jeremiah 13:11 — "For as the girdle cleaveth to the loins of a
man, so have I caused to cleave unto me the whole house of
Israel and the whole house of Judah, saith the LORD; that
they might be unto me for a people, and for a name, and for
a **praise**, and for a glory: but they would not hear."

Jeremiah 17:14 — "Heal me, O LORD, and I shall be
healed; save me, and I shall be saved: for thou art my
praise."

CONCLUSION

Our prayer is that something throughout this study has triggered a renewed zeal, a passionate love, and a holy longing to have a Biblical approach to music. May we fervently ensure that our music is godly and honors Christ in its message (the words), its melody (the tune), its method (the style), and its means (the instrumentation).

The Devil is certainly out to destroy it and violate our praise and worship of Almighty God. Our flesh is constantly struggling to be in control. The world is continually cramming its styles upon people. Therefore, it is no surprise that music is such a controversial issue among Christians and in churches around the world.

Nevertheless, God challenges us: *"That ye may approve* [examine, test, scrutinize] *things that are excellent* [to be of higher value and quality]; *that ye may be sincere and without offence till the day of Christ; Being filled with the fruits of righteousness, which are by Jesus Christ, unto the glory and praise of God."* (Philippians 1:10-11). It is healthy and vital for us to study what we believe and why we believe it. Music is such a crucial part of our worship and our lives and should be *"approved"* to ensure it is of the highest quality. God is worthy of our best. He is worthy of holiness. Nothing less! We trust this book has equipped you to scrutinize music honestly, thereby helping each of us to *"be sincere and without offense"* that we might be *"filled with the fruits of righteousness...."*

We desire to have a Biblical approach to music and for our music to be directly influenced by the application of Biblical principles. Some would call us "musical conservatives." We boldly embrace this title. Conservatism does not mean (as so many are lead to believe) *"a stubborn refusal to discard what is old and outworn, nor an old fogeyish prejudice against innovations of any kind. It really means a determination to retain what has been tried and proven to be good, and to refrain from the exploitation simply because it is new, of what is essentially cheap and silly."*[131]

As our dear friends Ron and Shelly Hamilton put it in reflection to this profound quote, *"Musical conservatives aren't against innovations of any kind. Musical conservatism really means 'a determination to retain what has been tried and proven to be good, and to refrain from the exploitation simply because it is new, of what is' worldly and sensual."*[132] We could not have worded any of this better ourselves! We simply echo a hearty **"Amen!"** to the above statements.

In reality, all of the material that we have studied together gives just a brief glance at what could be so many more pages of deeper study on this subject of music. We encourage you to get alone with the Lord and seek His face regarding these Biblical principles. The best thing you could do would be to ask the Holy Spirit, *"God, what music pleases You? Would You lovingly lead me to that which is wholesome and holy?"*

In Ephesians 5:18-20, we see that a life filled with the Spirit will lead to good, godly music! *"And be not drunk with wine, wherein is excess; but be filled with the Spirit; Speaking to yourselves in psalms and hymns and spiritual songs, singing and making melody in your heart to the Lord; Giving thanks always for all things unto God and the Father in the name of our Lord Jesus Christ."* A joyful song and a heart filled with praise and thanksgiving comes as a direct result of being in tune with the Spirit of God and allowing Him to fill your hearts and minds with His presence and His truth.

A Christian's lifestyle choices are extremely important to the Lord, because our choices will determine our godly or ungodly habits, and these habits will develop godly or ungodly character. Our musical choices will be the accompaniment of our lives. It will either build us up or tear us down. Please surround yourself and your children with Christ-honoring music that exalts the Word and name of God, uplifts your heart in a spiritual-building way, and glorifies the Lord in the beauty of holiness.

If you truly desire to know God's will when it comes to music and if you want to truly please Him in your choices of music, ask yourself, *"Am I filled with the Spirit?"* If we are letting distractions or worldly influences fill our lives, the topic of music may become more and more foggy and our standards may begin to slip away from where God wants them. Stay close to Him, stay in His Word, and allow His Spirit to fill you and guide you each and every day.

We must be careful. God warns, *"Cursed be he that doeth the work of the LORD deceitfully"* (Jeremiah 48:10). It has always been and forever will be wrong to do the work of the Lord through the wrong means. To promote or praise our holy God with unholy music is unacceptable. Secular music that has handicapped our nation (rock music and its styles) cannot be sprinkled with Christian lyrics and suddenly have God's blessing or approval. Music that satisfies the flesh is not what God wants us to be energized by.

It is our prayer that this study on the topic of music and the specific things that God led us to address has helped you gain a better understanding of His heart on the matter, giving you a more Biblical approach when it comes to your church music and the music playing in your everyday lives.

Again, this material was not compiled and presented to become enemies with other people and ministries or to haughtily look down at anyone. *(God forbid!)* Our hearts' desire is that the Lord would use it to create a Heavenly awareness and a holy appetite for Christ-honoring music. God cares about the music that we listen to and sing. His Word lays out many guidelines that **cannot** and **should not** be ignored. Just as David — a talented musician — was a man after God's own heart (I Samuel 13:14 & Acts 13:22), may we desire to be the same in our lives and with our music.

All we ask is that you mull over what you've read in your mind and meditate upon it in your heart. Maybe the Holy Spirit is not convicting you about an area where He wants you to change, to become more like Him, to please Him better. But...perhaps He is. In either case, we love you, and we desire that God would strengthen you and draw you closer to Himself through the Biblical principles we have studied together.

Please prayerfully consider surrendering the area of music over to God. As you let Scripture sift through your mind, it will help you know what music to keep in your life and what music should go. If your walk with God is strengthened and your life is changed in any small way through reading this book, we consider it worth it all!

The ultimate decision of the Christian regarding music should be as the Apostle Paul declared in I Corinthians 14:15: *"I will sing with the spirit, and I will sing with the understanding also."* Oh, that God's people would sing from the heart, that their music would be empowered by the Holy Spirit, and that their music (lyrics and instrumentation) would be based on Scriptural truth and meet God's standard of holiness as found in the Bible. This is what our Father desires of us. *"The true worshippers shall worship the Father in spirit and in truth: for the Father seeketh such to worship him. God is a Spirit: and they that worship him must worship him in spirit and in truth"* (John 4:23-24). *"Give unto the Lord the glory due unto his name; worship the Lord in the beauty of holiness."* (Psalm 29:2).

— ENDNOTES —

[1] *The Purpose Driven Church: Growth Without Compromising Your Message and Mission* by Rick Warren, published 1995, page 240.

[2] Testimony from *The Voice of the Martyrs* on March 19, 2007.

[3] *My Life and the Story of Gospel Hymns* by Ira D. Sankey, punished 1906, page 105.

[4] *Ibid.*, pages 169-170.

[5] *Ibid.*, pages 192-193.

[6] *The Band That Played On* by Steve Turner, published 2012, page 148.

[7] *Ibid.*

[8] *Ibid.* pages 152.

[9] *Ibid.*, pages 151-152.

[10] *Ibid.*, page 152.

[11] *Ibid.*, pages 151.

[12] *Ibid.*

[13] *Ibid.* page 152.

[14] *Born After Midnight* by A. W. Tozer, Chapter 31 "The Power That Shapes Us", originally published in 1959, re-published in 2015, page 153.

[15] *Notes and Queries* collected by the Oxford University Press, 1850, page 153.

[16] *Washington Times,* July 2, 1997; also, *The Virginian Pilot,* July 24, 1997; online source — https://scholar.lib.vt.edu/VA-news/VA-Pilot/issues/1997/vp970724/07240420.htm

[17] *Music and Medicine* by Dorothy Schullian and Max Schoen, published 1948, pages 270-271.

[18] *The Psychology of Music* by Max Schoen, published 1940, page 39.

[19] https://www.npr.org/2011/06/01/136859090/the-power-of-music-to-affect-the-brain

[20] *Music and Your Emotions* by Jay T. Wright, Ph.D., published 1952, page 88.

[21] *The Secret Power of Music: The Transformation of Self and Society through Musical Energy* by David Tame, published 1984, page 138.

[22] *Tuning the Human Instrument* by Steven Halpern and the Spectrum Research Institute, 1978, pages 25 & 43.

[23] *Music in Hospitals* by Willem Van de Wall, published 1946, page 15.

[24] *Ibid.,* page 106.

[25] *The New Life: Words of God for Young Disciples of Christ* by Andrew Murray, published in 1891. Also in other reprinted books by Murray.

[26] *Amazing Grace: 366 Inspiring Hymn Stories for Daily Devotions* by K. W. Osbeck, published 2002, page 193.

[27] *Music As a Psychotherapeutic Agent* published in "The Journal of Clinical Psychopathology" Volume 10, Number 3, July 1949 by Leonard Gilman and Francis Paperte.

[28] *Charles M. Alexander: A Romance of Song and Soulwinning* by Helen Cadbury Alexander and J. Kennedy Maclean, published 1920, page 62.

[29] *Harmony at Home* by Tim Fisher, published 1999, page 74.

[30] *The Big Beat: A Rock Blast* by Frank Garlock, published 1971, pages 43 & 45.

[31] *Inside Rock Music* by Vance Ferrell, published 2006, page 4-5.

[32] "Elvis Rocks But He's Not the First" by Christopher John Farley in *Time Magazine* on July 6, 2004. And *"What Was the First Rock 'n' Roll Record?"* by Jim Dawson and Steve Propes, published 1992.

[33] "Rock and Roll" by Greg Kot in the *Encyclopædia Britannica*, published online June 17, 2008, and also in print and in the *Encyclopædia Britannica Ultimate Reference* DVD, 2010.

[34] *Race, Rock, and Elvis: Music in American Life* by M. T. Bertrand, published 2000, pages 21–22.

[35] *American Hymns Old and New* by Albert Christ-Janer, Charles W. Hughes, and Carleton Sprague Smith, published 1980, page 364.

[36] *The Illustrated Encyclopedia of Music* by Paul Du Noyer, published 2003, page 170.

[37] *Creating Country Music: Fabricating Authenticity* by Richard A. Peterson, published 1999, page 9.

[38] See *The History of the Blues* by Francis Davis, published 1995.

[39] *Creating Country Music: Fabricating Authenticity* by Richard A. Peterson, published 1999, page 9.

[40] *The Roots of Rock 'n' Roll: 1946–1954* published by Universal Music Enterprises in 2004. And *What Was the First Rock 'n' Roll Record?* by

Jim Dawson and Steve Propes, published 1992.

[41] https://www.rockhall.com/roots-and-definition-rock-and-roll

[42] "The Development of the Blues" by David Evans in *The Cambridge Companion to Blues and Gospel Music,* edited by A. F. Moore, published 2002, pages 40–42.

[43] *It's Rock 'n' Roll: A Musical History of the Fabulous Fifties* by Gene Busnar, published 1979, page 45.

[44] "The Development of the Blues" by David Evans in *The Cambridge Companion to Blues and Gospel Music,* edited by A. F. Moore, published 2002, pages 40–42.

[45] "The Beat Goes Unevenly On" — https://www.npr.org/templates/story/story.php?storyId=15591120

[46] *Why I Don't Listen to Contemporary Christian Music* by Shelly Hamilton, printed 2015, page 27.

[47] *Ibid.,* pages 27-28.

[48] Quoted in *The Sound of the City: The Rise of Rock and Roll* by Charlie Grillett, published 1970, page 24.

[49] https://www.ibtimes.com/elvis-presley-quotes-20-sayings-singers-40th-death-anniversary-2578162

[50] *Rock & Roll: An Unruly History* by Robert Palmer, published in 1995, page 12.

[51] https://www.rollingstone.com/music/music-news/lennon-remembers-part-one-186693/

[52] Cited by John Blanchard, with Peter Anderson and Derek Cleave, in *Pop Goes the Gospel: Rock in the Church,* published in 1983.

[53] *Rock Reconsidered* by Steve Lawhead, published 1981, page 70.

[54] https://www.nytimes.com/2007/10/07/magazine/07Haynes.html

[55] *Closing of the American Mind* by Allan Bloom, published in 2008, page 73.

[56] *Sound Effects* by Simon Frith, published 1981, compiled from pages 12, 16, 19, and 164.

[57] *'Scuse Me While I Kiss the Sky: The Life of Jimi Hendrix* by David Henderson, published 1982, page 117.

[58] "The Oracle Has It All Psyched Out" by Frank Zappa in *Life* Magazine on June 28, 1968, pages 82-91.

[59] *Time* Magazine, January 3, 1969.

[60] Paul Kantner of the Jefferson Airplane, cited by Ben Fong-Torres, *"Grace Slick with Paul Kantner,"* The Rolling Stone Interviews, 1971, page 447.

[61] *The History of Rock* Magazine, August 1983 issue, page 60.

[62] Gene Simmons of the rock group Kiss, Interview, *Entertainment Tonight,* ABC, December 10, 1987.

[63] "The Oracle Has It All Psyched Out" by Frank Zappa in *Life* Magazine on June 28, 1968, pages 82-91.

[64] *Tuning the Human Instrument* by Steven Halpern and the Spectrum Research Institute, 1978, pages 44-45.

[65] *Your Body Doesn't Lie* by John Diamond, M.D., published 1989, pages 159-167.

[66] *The story of the piano begins in Padua, Italy in 1709, in the shop of a harpsichord maker named Bartolomeo di Francesco Cristofori (1655-1731). Many other stringed and keyboard instruments preceded the piano and led to the development of the instrument as we know it today.*

Mankind's knowledge that a taut, vibrating string can produce sound goes back to prehistoric times. In the ancient world, strings were attached and stretched over bows, gourds, and boxes to amplify the sound; they were fastened by ties, pegs and pins; and they were plucked, bowed or struck to produce sounds.

Eventually, a family of stringed instruments with a keyboard evolved in Europe in the 14th century. The earliest of these was a dulcimer, a closed, shallow box over which stretched wires were struck with two wooden hammers. The dulcimer led to the development of the clavichord, which also appeared in the 14th century. These were followed by the spinet, virginal, clavecin, gravicembalo, and finally, the harpsichord in the 15th century.

The harpsichord, however, was limited to one, unvarying volume. Its softness and loudness could not be varied while playing. Therefore, performing artists could not convey the same degree of musical expression as that of most other instruments. The artistic desire for more controlled expression led directly to the invention of the piano, on which the artist could alter the loudness and tone with the force of one's fingers.

Despite many improvements during the past 300 years, it is truly astonishing to observe how similar Cristofori's instruments are to the modern piano of today.

The piano is one of the most-popular musical instruments in the world. But when you look inside of it, you will quickly discover that it is among the more-complex instruments. You might also begin to wonder what type of instrument it is — percussion or stringed.

Inside a piano, there are strings, and there is a long row of uniformly rounded felt-covered hammers. In the traditional Hornbostel-Sachs system of categorizing musical instruments, the piano is considered to be similar to a lyre or a harp, having strings stretched between two points. When the strings vibrate, they produce sound. On a piano, however, those vibrations are initiated by hammers hitting the strings rather than by plucking or by moving a bow across them. So, the piano also falls into the realm of percussion instruments. As a result, today the piano is generally considered to be both a stringed and a percussion instrument.

Each of the 88 keys of a piano is attached to a hammer that strikes a string of varying length and thickness, with both dimensions of the string becoming smaller in size as the player goes from left to right across the instrument (most apparent in a grand piano). When a key is pressed, it sends its associated hammer into motion, accelerating it toward the string. If the string that is hit is long and thick, the pitch of the sound produced is relatively low; the key, in other words, was on the left end of the piano. If the string that is hit is thin and short, the pitch is higher, indicating that the key played was on the right half of the piano. After striking the string, the hammer rebounds and returns to its original position, ready for the next attack.

[67] *Music in the Balance* by Frank Garlock and Kurt Woetzel, published 1992, pages 67-68. PLEASE NOTE: This portion of the book originally stated: *"Although the guitar is not usually considered a rhythm instrument, as used by a rock group it definitely is. All four instruments can be classified as belonging to the rhythm family. The only one which offers the 'melody' on occasion is the lead guitar."* However, Frank Garlock and Shelly Hamilton decided to word that quote differently to what has been included in our book. We have the handwritten change in our original manuscript that they edited through for us.

[68] "Rock-n-Roll Pioneer Sam Phillips Dies," *USA Today,* July 30, 2003.

[69] *Drumming at the Edge of Magic* by Mickey Hart, published 1990, page 28, 20, 176.

[70] *Ibid.,* page 161.

[71] *Ibid.,* page 202.

[72] *Ibid.,* page 163.

[73] Pearl Primus, lecture, Mount Holyoke College, Holyoke, Massachusetts, Mary E. Wooley Hall, 1953; cited from Leonard J. Seidel, *Face the Music: Contemporary Church Music on Trial,* 1988, pages 42-43.

[74] *'Scuse Me While I Kiss the Sky* by David Henderson, published 1981, pages 250-251.

[75] *Drumming at the Edge of Magic* by Mickey Hart, published 1990, page 204.

[76] *Ibid.,* page 177.

[77] *Ibid.,* page 212.

[78] *Ibid.,* page 18.

[79] *Ibid.,* page 246.

[80] *Ibid.,* page 195.

[81] *Ibid.*, page 209.

[82] *Ibid.*, page 224.

[83] *Ibid.*, page 210.

[84] *Hole in Our Soul: The Loss of Beauty and Meaning in American Popular Music* by Martha Bayles, published 1994, page 130.

[85] *Drumming at the Edge of Magic* by Mickey Hart, published 1990, page 227.

[86] *Ibid.*, page 228.

[87] Ibid., pages 230-231.

[88] https://www.mickeyhart.net/news/there-no-world-music-conversation-grateful-deads-mickey-hart-457

[89] *Inside Rock Music* by Vance Ferrell, published 2006, page 43.

[90] *Ibid.*, page 42.

[91] https://www.mickeyhart.net/news/there-no-world-music-conversation-grateful-deads-mickey-hart-457

[92] *Drumming at the Edge of Magic* by Mickey Hart, published 1990, pages 230-231.

[93] *Ibid.*, page 174.

[94] Little Richard, *The Dallas Morning News,* October 29, 1978, page 14.

[95] *Rock & Roll: An Unruly History* by David Henderson, published 1995, page 53.

[96] *The History of Rock* Magazine, August 1983 issue, page 60.

[97] https://www.rockhall.com/roots-and-definition-rock-and-roll

[98] https://www.rollingstone.com/music/music-news/lennon-remembers-part-one-186693/

[99] *Why Should the Devil Have all the Good Music?* By Paul Baker (a pseudonym Frank Edmonton used as an author and disc jockey), published 1979, page xv of the "Introduction".)

[100] *Why I Left the Contemporary Christian Music Movement* by Dan Lucarini, published 2002, page 121.

[101] Cited from a sermon Frank Garlock preached in Bob Jones University Chapel on March 12, 2001.

[102] From Chapter 12 "There Is No Wisdom in Sin" of his book *Man: The Dwelling Place of God,* originally published in 1966.

[103] https://www.nytimes.com/2007/11/07/arts/music/07prais.html

[104] *The Music Within You* by Carol Merle-Fishman and Shelly, 1985, page 72.

[105] *Ibid.*, pages 89 & 96.

[106] *Why I Don't Listen to Contemporary Christian Music* by Shelly Hamilton, published 2013, page 42.

[107] *Fusses, Fights, and Funerals* by Ben Everson, published 2019, pages 162-163.

[108] *The Westminster Collection of Christian Quotations* edited by Martin H. Manser, published 2001, page 72.

[109] Printed in *USA Weekend* on November 8, 1985.

[110] Article by Cliff Jahr in *Ladies' Home Journal,* December 1985, page 98.

[111] *Ibid.*

[112] Amy Grant, *USA Weekend,* November 8-10, 1985.

[113] *Why I Don't Listen to Contemporary Christian Music* by Shelly Hamilton, published 2013, pages 99-103. Excerpt used by permission from Mrs. Shelly Hamilton.

[114] Attributed from *The Rolling Stones* Magazine. However, his teachings and numerous books on psychedelic experiences clearly prove that this is what he believed and practiced.

[115] *Hole in Our Soul: The Loss of Beauty and Meaning in American Popular Music* by Martha Bayles, published 1994, page 130.

[116] "Elvis and Gospel Music" by Cheryl Thurber in *The Gospel Music Magazine,* published 1998.

[117] Quote pulled directly from the DVD *Elvis on Tour.*

[118] *The Sound of Light: A History of Gospel Music* by Don Cusic, published 1990, page 96.

[119] https://www.psychologytoday.com/us/blog/in-excess/201405/going-song

[120] Derived from his 1949 play *The Cocktail Party.*

[121] https://www.christianitytoday.com/ct/2006/julyweb-only/127-52.0.html

[122] *Can Rock Music Be Sacred?* by Frank Garlock, 1974, page 39.

[123] *Why I Don't Listen to Contemporary Christian Music* by Shelly Hamilton, published 2013, page 57-59. Excerpt used by permission from Mrs. Shelly Hamilton.

[124] http://www.gospelmusic.org/ccm-united-music-moments-and-memories/

[125] The concert can be watched on YouTube here: https://youtu.be/cj5Nq5sWJA0.
And here: https://youtu.be/TzfjelOSmQg

[126] *The Evolution of the English Hymn* by Frederick John Gillman,

published 1927, page 30.

[127] *Ibid.*, read pages 214-220 for context.

[128] *Ibid.*, pages 302-303.

[129] https://www.npr.org/sections/health-shots/2013/07/09/200390454/when-choirs-sing-many-hearts-beat-as-one

[130] *Why I Don't Listen to Contemporary Christian Music* by Shelly Hamilton, published 2013, taken from pages 89-99.

[131] Winthrop H. Brooks, President of the *Brooks Brothers,* the oldest men's clothier in the United States, from 1935-1946.

[132] *Why I Don't Listen to Contemporary Christian Music* by Shelly Hamilton, published 2013, page 85.

ABOUT THE AUTHORS

Caleb Garraway was born into a Christian home on July 20, 1986, and was born into the family of God on November 9, 1994. At the age of 11, he was called to preach through the preaching of Dr. Jack Hyles at Pastor's School in Hammond, IN. When he was 16, God called him to enter the field of evangelism. While  attending Oklahoma Baptist College, Caleb traveled with the men's singing group for four years and also worked at the Windsor Hills Baptist Church for two years. He entered full-time evangelism in the beginning of 2009.

Katie was born on November 9, 1985, and was blessed to be able to grow up in a Christian home as a Pastor's daughter. She accepted the Lord as her Savior in 1991 and surrendered her life to the Lord's work in 1997. Through the years, God has allowed Katie to use her musical gifts in the local church as pianist, singer, children's choir director, and teacher. She has written many songs and arranged many hymns and hopes to continue this much needed ministry as the Lord allows.

Caleb and Katie were married on March 20, 2010. They traveled out of Oklahoma City until God providentially led them to Marion Avenue Baptist Church of Washington, Iowa, in May 2012. After much prayer with Pastor Joseph Brown, Caleb launched *Remnant Ministries.*

Remnant Ministries seeks to stir up the hearts of Christians around the world in two areas: to passionately reach our generation with the Gospel before it's too late and to enthusiastically stand with confidence and conviction upon the principles and precepts of God's Word. To God be the glory, thousands have been saved and touched by the Lord through this ministry.

Caleb and Katie have written a number of other books including: *America: A Journey of Faith & Freedom, Baptists and the American Revolution, Found Fully Faithful, Her Knight in Shining Armor, Let God Write Your Love Story, Men on Fire, Modesty: An Issue of the Heart, Not I But Christ, Thriving As a Busy Mom, The Secret of the Lost Scrolls,* and *Our Blessed Book* (a practical study on the King James Bible).

The Garraways have been blessed with four children — David, Jonathan, Alyssa, and Julianna.

For additional copies of this book, or to schedule the Garraway family to come and conduct a local-church evangelistic revival, an "American Heritage Conference," a "Revive America Crusade," or a "Revive America Sunday" at your church, please contact Caleb at:

Evangelist Caleb Garraway
(917) 412-0059
www.remnantministriesonline.com
calebgarraway@gmail.com

For questions, comments, or additional copies of this book, please contact us:

✉	**WRITE**	Remnant Ministries c/o Caleb Garraway 215 S. Marion Avenue Washington, IA 52353
☎	**CALL**	917.412.0059
⌨	**EMAIL**	remnantministriesonline@gmail.com
🖱	**GO ONLINE**	www.remnantministriesonline.com

$17.99
ISBN 978-0-9914963-4-1
51500>

9 780991 496341